IF BY YOUR ART

If

by your art

Testament to

PERCIVAL HUNT

University of Pittsburgh Press
1948

PRINTED IN UNITED STATES OF AMERICA BY
LANCASTER PRESS, INC., LANCASTER, PENNA.

HUNT, PERCIVAL, professor of English; born Cedar Falls, Iowa, January 9, 1878; son of Henry Clay and Helen Marr (Garrison) H.; A.B., University of Iowa, 1900, A.M., 1904; Litt.D., University of Pittsburgh, 1938; unmarried. Fellow in English, University of Iowa; associate professor, same, acting head of department, 1916–19; professor and head of department of English, University of Pittsburgh, 1922–41. Professor-at-large since 1941. Department of English. Member of Modern Language Association of America, English-Speaking Union, Phi Beta Kappa, Sigma Chi. Republican. Clubs: Faculty, Pittsburgh Athletic Association. Author: (monographs) An Outline of Composition, 1930; Student Themes, 1938. Contributor magazine articles to Poetry, Teaching, etc. Home: Schenley Apartments, Pittsburgh, Pennsylvania.

Who's Who in America, 1948–1949

THE TEACHER

I

A GOOD teacher must know his subject. He needs to find in it large meanings and needs to master its details. He need not be a scholar, though he may well be. He is, however, master of what he teaches and why he teaches it and how to let his students into what he has.

He needs power to communicate his facts and his intangibles. He finds a way to go. He has the details, and the meaning, and he unifies these for his students (according to their abilities) into a common understanding, a common if uneven grasp of what he teaches. He builds a bridge. The way he takes is not "method" got from a book or from another teacher. He gains freshness from books and from knowing another person's way, but in the end, he is alone. He follows his own clear-cut, personal, vital path toward the vital in others.

These two seem to me the foundation. To name them is to bring up what is the basis, and almost to say what is quite granted (if not always practiced).

II

A good teacher holds to a few ideas he believes, a few guides, some constants he serves because they are to him the best. These constants will deepen, will simplify, with growing wisdom. He will need, by thought, reading, watching, trying-out, to better them as his experience goes on. Anyhow, he has a few guides he follows and cannot put away unless he finds better ones.

A good teacher needs more than ideas. He needs feeling about these ideas and about his students. He needs to realize the humanity of those he teaches; they, like him, are more than holders of facts. This feeling never sags into flatness of sentimentality. It is not false, professional, or casual. It can use severity in method and can require much, but it keeps its humanity. The teacher is trying to give what is real to others who are, he judges, capable of right thinking and right feeling.

Then, the teacher must work, in season and out, never "slothful in business." He just has to keep at it; he must hold, unendingly, to his purposes, and must, unendingly, preserve his feeling of a common and human bond.

III

A good teacher is a good man, teaching.

PERCIVAL HUNT

Reprinted from *Pitt,* a quarterly of fact and thought at the University of Pittsburgh, winter 1942–43

CONTENTS

[xi]

Contents

PERCIVAL HUNT

PERCIVAL HUNT is tall and slender and straight. A strong wind, it seems, might blow him away. He is a solitary man who, one of his colleagues told me, commutes to work from another star. He is austere and silent, yet filled with good will and affection. In his eyes is usually a suggestion of humor. If you see him even from across the street, you need not be told that the whole of him is opposed to gush or sweet pathos. But you would need a long time in which to realize how much kindness is in him.

Percival Hunt and I were undergraduates in the same class at the State University of Iowa. He was top scholar in the class. Since those days his manner, kindness, residence on another star, and habit of much work have but little changed.

The man is the best teacher of English I have known. To the teaching of any subject—Shakespeare, Chaucer, composition—he brings the same good sense, order, insight, and subtlety of humor. His students with enthusiasm generally agree that he is "best."

What is Percival's secret of teaching? At the beginning of a course by his sheer presence he tells his class that he possesses joy of living and that he hopes they, each one, possess their own individual joy of living. Then day after day as he talks the wonder of "going to college" opens for those students. Yet no course of his is a holiday-errand. In his class you must be you; simply, honestly, gladly be you. Tomorrow you will be a more satisfactory person to yourself. No one can tell you how to change in such a way. But you may begin by being now honestly what you are: a bright or a dull person, a selfish talkative sham, or a seeker of loveliness in human personality and in the outdoor world. When you write a theme or a paper, you are to make it an expression of yourself. Also you are to keep your mind open and sensitive. In this way you may find more of heaven in these days than you suspected was in them.

Part of Percival's secret, then, is to waken in his students a desire to be themselves, to be the best selves of which they are capable. A fresh high aim stirs in them. Many of us can cause a temporary flare of this kind. In Percival's class, however, the flare is not temporary. He sustains the aim—that is the main part of his secret. Creativeness bubbles up. Themes, verses, stories—no amount of effort among his students is too much effort. His quiet approval or word of praise becomes for them the joy of living; and even if the approval is slight they feel his kindness and begin again, this time to do better.

Percival Hunt is all teacher. He is a great soul.

JOHN G. BOWMAN

Hardin Craig

PERICLES PRINCE OF TYRE

THE accepted view of the authorship of Shakespeare's *Pericles* can be found in any current edition of the play. It is said that the play is only in part by Shakespeare; that the drama was not included in the 1623 edition of *Comedies, Histories, and Tragedies* sponsored by Shakespeare's fellow actors in the King's Company, John Heminges and Henry Condell, who were in position to know and probably omitted *Pericles* because it was not a genuine Shakespearean play; and that the play itself shows the hand of two authors. Dryden, however, accepted *Pericles* as Shakespeare's, for *Pericles* had been printed six times with Shakespeare's name on the title-page and had been widely recognized as his. The play was rejected by Pope, whose perfectionism would not countenance so irregular a poetic work. Malone accepted *Pericles* with qualifications, and Steevens took it into the canon of Shakespeare's works. Delius in a well-known article, "Über Shakespeares Pericles Prince of Tyre," [1] advanced the theory that George Wilkins was the original author of *Pericles,* that Acts I and II remain as Wilkins wrote them, and that Shakespeare rewrote Acts III, IV, and V. Finally, the Reverend Frederick Garde Fleay [2] accepted Delius' division of the play and said with metrical circumstance that Shakespeare's hand cannot be traced in Acts I and II. He went further and declared that

---

[1] *Shakespeare Jahrbuch,* III (1868), 175–204.
[2] New Shakespeare Society, *Transactions,* 1874, Pt. I, pp. 195–209.

[1]

the coarse portions of Act IV, viz. scenes ii, iv, vi, cannot have been written by Shakespeare. These opinions have in general remained current.

Malone's genius for being right caused him to accept *Pericles* as Shakespeare's in spite of its being "irregular and lawless," although it is evident that he did not like the plot of *Pericles* or the idea of Shakespeare's being responsible for the "fabric of the drama." He does, however, see that Shakespeare "bestowed some decoration on its parts."

Not too much attention is to be paid to Fleay's determinations in so far as they are based on moral considerations, or to Malone's objections to the plot. Fleay manifests a desire to bestow on Shakespeare a Victorian deliverance from the charge of having treated a plot with incest in it and of having laid some of his scenes in a brothel. Of the latter charge Shakespeare was already guilty, as *Measure for Measure* shows; and, as to the former, the plot of the old romance of *Apollonius of Tyre,* with its story of the sin of Antiochus, had been for centuries one of the most popular stories in the world. As to what Malone objected to as the "fabric of the drama," Shakespeare had nothing to do with it; the plot came to him ready-made, and he tells the story, all of it, very fully. Indeed, it was the necessity laid upon him to put a long and rambling narrative on the stage which caused him to invent a new kind of drama, namely, the dramatic romance, or tragicomedy, as it is sometimes called. Further than choice of detail for purposes of emphasis, Shakespeare allowed himself no freedom in the dramatization of his theme. So far as the parts Fleay rejected on grounds of delicacy are concerned, such refinement of taste had hardly appeared in the world when

[2]

Shakespeare lived. Malone, at the end of the eighteenth
century, was concerned about Shakespeare's writing on such
themes, and George Lillo in the prologue to his *Marina,* an
adaptation of *Pericles* (1738), comes perhaps unnecessarily to
Shakespeare's defense:

> Though some mean scenes, injurious to his fame,
> Have long usurp'd the honour of his name;
> To glean and clear from chaff his least remains,
> Is just to him, and richly worth our pains.
> We dare not charge the whole unequal play
> Of Pericles on him; yet let us say,
> As gold, tho' mix'd with baser metal shines,
> So do his bright inimitable lines
> Throughout those rude wild scenes distinguish'd stand
> And show he touch'd them with no sparing hand.

These criticisms on grounds of plot miss the point. Shakespeare was bound to follow his plot and probably had no objection to doing so; his moral refinement appeared in the way
he handled it. After all, Pericles (or Apollonius) is righteous
as well as clever, Antiochus is deeply censured, and the chas-
tity of Marina shines out with peculiar luster because of her
obscene surroundings. Shakespeare and his contemporaries
would have had no objection to this widely current story,
whose popularity was due no doubt to its obviously moralistic
quality.

The story of Apollonius of Tyre gained currency throughout Europe [3] from a sixth-century partly Christianized Latin

---

[3] There are numerous studies of *Apollonius of Tyre.* For our purposes it will be sufficient to cite S. Singer, *Apollonius von Tyrus: Untersuchungen über das Fortleben
des antiken Romans in spätern Zeiten.* Halle a. S., 1895, and Albert H. Smyth, *Shakespeare's Pericles and Apollonius of Tyre: A Study in Comparative Literature.* Philadelphia, 1898. In these studies is summarized most of the work of earlier scholars.

version thought to have been based on a third-century pagan
Latin version, based in turn on a lost Greek romance. The
story enjoyed the widest currency, appeared in Old Spanish,
Old French, Middle German, and surprisingly enough, in
ninth or tenth century Anglo-Saxon, both in poetry and
prose. *Apollonius of Tyre* is in *Gesta Romanorum,* a fact
which of itself is a warrant of wide currency. A "Cronica de
Apollonio" appeared in Godfrey of Viterbo's *Pantheon* (ca.
1184), another channel of wide distribution, and from *Pantheon* John Gower derived his story in *Confessio Amantis*
(Bk. VIII, ll. 271–1962). The play of *Pericles* is based on
Gower's poem together with Laurence Twine's *The Patterne
of Painefull Adventures: Containing the most excellent, pleas-
aunt and variable Historie of the strange accidents that befell
vnto Prince Apollonius, the Lady Lucina his wife, and Tharsia
his daughter.* This book was entered in the Stationers Register in 1576.

The surprising, if not unique, feature of the *Pericles* situation is the appearance of a prose tale professing to be based on
the play itself: *The Painfull Adventures of Pericles Prince of
Tyre: Being the true History of the Play of Pericles, as it was
lately presented by the worthy and ancient Poet Iohn Gower*
(1608). It is a quarto of forty pages, the only known copies of
which are at the British Museum and at the Stadtbibliothek
in Zurich. The latter copy contains a dedicatory epistle (wanting in the B.M. copy) by George Wilkins to Henry Fermor,
J. P., of Middlesex. Wilkins was himself a dramatist, and the
discovery that he was the author of *The Painfull Adventures*
brought him into consideration as a possible collaborator
with Shakespeare in the authorship of *Pericles.* That question

[4]

has engaged, and still engages, much attention; but we shall not consider it at this time.

J. Payne Collier interested himself in Wilkins' novel, cited the main facts of publication, and put forward an apparently unfounded claim that the Alleyn papers give ground for supposing that there was a Pre-Shakespearean play, now lost, on the subject of Pericles. He put forward also a very interesting idea,[4] later adopted by Sir Edmund K. Chambers,[5] that the version of the play of *Pericles* followed by Wilkins in writing his novel was a longer and more complete version than that of the only text we possess, namely, the quarto published in 1609 (twice) and in 1611, with later printings until it was included in the second issue of the Third Folio (1664). That a better version once existed was only to be expected, since the quarto is obviously an abridged and somewhat mutilated stage version of the original play.

When such so-called "bad" quartos were first observed, they were usually thought of as first sketches of plays subsequently completed in longer and more perfect forms. It is, however, noteworthy that neither Malone nor Collier was under any delusions as to the nature of the quarto of *Pericles*, which is so corrupt and so abridged as to be obscure. It has long been known that these abridged and imperfect quartos are usually, perhaps always, stage versions got together for acting by companies on the road from longer and more perfect originals.[6]

---

[4] See Collier's introduction to Twine's *The Patterne of Painefull Adventures* in Hazlitt's *Shakespeare's Library*, Pt. I, Vol. IV, pp. 229–42.

[5] See *William Shakespeare: A Study of Facts and Problems* (2 vols. Oxford, 1930), I, 523–6.

[6] See Alfred Hart, *Stolne and Surreptitious Copies: A Comparative Study of Shakespeare's Bad Quartos*. Melbourne and London, 1942; also Chambers, *Op. cit.*, Vol. I, chs. iv–viii *et passim*, with bibliographical references.

There is no known copy of the original play of *Pericles,* and surely Heminges and Condell had no copy at hand for inclusion in the First Folio or else regarded *Pericles* as not by Shakespeare.

By virtue of Collier's discovery it is possible to see that the lost original of *Pericles* must have told the story of Apollonius of Tyre more fully and clearly than it is told in our quarto version, and we must believe that the lost original was also much more correct in verse and better in style. Nevertheless, in many passages throughout the quarto text, the style of *Pericles* is very good indeed. The last three acts seem to have been written in Shakespeare's late manner, when it had become his practice to disregard metrical regularity, overuse ellipses, condense his thought until the language groaned under the weight, and introduce flashes of imagination in the form of figures of speech drawn from unexpected sources—such a style, indeed, as is to be found in the later plays from *Macbeth* to *Henry VIII.* It is not to be wondered at that a text possibly taken down from the words of actors in a road company would lack much of the beauty and clarity, perhaps splendor, of Shakespeare's first romance.

As evidences of an older and more perfect original, consider the following cases cited by Collier. In the original story as given by Gower and Twine, Marina (Thaise in Gower and Tharsia in Twine) is made to argue vigorously with the original of Lysimachus; but in *Pericles* she says only (IV, vi, 82–5):

Do you know this house to be a place of such resort, and will you come into't? I hear you are of honorable parts, and are the governor of this place.

[6]

And later (ll. 96–8):

> If you were born to honour, show it now;
> If put upon you, make the judgement good
> That thought you worthy of it.

Collier points to a very brilliant passage in Wilkins and says rightly that we have in it the thought and language of Shakespeare. His conclusion is that Wilkins has reproduced in prose a speech of Marina which appeared in the original version and has been lost in our quarto:

> If, as you say, my lord, you are the governor, let not your authority, which should teach you to rule others, be the means to make you misgovern yourself. If the eminence of your place came to you by descent, and the royalty of your blood, let not your life prove your birth a bastard: if it were thrown upon you by opinion, make good that opinion was the cause to make you great. What reason is there in your justice, who hath power over all, to undo any? If you take from me mine honour, you are like him that makes a gap into forbidden ground, after whom too many enter, and you are guilty of all their evils. My life is yet unspotted, my chastity unstained in thought: then, if your violence deface this building, the workmanship of heaven, made up for good, and not to be the exercise of sin's intemperance, you do kill your own honour, abuse your own justice, and impoverish me.

Chambers cites other passages from the prose of Wilkins which as evidences are still more convincing; they seem to be lost Shakespearen speeches reported by Wilkins. So that one concludes that *Pericles* as first written was a longer and nobler work than it is in the version preserved.

Pericles is a dramatic romance and was evidently the first

[7]

of Shakespeare's dramas written with the new technique.[7] It was notoriously popular, so much so that Ben Jonson despised it and spoke in his ode, "Come leave the loathed stage," of

> . . . some mouldy tale
> Like Pericles.

This may be set off by abundant praise from many quarters, by enthusiastic title pages, and by the fact that Wilkins and his publisher prepared for sale the prose version in order to take advantage of a popular interest.

The extant quarto text would leave us wondering how this could have been so, but, if we imagine a greater lost version, we can see that *Pericles* was indeed the first of the glorious group of romances with which Shakespeare closed his dramatic career. No convincing study of Collier's hypothesis has been made, and the ground is of course uncertain, particularly because Wilkins in writing his novel made use of Twine's *The Patterne of Painefull Adventures* as well as of the play. Nevertheless, it is entirely probable that *Pericles* as originally written was a much more workmanlike and beautiful dramatic achievement than is the quarto text.

Shakespeare was confronted by the necessity of putting a Greek romance, with all its vagaries, on the Elizabethan stage, and the thing that he did was significant and influential. In the first place, he wrote the play in a leisurely style, a style

---

7 As to the date of composition, the late Professor T. S. Graves, "On the Date and Significance of *Pericles*," *Modern Philology*, XIII (1916), 545–56, advanced arguments, rejected rather summarily by Sir Edmund Chambers, that *Pericles* belonged to the year 1606, and there is some probability in the case he makes out. There is, besides, a suggestion of an early date in the fact that Twine's *The Patterne of Painefull Adventures* was republished in 1607 as if in response to the popularity of *Pericles* on the stage.

which gave opportunity for thoughtful comment and noble sentiment. The first two acts were certainly written in a consciously simple and archaic style. There are many notable passages in *Pericles* as it is and apparently much poorly reported great poetry. A considerable number of these distinguished passages are found in the first two acts. Critics who believe that these two acts were not written by Shakespeare but by George Wilkins or another point out these excellences and, under the belief that they are too good to have been written by anybody but Shakespeare, justify themselves by supposing that Shakespeare wrote the last three acts and "touched up" the first two. The number of these exceptionally beautiful passages is considerable, and no two critics seem to agree as to which passages they are. These critics may be right in their theory of revision, and I do not mean in this paper to enter very deeply into the vexed question of the authorship of *Pericles*. An honest reading of the play will reveal at least this fact, that the style of the first two acts and that of the last three are obviously different. The late Professor G. L. Kittredge [8] said emphatically, "That *Pericles* is not all Shakespeare's is an obvious and undisputed fact. In style and meter it falls into two strongly contrasted parts: (1) Acts i–ii and (2) Acts iii–v. Most of the second part is certainly Shakespeare's work in his latest period. The first part cannot be his, except perhaps for an occasional touch." The author goes on to say that the problem is insoluble. Its insolubility rests perhaps ultimately on the fact that there is so far no way of telling what experiences the quarto text went through in arriving at its present form.

---

8 *The Complete Works of Shakespeare,* edited by George Lyman Kittredge (Boston, 1936), p. 1377.

The first two acts have dignity and simplicity and have, besides, a certain spectacular quality which is in harmony with the dramatic conception as a whole. It has been suggested that Shakespeare completed a play which he himself had begun at an earlier time in his career, but usually that Shakespeare completed the work of another dramatist by writing the last three acts and revising to a considerable extent the first two. There is, however, still another possibility, scarcely more. The first two acts of *Pericles* are consciously archaic and have frequent echoes of Gower. Shakespeare may have begun the play in an old-fashioned style, used for its romantic effect, and may have abandoned that style or relaxed it when he came to the more immediately dramatic story of Marina. In dramatizing the story of Apollonius of Tyre the author sought to reproduce the quaintness of old romance.

Shakespeare dominated the enterprise, and the Gower prologues are certainly his. They are of one piece and are the chief device by which was made possible the dramatizing as one story of a set of episodes with wide gaps of both time and space between them. The Gower prologues must be part of the original plan and must have added a most attractive feature to the play. Gower stood high in the age, was regarded as a great poet, and was well attuned to the morals of the time. *Confessio Amantis* had been printed by Caxton and twice by Berthelette. It was an Elizabethan storybook whose archaic language and style added to its charm. But that charm was not exactly what it is now. Gower was a careful and harmonious metricist and wrote a language which preserved the grammatical features of Middle English. Final *e* was pronounced or elided according to the same prosodic rules that Chaucer followed, and, like Chaucer, Gower suffered in his poetical reputation from the fact that about the time of his death the grammar of Middle English went to pieces. Readers no longer understood when the final *e* was to be pronounced and when it was not. The consequence was that Gower's lines sometimes would not scan, and he, like Chaucer, was supposed by critics to have been unable to write metrically correct verse. In point of fact, Gower was a careful writer of meter and was consistent in his grammar.[9] For example, George Gascoigne in his *Certayne Notes of Instruction concerning the making of Verse or ryme in English* [10] says of Chaucer,

Also our father *Chaucer* hath used the same libertie in feete and measures that the Latinists do use: and who so ever do peruse and well consider his workes, he shall finde that although his lines are not alwayes of one selfe same number of Syllables, yet beyng redde by one that hath understanding, the longest verse and that which hath most Syllables in it, will fall (to the eare) correspondent unto that whiche hath fewest sillables in it: and like wise that whiche hath in it fewest syllables shalbe founde yet to consist of woordes that have suche naturall sounde, as may seem equall in length to a verse which hath many moe sillables of lighter accentes. . . . I had forgotten a notable kinde of ryme, called ryding rime, and that is suche as our Mayster and Father *Chaucer* used in his Canterburie tales, and in divers other delectable and light enterprises.

Dryden in *Preface to Fables, Ancient and Modern* says, "Chaucer, I confess, is a rough diamond, and must first be polished, ere he shines. . . . You have here a specimen of Chaucer's language, which is so obsolete, that his sense is

---

9 See *The English Works of John Gower*, edited by G. C. Macaulay, 2 vols. E.E.T.S., Extra Ser., Nos. 81, 82, Vol. I, pp. xcvii–cxxvii.
10 *Complete Works*. 2 vols. Cambridge, 1907, I, 467–72.

scarce to be understood; and you have likewise more than one example of his unequal numbers. . . . Yet many of his verses consist of ten syllables." Both Gascoigne and Dryden are greatly puzzled at what they find in the study of Chaucer's meter. Gascoigne, it will be observed, finds a certain regularity in the disorder and dubs it "ryding rime." Similar difficulties would be found in the case of Gower, although, since he wrote prevailingly four-beat couplets, the difficulties would be slightly less.

Shakespeare's problem in imitating Gower in the prologues is thus indicated. Many of Gower's four-foot lines came through without metrical change, but, in other cases, the loss of final *e* in pronunciation tends to throw heavy syllables together and to increase the number of trochaic feet in the verse. These two are the chief irregularities reproduced in the Gower prologues in *Pericles*. Some lines in Gower when read in a modern way seem to lack a syllable or a foot, and they too are imitated. In other cases, the pronunciation of syllables which would have been elided in Middle English verse causes the line to have a sprawling quality. Then too the numerous extra syllables at the ends of Gower's lines tend to disappear so that in the imitation the verse tends to end in accented syllables and therefore seems less fluent. Gower moreover had his own metrical irregularities, and these too no doubt make their contribution to Shakespeare's gentle travesty of Gower. Almost any parallel passages will illustrate Shakespeare's attempt to reproduce the metrical effect of Gower as Shakespeare read him. For example, consider *Confessio Amantis*, Bk. VIII, ll. 1122–30, and *Pericles* III, ii, 68–75:

I Kynge of Tyre Appollinus
Doth all men for to witte,
That here and see this letter writte,
That helpeles without rede
Here lieth a kynges doughter dede,
And who that happeth her to finde,
For charitee take in his mynde,
And do so, that she be begraue:
With this treasour, whiche he shall haue.[11]

Cerimon reads from the scroll:

Here I give to understand,
If e'er this coffin drive a-land,
I, King Pericles, have lost
This queen, worth all our mundane cost.
Who finds her, give her burying;
She was the daughter of a king:
Besides this treasure for a fee,
The gods requite his charity.

It is possible that the prologues in pentameter before the fourth scene of the fourth act, the first scene of the fifth, and the epilogue were suggested to Shakespeare by the hymn to Venus, which follows the story of Apollonius in *Confessio Amantis*. They are freer in movement and less archaic in style than other speeches by Gower.

The Gower prologues are, as already said, the chief means by which the old romance, *Apollonius of Tyre*, was put on the Jacobean stage as Shakespeare's *Pericles*. Gower's speeches are charming in their quaintness, sometimes poetically beautiful, and, with their accompanying dumb shows, preserve a

---

[11] The text followed is that of Berthelette reproduced in Chalmers, *English Poets* (London, 1810), p. 258.

richness of detail in the writing of the play which the extant text has in large measure lost. Indeed, *Pericles,* as we have it, might be likened to a beautiful building slightly ruinous. Never cathedral-like, never awe-inspiring, never lyrical or gay, *Pericles* had, and still in some measure has, romantic peace and calm; it was never austere or gloomy.

One of the many meanings of the word "romance" fits it perfectly: "a fictitious and wonderful tale, whose interest lies, not so much in the depiction or analysis of real life or character, as in picturesque and surprising incident which reveals under trial the triumphant purity of woman and the fortitude of man." Like all romances of its kind, *Pericles* secures its credibility from the tacit popular belief that, in old times and faraway lands, life may be at once gentle and adventurous, fortunate and calamitous, disordered and beautiful. It is the romantic style of *Pericles* (so marvelously present in *The Winter's Tale*) that has been disastrously injured in our bad version. And yet, as may be easily seen, Shakespeare exercised great dramatic and literary skill in transforming a rambling and episodic plot, extending through two generations and occupying many places, into a single action. Dryden called it a "ridiculous and incoherent story," because it certainly defied the precious unities of time, place, and action.

HARDIN CRAIG
University of North Carolina

Putnam Fennell Jones

SATAN AND THE NARRATIVE STRUC-
TURE OF *PARADISE LOST*

IN this paper I should like to comment on the old controversy over Satan's role in *Paradise Lost*. I do not offer
any new interpretation. I merely wish to suggest that the
dispute was as much Milton's fault as anybody's, since it had
its basis in the narrative structure of his poem.

We may glance briefly at the controversy itself. The point
at issue, of course, is whether Satan is the hero of *Paradise
Lost*, or whether the role belongs to Man, as personified in
Adam and Eve. John Dryden first raised the question in 1697,
less than twenty-five years after Milton's death. In the preface
to his translation of the *Aeneid* he remarked that Milton
would have held a higher place among epic poets "if the
Devil had not been his hero, instead of Adam." Lord Chesterfield supported this view in a letter to his son: "I assert with
Mr. Dryden that the devil is in truth the hero of Milton's
poem; his plan, which he lays, pursues, and at last executes,
being the subject of the poem." [1] Samuel Johnson, however,
disagreed. After stating that Milton intended Adam as the
hero of *Paradise Lost*, he rebuked Dryden in these words:

> Dryden petulantly and indecently denies the heroism of Adam,
> because he was overcome; but there is no reason why the hero should

---

[1] *The Letters of Lord Chesterfield*, edited by Bonamy Dobrée (London, 1932), IV, 1306.

not be unfortunate, except established practice, since success and virtue do not necessarily go together. . . . However, if success be necessary, Adam's deceiver was at last crushed; Adam was restored to his
maker's favor, and therefore may securely resume his human rank.[2]

The romantic movement, with its revolutionary sympa-
thies, was naturally on Satan's side. Blake sounded the key-
note in his *Marriage of Heaven and Hell* (1790): "The reason
Milton wrote in fetters when he wrote of Angels and God,
and at Liberty when of Devils and Hell, is because he was a
true Poet, and of the Devil's party without knowing it." [3]
Shelley elaborated Blake's notion in his essay *On the Devil,
and Devils:*

Milton's Devil as a moral being is as far superior to his God, as
one who perseveres in some purpose which he has conceived to be
excellent, in spite of adversity and torture, is to one who in the cold
security of undoubted triumph inflicts the most horrible revenge upon
his enemy,—not from any mistaken notion of bringing him to repent
of a perseverance in enmity, but with the open and alleged design of
exasperating him to deserve new torments.[4]

Byron also regarded Satan as the hero of Milton's epic, though
for different reasons. Writing to Francis Hodgson in 1821,
he argued that in a tragic poem the hero must be guilty in

---

[2] *The Works of Samuel Johnson,* edited by Arthur Murphy, 3rd American ed. (New
York, 1851), II, 42; *The Lives of the English Poets,* "Milton." Addison, in the first
of his papers on *Paradise Lost* (*Spectator* No. 267, Jan. 5, 1712), had reached a similar conclusion: "The principal actors are man in his greatest perfection, and woman
in her highest beauty."

[3] *The Poetical Works of William Blake,* edited by John Sampson (Oxford University Press, 1914), p. 249.

[4] *The Complete Works of Percy Bysshe Shelley,* edited by Roger Ingpen and Walter
E. Peck (New York, 1927–1930), VII, 91; Shelley repeated this passage almost ver-
batim in his *Defence of Poetry* (*op. cit.,* VII, 129). Earlier, in the preface to *Prometheus Unbound,* he had compared Prometheus with Satan and had asserted that
Satan was the hero of *Paradise Lost.*

order to excite feelings of terror and pity, which is the purpose of all tragic poetry. "Is Achilles a *good* character?" he asked. "Or is even Aeneas anything but a successful runaway? Who is the hero of Paradise Lost? Why, Satan." [5]

During the latter half of the nineteenth century the Satanist position was defended by such eminent Milton scholars as David Masson and Sir Walter Raleigh. In his great *Life of Milton* Masson wrote:

> If the "hero" of an epic is that principal person who figures from first to last, and whose actions draw all the threads, or even if success in some sense, and command of our admiration and sympathy in some degree, are requisite for the name, then not wrongly have so many of the critics regarded Satan as "the hero" of Paradise Lost. [6]

Raleigh added his voice in 1900:

> Milton lavished all his power, all his skill, and, in spite of himself, the greater part of his sympathy, on the splendid figure of Satan. He avoids calling *Paradise Lost* "an heroic poem"; when it was printed, in 1667, the title-page ran merely—*Paradise Lost, A Poem in Ten Books.* Had he inserted the word "heroic," the question as to who is the hero would have been broached at once. And to that question, if it be fairly faced, only one answer can be given,—the answer that has already been given by Dryden and Goethe, by Lord Chesterfield and Professor Masson. [7]

In our own century Lascelles Abercrombie has given the strongest statement of the Satanist credo. Though admitting that it is perhaps injudicious to use the word "hero" in connection with Satan, he says:

---

[5] *The Works of Lord Byron: Letters and Journals,* edited by Rowland E. Prothero (London, 1924), V, 284.
[6] *The Life of Milton* (London, 1859–1894), VI, 554.
[7] *Milton* (New York, 1900), p. 133.

It is surely the simple fact that if *Paradise Lost* exists for any one figure, that is Satan; just as the *Iliad* exists for Achilles, and the *Odyssey* for Odysseus. It is in the figure of Satan that the imperishable significance of *Paradise Lost* is centered; his vast unyielding agony symbolizes the profound antinomy of modern consciousness. And if that is what he is in significance it is worth noting what he is in technique. He is the blending of the poem's human plane with its supernatural plane. The epic hero has always represented humanity by being superhuman; in Satan he is grown into the supernatural.[8]

So much for the Satanist side of the controversy. We may glance now at the opposite interpretation, which sees Man as the hero of *Paradise Lost,* Satan as the antagonist. This anti-Satanist point of view has gained favor rapidly during the past few years, largely as the result of modern scholarship.

Such twentieth-century students of Milton as Emily Hickey,[9] Denis Saurat, Martin A. Larson, E. M. W. Tillyard, Charles Williams, and C. S. Lewis have been willing to grant that Satan is a brilliant and impressive poetic creation, but they deny that Milton intended him to be the hero of *Paradise Lost.* Saurat, for instance, though agreeing with the romanticists' assertion that Satan contains elements of Milton's character, concludes that "Satan is not the hero of the poem: he is intellectually condemned, in spite of all the poet's—and the reader's—sympathy." [10] Larson notes that Satan accumulates weaknesses until he is submerged in deceit and treachery, the

---

8 *The Epic* (London, 1914), p. 105. Cf. James Holly Hanford, *The Poems of John Milton* (New York, 1936), p. lxxi: "Satan is the most gloriously conceived of epic heroes, for he *is* the hero of *Paradise Lost,* as Dryden affirmed, if we mean by that the most active and most memorable character in the poem." The most recent defence of Satan is that of G. Rostrevor Hamilton, *Hero or Fool? A Study of Milton's Satan* (London, 1944).

9 "Is Satan the Hero of *Paradise Lost?*" *Catholic World*, XCVI (1912), 58–71.

10 *Milton, Man and Thinker* (New York, 1925), p. 219.

[18]

weapons of the weak and contemptible; during the course of the poem he exhibits hypocrisy, envy, hatred, dissimulation, and self-contradiction, and in the end his "self-assertiveness and Stoic self-sufficiency have wholly vanished." [11] Tillyard takes much the same position in describing Satan's function in the poem: "There is not the slightest reason to doubt that Milton intended Satan to be a terrible warning embodiment of the unrestrained passions, inspiring horror and detestation rather than sympathy." [12] Charles Williams and C. S. Lewis, who have given us the most recent and probably the most illuminating comment on Milton's epic,[13] emphasize the absurdity of the predicament in which Satan places himself by his decision to rebel. Satan's motive for revolt is, in his own words, a "sense of injur'd merit" (I, 98) because "he felt himself impaired" (V, 662) by God's appointment of His Son to rule the angels. Lewis comments:

This is a well known state of mind which we can all study in domestic animals, children, film-stars, politicians, or minor poets; and perhaps nearer home. Many critics have a curious partiality for it in literature, but I do not know that any one admires it in life. When it appears, unable to hurt, in a jealous dog or a spoiled child, it is usually laughed at. When it appears armed with the force of millions on the political stage, it escapes ridicule only by being more mischievous. . . . No one had in fact done anything to Satan; he was not hungry, nor over-tasked, nor removed from his place, nor shunned, nor hated —he only thought himself impaired. In the midst of a world of light and love, of song and feast and dance, he could find nothing to think

[11] *The Modernity of Milton* (University of Chicago Press, 1927), pp. 210–216.
[12] *Milton* (New York, 1930), p. 271.
[13] Charles Williams, Introduction to *The English Poems of John Milton* (Oxford University Press, 1940); C. S. Lewis, *A Preface to Paradise Lost* (Oxford University Press, 1942).

of more interesting than his own prestige. And his own prestige, it must be noted, had and could have no other grounds than those which he refused to admit for the superior prestige of Messiah. Superiority in kind, or Divine appointment, or both—on what else could his own exalted position depend? . . . A creature revolting against a creator is revolting against the source of his own powers—including even his power to revolt. . . . It is like the scent of a flower trying to destroy the flower. As a consequence the same rebellion which means misery for the feelings and corruption for the will, means Nonsense for the intellect.[14]

The foregoing summary of the Satanist dispute shows that whereas the Satanists have argued mainly from the effect Satan makes on a reader, the anti-Satanists have dwelt on Milton's probable intention in the poem. Both sides may well be right, especially if we accept their different bases of interpretation. What is interesting, however, is that such a discrepancy should exist at all—the discrepancy, that is, between Milton's apparent intention in *Paradise Lost* and the effect the poem has had on so many competent readers. I believe the explanation lies in the structure of Milton's epic.

But first, what do we know about Milton's intention in the poem? On the basis of the evidence it would appear that Milton's purpose was to deal, in an epic poem of classical structure, with the earliest crisis in man's spiritual history— that is, in man's relations with God. This seems clearly indicated in the opening lines of the poem, where Milton states his topic in the conventional epic formula:

> Of Man's First Disobedience, and the Fruit
> Of that Forbidden Tree, whose mortal taste

---

[14] Lewis, *op. cit.*, pp. 93–94.

Brought Death into the World, and all our woe,
With loss of Eden, till one greater Man
Restore us, and regain the blissful Seat,
Sing Heav'nly Muse. . . .

Besides, we have Milton's explicit statement, in the "Argument" to Book I, that "this first Book proposes, first in brief, the whole Subject, Man's disobedience, and the loss thereupon of Paradise wherein he was plac't." It is also worth noting that in all Milton's preliminary jottings on the subject (preserved in the Cambridge manuscript of his minor poems),[15] the fall of man is the central theme; in the fourth and last draft of his plan the title is given as *Adam unparadiz'd*. There seems little question as to who Milton thought was his central figure, or "hero."

What about Satan, then? How was he meant to fit into the story of man's fall? The evidence suggests that Milton intended Satan as an example—as a blueprint, so to speak—of the workings of evil.[16] That is, he is presented to us not only as the originator of evil, but also as the first victim of its power to destroy. He shows throughout the poem a progressive deterioration of moral and intellectual fibre corresponding to his outward loss of brightness, and we are expected to see in this deterioration the consequences of sin—consequences which will be visited upon Man if Man chooses to disobey

---

[15] See *Facsimile of the Manuscript of Milton's Minor Poems*, edited by William Aldis Wright (Cambridge University Press, 1899), plates 33, 38; *The Works of John Milton*, Columbia Edition (New York, 1931–1938), XVIII, 228–232.

[16] See Tillyard's comment above. Note also the exact correspondence between Milton's presentation of Satan in *Paradise Lost* and his analysis of the effects of sin in Chapter XII of the first book of *De Doctrina Christiana*. This summary of Milton's theology was written between 1655 and 1660; when it is remembered that *Paradise Lost* was begun in 1658, it will be seen how closely the two works are linked in time as well as in thought.

God's command. Thus in plan, at least, Satan is a subordinate element in the development of Milton's theme.[17] He is intended to inform the reader of the issues at stake when Adam and Eve make their crucial choice. He prepares the way for our comprehension of the human story, but he himself is not the story.

We may now attack our problem, which is to explain how Satan, a subordinate character, got so badly out of hand as to be regarded by many readers as the hero of the story. I shall limit my discussion to one feature of Milton's narrative pattern that probably did more than anything else to create a misunderstanding of Satan's role in *Paradise Lost.* I refer to his method of opening the story.

Immediately after the invocation Milton plunges us down to hell, there to witness Satan's recovery after his bitter defeat in heaven, there to hear his ringing speeches as he rallies his legions, there to watch him as he promises renewed warfare against heaven and heaven's King. This continues throughout Books I and II. Satan is constantly before us. We see him reaffirm his leadership in the council at Pandaemonium; we hear him undertake to scout out the new world; we share his encounter, at hell's gates, with the horrible figures of Sin and Death; we accompany him on his perilous journey through chaos towards the world. By the time we have finished Book II, Satan is so firmly implanted in our imagination, his hopeless campaign has become so real to us, that from that point

---

[17] For a different view see Elbert N. S. Thompson, "Epic Structure of *Paradise Lost,*" *Essays on Milton* (Yale University Press, 1914), pp. 82–108. Thompson asserts that the poem consists of two plots in a "sequential relationship"; the first deals with Satan's revolt and has Christ for its hero, while the second describes Man's fall and has Man for its hero (pp. 85, 95, 101).

onward we tend to see the story in terms of the struggle between Satan and God. I do not mean that we are necessarily
on Satan's side. I only mean that whether we are for him or
against him, he has captured our attention and our interest
so irrevocably that no character introduced later can hope to
dislodge him from the forefront of our minds.

To put the matter more technically, Milton here violates
the laws of emphasis, of attention, and of narrative technique.
First position is both strongly emphatic and extremely favorable to attention. The experienced storyteller is well aware
of this fact and uses his opening to establish his theme and
his main character in the reader's mind. He knows he cannot
do this by merely naming his theme and his character, as
Milton does in the first few lines of *Paradise Lost*. He must
do much more than that. He must present his main character
in action, dramatically, so that the reader can grasp him with
his emotions as well as with his intellect, can understand and
perhaps sympathize with his problems and his desires. There
is no question but that Milton contrived a dramatic, vivid,
and interest-fraught opening for his epic. The trouble is that
he focused that interest on the wrong character.

Man, the stated hero of the poem, does not appear until
Book IV. This late presentation makes him seem subordinate
in importance, a sort of pawn in a celestial game of chess. Milton does his best to present Adam and Eve attractively, and
it must be granted that he succeeds rather well.[18] But Satan
has been given too much of a start, too much of our attention,
in the first two books. By contrast Adam and Eve seem prosy,

---

[18] See C. S. Lewis, *op. cit.*, Chapter XVI, for a penetrating analysis of Milton's characterization of Adam and Eve.

earthbound—little people mixed up in a battle of titans. The effect is unfortunate, and Milton is hampered by it throughout the rest of the poem. He never quite makes us feel that this is the story of Man.

One other defect of Milton's opening is that it cannot be related to the close, or the close related to it. Except in the first half-dozen lines it does not provide a starting point to which the ending can return, in the ideal circular pattern. The poem begins with Satan, ends with Man. It starts in hell, ends on the outskirts of Eden. It is as if a symphony should open in one key, close in another. The effect becomes confused and unsatisfying.

These faults in Milton's opening show up more clearly if we compare Book I of *Paradise Lost* with the corresponding book in the *Iliad,* the *Odyssey,* or the *Aeneid.* Much has been written about Milton's familiarity with the classical epic, and especially about his use of classical epic devices in *Paradise Lost.* Yet at the point where exact imitation would have done him the most good, he apparently missed or chose to disregard the lesson that Homer could have taught him.

The opening of the *Iliad* is probably the finest piece of craftsmanship in the whole realm of narrative literature. Homer knew that the mere stating of a theme and naming of a character do not, in themselves, make an adequate beginning for a story. Both theme and character must be given dramatic reality, must be made to live in the imagination of the reader. Not only that, they must be made to live with such exact shadings of proportion and emphasis that there can be no doubt as to which are the major elements and which are the minor. The opening of the *Iliad* fulfils these requirements.

After stating his theme, the wrath of Achilles, Homer proceeds to develop it dramatically. He takes us into the assembly of the Greeks; he lets us watch and listen as Agamemnon deprives Achilles of his meed of honor; we are with Achilles in his tent as Briseis is led away; we understand his resentment, and we share it, because we were witnesses to the whole transaction. For us, the wrath of Achilles is not a matter of vague and distant report. It is immediate, concrete, and real.

Of course the gods are involved, as they are involved in all the affairs of mortals. But the Olympians and their quarrels are kept secondary, are deftly subordinated to the fundamental human theme. We enjoy the blandishments with which Thetis wins Zeus to Achilles' side; we are amused as the thunderbearer checks Hera's nagging. But we are not misled. We know that this is not the main story. It is merely the background for a tale of human beings.

The same observations apply to the *Odyssey,* and in a lesser degree, to the *Aeneid.* The man who is *said* to be the central figure in the story is *shown* to be the central figure; what is said to be his main concern is set forth, in narrative, as the theme of the story. The gods appear, as they are expected to, but they do not usurp the stage, do not crowd the human actors into the wings. The audience does not have to ask, Who is the hero, who the adversary?

As I have shown earlier, this is a question which readers of *Paradise Lost* have never found easy to answer. I have indicated my belief that the fault is Milton's. Had he followed the model set for him by Homer, he would not have left his theme and his main character hanging in the air while he concentrated his attention—and ours—on a struggle among the gods. He would have managed somehow to place the emphasis where it belongs, on the man and woman and their problems.

I realize how presumptuous it is to ask for any change in one of the world's acknowledged masterpieces. In all likelihood the first two books of *Paradise Lost* contain the greatest poetry Milton ever wrote. It would be folly to deny the dramatic power, the intensity, the majestic sweep and splendor of that part of Milton's epic. I only suggest that in terms of Milton's whole purpose the beginning is inappropriate. What the beginning should have been I do not know. I feel, however, that it should have had some relation to the exquisite five lines that close the poem—that quiet, richly human passage in which Adam and Eve bid farewell to Eden:

> Some natural tears they dropp'd, but wip'd them soon;
> The World was all before them, where to choose
> Thir place of rest, and Providence thir guide:
> They hand in hand with wand'ring steps and slow,
> Through Eden took thir solitary way.

PUTNAM FENNELL JONES
University of Pittsburgh

Henning Larsen

ORIGO CRUCIS

ENGLISH influence on the culture of Medieval Norway and Iceland has been fully recognized for half a century. Ever since the appearance of Sophus Bugge's *Studier over de nordiske gude- og heltesagns oprindelse,* 1881–1889, innumerable studies have stressed West European influence in general and English in particular upon Norse culture and Norse life. The study of loan-words has yielded convincing proof that an unbroken contact existed between England and Norway from prehistoric times until well into the thirteenth century. These results have been corroborated by studies of the art of writing and book making, which unquestionably reached the Norse from England. Archeological and numismatic investigations lead to similar results.

If these findings of philology, history, and archeology are correct, we should expect, also, a strong literary influence of England upon Norway and Iceland. To some extent our expectations are fulfilled, but by and large the evidence is surprisingly slight.[1]

The explanation is, I believe, fairly simple. The power of Old English poetry was largely spent before Viking settlements became strong. Old English prose left a greater mark, though not a prominent one, for by the time Christianity was

---

[1] What material we have is presented by H. G. Leach: *Angevin Britain and Scandinavia,* Cambridge, 1921, and M. Schlauch: *Romance in Iceland,* New York, 1934.

[27]

firmly established in the North and book making had become common, the Norman Conquest had broken the continuity of vernacular literature in England. The early missionaries knew Alfric and the homilists, and they carried with them the books of the day; but, if the established Norse church of the twelfth and thirteenth centuries turned to England for additions to her libraries, she would be supplied with Latin or Anglo-Norman books. The bulk of Old Norse Christian literature obviously goes back to Latin sources; and to trace the route over which a medieval Latin book passed is usually a difficult (if not impossible) task. Some came to Norway via England, others presumably directly from France or Germany.

Some evidence of English influence we do find. A case in point is the tradition of the true cross. The Norse legends are so intimately related to English versions that the only reasonable conclusion is that the Norse compilers got their materials from England.

The most interesting parallel is that between the *Hauksbók* version of the *Origo Crucis* and the Middle English poem *Cursor Mundi*.[2] The story of the origin of the cross is well known in late Old English and in Middle English literature. Close analogues to the *Cursor Mundi* version are: the *Canticum Creatione,* a thirteenth-century poetic combination of the *Vita Adae et Evae* and the *Origo Crucis,* well known to American students from Emerson's *Reader,* the *South English Legendary,* and the *Northern Homily Cycle.* The Old Norse text is much closer to that of *Cursor Mundi* than is any of the

---

2 The *Origo Crucis* is found in many manuscripts. The story was first published by R. C. Unger: *Heilagra Manna Sögur.* Christiania, 1877, I, 298 ff. from MS 544 qv., i.e. *Hauksbók.* F. Jonsson edited the whole MS, Copenhagen, 1892–1896.

English analogues. It is also much closer to *Cursor Mundi* than it is to any continental version I have found.[3]

The introduction of the *Hauksbók* version, about fifteen lines, has no counterpart in the Middle English text. This is to be expected, for the Norse version is an isolated story, while that of the *Cursor Mundi* is woven into the story of Genesis, placed in its proper chronological place in relation to the life and death of Adam. After the introductory lines, there is such difference only as would be expected between a prose and a poetic composition.

Briefly told the story runs as follows:

Adam weary of life leans on his pickax and complains of his unending existence. He directs Seth to go to Paradise to ask the guardian Cherub for the oil of mercy promised him by the Lord at the time of the expulsion from Eden. Seth follows the trail of Adam and Eve (so sinful were they that their footprints left a burnt trail through green plains). At the gate of Paradise Seth finds the angel, who for the present denies him the oil of mercy. Seth is sent three times to look in at the gate. He sees, the first time, the beauty of the garden, the fountain of life, the source of the four rivers, and over the fountain a great spreading tree stripped of bark (Seth thought of the burnt trail and wondered whether the tree also had suffered for Adam's sin). The second time, he sees a serpent that encircled the tree. The third time, he sees that the tree stretches to heaven, and in its very top is a child in swaddling clothes. He

---

[3] On the English texts and their place in the development of the cross legends see Arthur S. Napier: *The History of the Rood-Tree*, E. E. T. S. 103, London, 1894; Richard Morris: *Legend of the Holy Rood*, E. E. T. S. 46, London, 1871; and J. E. Wells: *A Manual of Writings in Middle English*, pp. 316 ff.

sees also a root extending to Hell below where rests the soul of his brother Abel.

The angel explains that the child is to cleanse the sins of Adam and Eve when the due time comes; he is the promised "oil of mercy."

When Seth departs the angel gives him three pippins of the tree of knowledge to be placed under the tongue of Adam in burial. Seth reports the angel's instructions to Adam, who laughs with joy at prospective death. Adam died, was buried, and from the three pippins placed in his mouth spring three sprouts—a cedar, a cypress, and a pine—three trees in one, representing the trinity.

At this point the Old Norse story gives a brief summary of the history of the rood till the time of the crucifixion. The *Cursor Mundi* breaks off, to resume the account fully in the proper chronological place—in the account of Moses, of David, of Solomon, of the crucifixion, and of the invention (St. Helena).

The closeness of the *Cursor Mundi* and the *Hauksbók* can only be suggested here.

Cursor Mundi	*Hauksbók*
Adam had pastd nine hundret yere	Adam hafði lifat. ix . . c. vetra ok. ii. ok xxx.
He lened him þan upon his hak	hann studdi sik ved oxi sinni
With Seth his sun he gat to spak, Sun, he said, þou most now ga to paradis þat i com fra til Cherubin pat es the yateward	Hann killaði þa til sin Seth . . Sun min ek vil senda þik til Paradisum til Cherubin engils . . .
Yai, sir wist i widerward	Ek vil giarna fara . . ok visa mer vegenn ok
Fader, he said, sai me þi will, Quat sal i sai þat engel till?	seg mer, hvat ek skal englinn segia.

Adam gives Seth explicit directions:

Toward þat est end of þis dale
Find a grene gat þou sale

Hann skyldi ganga i austr ok
'mantu hitta einn dal firir þer ok
þar upp hefiaz vegr grœnn'

Adam tells him to follow the burnt trail:

Throu þe gretness of our sin
Moght na gres grove siþen þarin

En sva voru storar syndir okrar,
at allri siðan vox þar grœnt gras.

Seth addresses the angel at the gate, is questioned in turn, and replies:

[He] tald him of his fader care

to send him word wen he suld dei
to live noght he na langar drei;

Faðir minn Adam moðr af elli er
nu leiðiz at lifa, sendi mik hingat . .

Quen cherubin þis errand herd
Mikelik he him answerd:
Ga to the zatte, he said, and lote
þi hed inwar . .

Englinn svaraði: Gakk til paradis
dura ok rett inn hofuðit . . .

Quen seth a quil had loked in
He sagh sua mikil welth and win
It es in erth na tung may tell,
þat flour, þat frutte, þat swete smell

þa sa hann sva mikil fegrð at engis
mannz tunga matti or leysa i ymsum
kynum avaxtar ok blomstrs, fuglasong,
ok utologium ilmum of sœtum þef.

The descriptions run parallel to the end where Seth looks down into Hell:

And to the rote he cast his ey
He thought it raght fra erth til Hell
Quar under he sagh his broper Abel

þa sa hann rœtr apaldrsins
smiuga i gegnum iorðina allt niðr
til helvitis ok þar kendi hann salu
Abels broður sins.

The angel explains to Seth the significance of his visions and gives him a message for Adam:

þi fader, he said, þan sal þou say
þat he sal dei þe þrid day
. . .
but þo sal tak þis pepins thre,
þat . I . tok o þat appel tre
And do þam under his tong rote
þai sal til mani man be bote;
þai sal be cedre, cipresse, and pine,
O þam sal man have medicen.

þa fekk engilinn honum. iii.
korn or epli þui er faðir hanns
hafði etið, ok sagði honum:
Innan þeirra þriggia daga er
þu kemr heim man faðir þinn
andazt, skalltu þa þessur korn
leggia undir tungu rœtr honum dauðum.
Enn þau muner vaxa i .vii. [leg. þriá]
appaldra stora. Man einn verða cedrus,
annarr cipressus, riði pinus.

[31]

These trees, or sprouts, signify the trinity. Seth reports the angel's words to Adam:

Adam was for þis tiþand blith
Sua glad was he never sith;
Quen he herd he suld live namore,
þan he logh, but never are.

þa gladdiz faðir hans ok ló
viðr. Enn a ollum lifdogum
Adams . . sa engi maðr hann lægia
fyrr en þa.

The account of the death and burial of Adam and of the sprouting of the pippins runs parallel in the two texts. Here the parallelism ends and the two accounts follow different plans.

There is no single word or idiom of the Norse that suggests direct translation from *Cursor Mundi;* nor are there any idioms that would make such a theory impossible. More probable is a theory of a common source. This may have been either in Latin or English. That the Old Norse parallels only the account of the origin of the cross raises the question whether the same source had also some continuation dealing with the history of the rood tree. That the *Cursor Mundi* depended on two sources is certain from the findings of Napier.[4] The brief account of the history of the rood in *Hauksbók,* proportionately much shorter than the story of the origin, agrees in detail with none of the English versions. The whole history of the rood tree from Adam's burial to Christ's crucifixion covers only twenty-seven lines. The author of the Norse may have found it appended to the *Origo,* or he may have added it (to complete the picture) from another source.

The peculiarities of the *Hauksbók* account [5] warrants a summary.

---

[4] *Op. cit.,* pp. xxiii ff. and pp. 63 ff.
[5] Those who wish to check with the English can turn to Napier's parallel summary of two groups of MSS. *Op. cit.,* p. xxxvi.

The three wands grow from Adam's grave in Hebron. When Moses is to liberate Israel from Egypt, the Lord cuts two of the wands giving Aaron one and Moses one. With these wands they perform their miracles. The third sprout remained and continued to grow until Solomon had it cut for use in the construction of the temple. The usual failure is recorded, and the beam is deposited near the temple. Solomon's queen, called Sibilla by some and Saba by others, after returning to Ethiopia, warns Solomon that a man is to be hanged on the beam whose death will mean the destruction of the Jews. To save his people Solomon has the beam loaded with lead and sunk in a pond. It appears at the surface in time to be used for the true cross; and the prophecy is fulfilled.

HENNING LARSEN
University of Illinois

Frederick P. Mayer

GEORGE MEREDITH: AN OBSCURE COMEDIAN

[Reprint from THE VIRGINIA QUARTERLY REVIEW, published by the University of Virginia, October, 1925.]

WHEN I was very young, people used to tell me—good people all of them, but ill advised—that some day I would close my Byron and take up my Wordsworth, and that some day I would give over my Meredith and take up my Hardy. Well, I was a perverse child; I dug up the crocuses in the back lawn because somebody wanted to plant them and watch them grow, and I never ate spinach because I was told it was good for me. So, it took a long time to close my Byron; indeed, today there are still times when all Wordsworth's seeing into the heart of things cannot give the kindly ache that Byron's growing pains leave with me.

> The isles of Greece, the isles of Greece!
> Where burning Sappho loved and sung

has my fancy, and the old perverseness may be the cause, for I can remember that fine old Englishman—my teacher—waggling his funny goatee at me and letting his voice boom in the empty classroom and saying, "Ah, you are young, and Byron is young, but the day for your Wordsworth will come, and he will mean more to you—much more." And so I determined never to let it come, but it has, like age; for it slipped upon me when I thought least about it.

[34]

So it is with my Meredith flair, but not quite. My love for *The Egoist* came late, because of necessity it began late, and so it is more of the mature Me than the Byron mood. I see now, of course, that Meredith would never do, if he were alone in the world of the novel, and Hardy might, although I had rather die than live to see that come. I can readily admit that nobody talks in real life like Sir Willoughby or Clara, and I can see that Meredith writes description as it should not be written—with a full measure of self in his trees and his hills and his people. I know all this is true, and I admit it, but I do not think that the old perversity is the reason I say that to me, Meredith, with all his faults, is great as Hardy and Dickens and Wells and May Sinclair never can be. He is unreal; he is great because of it, and he is obscure because of it. Let me explain.

To the critic, George Meredith seems to have been—and he is still—a perennial puzzle, almost as great a mystery as Laurence Sterne and his infamous *Tristram Shandy*. It seems that the reviewers of Meredith's novels come—as most critics do and should never—with a definite idea of the way Meredith should have written his books, and when they find he has not followed their ideas of comedy, or novel writing, or description of persons or place, or what not, they judge with the peculiar severity of men who feel they have been laughed at. To look at life and writing with the eyes of Meredith they refuse, and the acceptance of his viewpoint is the one thing needed for an understanding of the man. Obscure he is, at times, but the major obscurity of the reviews comes from a failure on the part of the critic to adjust himself to the task at hand. Such criticism is like an English churchman of the zealot sort giving his opinion of that delightful rattlebrain, Laurence Sterne.

There has been much discussion of the comic spirit in Meredith and how he uses it to reduce abnormality to sanity; there has been wise and unwise talk of his feminism, with little understanding of what it means. There has been unthinking praise for his boy portraits; his ability at descriptive analysis has been cheered, but all is far wide the mark and yet quite near. It seems to me that there is a better solution for these questions.

As one reads the novels of George Meredith, there comes a growing sense of the utter uselessness of judging him as a novelist on the old terms of romanticist and realist, writer of romance or manners, builder of characters or plots. He seems somehow aloof from the grasp of the pigeonhole cataloguer. There grows a sense that he must be read as poetry is read and judged, and more particularly, that he must be read as we read (or should read) Theocritus, "Daphnis and Chloe," "Aucassin et Nicolette," "Gawain and the Green Knight," "Astrée," "Shepherd's Calendar," "Hermann and Dorothea," "Idylls of the King," and the rest of that literature of unreality that we call "pastoral." Poetry takes its rise from this old field of writing. The play instinct, or rather the pleasure instinct, the looking to the beautiful, the smiling attitude towards life and what passes as living, in short, the true art attitude of life remoulded by retrospective artistic mentality, is found in pastoral verse and prose pictures. Pastoral verse was great because it was free from life as life is really lived; it looks at life as it has been lived, and the knocks and bumps on the nose that come from being too near the actual living are all far enough gone to seem pleasant, valuable to think about, and just a bit trifling after they are gone. In true pastoral literature, there is a looking back on youth and young love as something which is funny, but which dare only be gently smiled at, because it is real, and the most beautiful thing the observer has ever known. It is middle age, wise and tolerant, looking back on twenty-two; it is the spirit that makes grown women like rather mawkish stories when they should know better. "There hath passed away a glory from the earth." It may not have been a very flaming glory, but while it lasted it meant everything. This *pastoral* quality is what I find in Meredith; he would sneer at this, politely, but it is true. Men do not usually know themselves, or care to admit themselves revealed. The world of Meredith is a pastoral hillside; there are bows on the sheep and on the trees, and he put them there because they meant something. He has not lost his good sense in painting a play world; he is showing the real world by means of it. He looks back on youth and finds it pleasant; he sees very young love and is not dismayed.

In serenity, aloofness, playing with reality and so being unreal, making the picture perfect and beautiful in defiance of truth and simplicity, smiling and laughing gently at human passion and extra-serious endeavour, George Meredith was a man who viewed life, in his novels at least, with pastoral vision. This is the unity of attitude that, I believe, offers some means of understanding and appreciating George Meredith. Meredith demands, as every writer does, that we look at men and women with him. Doing that, obscurity due to our own perverseness dies. To read Meredith well, we must accept his detached attitude.

[37]

Meredith has the pastoral attitude, even if he does lack the ancient pastoral machinery. He has tranquility, and a comic sense that arises from events as they happen, not as they are made comic by the sharp brilliance of the writer. This brilliance he has been accused of, but it is a false accusation. He sees the essential humor in situations, even serious ones, and by his art he draws that humor out. He decorates, but that is for the atmosphere of his world, not for making funny a thing that is not essentially so. His is a philosophic humor, and his phrases only give us this humor; they do not grin apishly.

Having this aloofness that sees the true essence of situations, having an art that is, like the pastoral, based on a re-shaping of events from their real dimensions into those of the art world, Meredith approaches greatness.

The change of reality to a convention of the artist's is to some degree always a necessity and commendable as such. The pastoral picture is not wrong because it has its set form or its artificiality. All art is by nature artificial, and the reason for the production is the pleasure that the artist takes in the creation. Pleasure, individual delight, is the reason that we get artistic work done. There is relief in reshaping ugly reality into art forms and that relief is pleasure.

The comedy in the prose of George Meredith, in fact, the whole comic machinery which is the background for his stories and their ideas, springs from the *attitude* in the mind of the author, the attitude which has arbitrarily been designated "pastoral." The attitude in the mind of the writer is given expression in what we call "Meredithian comedy"; to know the attitude is the first step in understanding that comedy which has seemed so difficult to know.

[38]

It is a commonplace of conservatism in literary judgment today that we are afraid of novels that do not show life as it is. In everything else but our world of letters, we are trying to forget reality, by vacations from real work, by amusements when the day's work is over. Motion pictures and the automobile ally with each other to make us feel that unpleasant and even accepted reality are far, far away. In the churches we talk about the vanity of this world and not setting our hearts on the things that are really round about us. But let the novelist say, "I am not painting life as it is; I am painting life as it looks to me; I have distorted that man's face to let you know him better. I have made a pretty world to show how comic men would be if they lived in it," and we are suspicious. If it is a play, we laugh with Pierrette and we love Harlequin. But we are severe with the novelist. We say, "Sir, stay at your pile. We want kindling, not shavings."

Meredith refused to chop kindling. He is, as a writer, not interested in the details of life; if we have not observed it enough to recognize it, he throws the burden of our lack of knowledge upon us. His is a strange world but very simple. If we see this, if we fit ourselves to the convention, Meredith in his bigger phases will not be incomprehensible. The realist objects, "People do not act that way." No, but let them, and see what results. "There never were trees like that." No, but it might have been better if there had been. "People are never so wholly one thing." But you never cleared away enough of the details to find out. In a hall of mirrors, do not look for likeness. Art is a hall of mirrors, a world of unrealities that tries to show, in Meredith's way, human traits, frailties, abnormalities, and the comedy of these rather stupid beings that we call men—stupid, roughshod, but interesting, appends the writer of *The Egoist*.

To have Heaven, we must postulate a hell. To show how comedy, a laughing at pose, at ridiculous pretence, can clear away the worst personal abnormality, we must allow the evil to run unchecked to its peak. Then follows reversal, correction, the full picture of the joke in the evil, and the excess seems all the greater and the more ridiculous. We are interested in seeing egoism at work. What is it? How does it thrive? What is its chief trait? How do we know an egoist? To find this, build the perfect world (unreal) for the production of egoism at its worst. Let us have Sir Willoughby, a man of many inherited aristocratic progenitors. Let him have money and a sense of family pride. Let him be handsome, and let him excel in brain and brawn. Let women worship and men applaud. Then let the egoist fall in love and win, and cast the gain aside. Let him then love again, and let him be cast aside but let him seem to win, and thus save his self-respect. Let him, wary, hurt in pride, love again and meet what—? A mere woman, a handful of feminine grace would never do. Let him meet a perfect woman, but a young girl, beautiful and with her eyes open, untricked by infatuation or inherited adulation. Let her love him—almost—and then let her make the egoist look himself—almost—in his unpleasantly satisfied face. This is the very seat of comedy, life as it might be if we watched close enough, life with its laughable upsettings that lie so near to disaster that we are not sure what we are feeling. Why do we enjoy Sir Willoughby philosophically riding to his fall? It is true that he would never have ridden so in real life, but within him, in his real self, in his real world, unobjectified, he rode and does ride, hard to his tripping. So runs an outline of *The Egoist,* and its method suggests the method used in all the novels.

Comedy, in Meredith's view, has some of the elements of the "pastoral"; it is a *"game played* to throw *reflections* upon social life." Comedy, in the Meredith sense, has no thesis beyond his curiously Faust-like conception of the Earth Spirit which broods over affairs in a non-deistic, unalterable governance. Comedy comes from any discrepancy between the normal which the Earth and its pure workings would have and the abnormal which man in his foolish pretensions puts up as a gratification to himself. It is the emanation of earthly things; it comes, when it is perceived, as a correction of departures from the sane world of living; it gives earthly things their true importance and allows them their dignity; it limits emotion of the delicate sort to sentiment, and emotions of the passionate sort to authenticity and sanity. It is, once again, an emanation of earthly things, and is so concerned with unreal atmospheres finely drawn from reality. Its language is the language of conceits (in the word's oldest and best sense) because anything intellectually perceived after it is emotionally over is a conceit. It re-creates not for play but for reality. By being a realization of the subtle undercurrent which moves details it is more significant, in its true power, than the details themselves can ever be. Doing this it is back with the world of sheep and shepherdesses, where cultivated society of a simple sort played with reality and so learned its inner meaning, and saw by an enjoyable use of its leisure time what life and living can be to thoughtful men. This is the pastoral element in George Meredith and his Comic Spirit.

[41]

Style and subject matter are irrevocably linked in Meredith, and in looking for errors in one it is imperative that we look for their reason in the other. Style is the man in the very genuine sense that it is his most intimate disclosure of himself to an outer world. What he says is no more important than how he says it; the thing he is thinking about usually determines his method of articulation. This is where we need an understanding of Meredith's unified attitude towards life and his art to see through the technical obscurities. The pastoral attitude, we have seen, is an artificial shaping of reality; it is art transfusion in its most severe form; it implies by its very nature a set style, formal, involved, artificial, to make its idea adequately presented to a disbelieving world. It is not any more possible to present an art conventionality of thought in bald, true-to-nature style than it is to present a strong picture of glaring realities of passion and sentiment in terms of "Euphues." Meredith must frame his picture with a style that makes it appear beautiful and real; to make his convention seem real, he must use a conventional style. In an office building we do not notice as unfitting the click of a typewriter; in a church or cathedral the machine is blatant and conspicuous.

Knowing and believing as we do, that the art of Meredith is a convention and that the style must agree, we see his complexity and his playing with an idea and decorating it with elaborate metaphors and witty aphorisms are not out of place or unreal; they concur in the thing to be done. Meredith seldom comes clearly to the point and says a simple thing simply. He twists, intellectualizes an unintellectual idea, if this be possible. Speaking of Laetitia, Meredith tells us that she gave up hope of marrying Willoughby. He says, "she quietly gave

a wrench to the neck of the young hope in her breast." This
has been blamed stylistically; it is ugly, unsympathetic. It
takes time off for a smart figure. But we are not weeping with
Laetitia or over her at any time. She is slavish in her adoration
of Willoughby. She needs comic scourging and she gets it.
After all, dirt-eating love is humorous. It may be real, painful, but viewed from the detachment of "well, what does it
matter in a hundred years," it is comic, and Laetitia herself
would be the happier if she could laugh. We are in reading
aloof with the author, and the style supports the attitude of
the art Meredith deals in. Meredith tells us by his attitude, as
expressed by his style, "Let us bandy words and see how funny
pompousness is." And so the style plays and decorates simplicity to show that, after all, simplicity is not the end hoped for.
Simplicity and straightforwardness in *The Egoist* would be
like Meredithian involutions in "The Village Blacksmith."

There is a time for weeping and a time for laughter; there
is a time for simplicity and a time when an embroidered style
is good. To the realist the love scene in *Feverel* is a sentimental exhibit of triviality. Of course it is, but granted the
attitude of the writer, such a scene is in keeping, and in terms
of Meredith's gentle comedy is the very antithesis of sentimentality. It is sentiment; it is an almost perfect pastoral—but
it does not drip. Young love always did border on the bound-
ary of sentiment and sentimentality, but being in that border-
land it is not posing or getting over-sweet. This Meredith saw.
By changing the tone of the scene to a delicate burlesque
through his own twitches of the words, Meredith says something about eighteen and twenty. He doesn't enter in, except
by feeling with the young people keenly enough to know the

world in which they are living. In attitude he has passed forty, but he does not mimic with the heavy-footed chuckle of the boy story, typified by Booth Tarkington's *Seventeen,* which lacks the intellect to be graceful. Meredith is too much of a gentleman to do the last and too wise to enter in. His pastoral reconstruction says, "It is beautiful for this to happen to Lucy and Richard," that is, for Lucy and Richard, but it is comic or very near it in its hyper-intensity and its extravagance. If Richard poses in his love, Meredith goes a step more. "Fool, you are comic in trifling with what you feel." And down comes the imp host to plague a posing Richard, who is, then, by the way, Sir Willoughby Patterne.

Meredith is a feminist because it is, for the most part, only women who are able by natural sensibilities and perceptions to see the world on play terms, to look at living as something to be enjoyed as a strange art, instead of something which must be fought because it is difficult. Women have by nature the pastoral attitude; a woman can enjoy an embarrassing situation because she sees it in terms of its ultimate value in the general scheme of things. A man resents embarrassments; he is a hard person to make see the fun in it; he can never quite free himself from the immediate sting of the incident. Some few men, with larger capacity for imagination, can, and Meredith is one of these. He turns to the world of woman for his attitude—this world and the pastoral are nearly one—because he finds there understanding and a large field for artistic imagination. He is by nature feminine; whatever he may say in favor of the new feminism that meant so much in the mid-nineteenth century and earlier is above and beside this first essential of character. For its very life, his art was dependent upon the cultivated society which woman demands and gets.

It is this love of the society which women are capable of producing that makes Meredith a feminist in the active sense of the word. He has the intuition, the analytic probing, the delicacy of wit and understanding, the fineness of feeling, the subtle sting, the cold sufficiency in looking an ugly situation in the face, the love of play that we commonly call feminine. The pastoral separation from the engrossing realities is hard for a man to get; a woman gets it rather easily—or rather, it is born in her. She has, too, the love of looking back on pleasant scenes and happenings. She is more tolerant of youth because she got more enjoyment from it. All this is in Meredith. His feminism lies in his mental make-up. The other side of the feministic argument—that of a definite thesis for feminist reform—is a corollary to this. One cannot have the feminine point of view without understanding women keenly. Meredith knows his women and feels with them—hates their dependence, their necessity for keeping quiet when they should have the right to say something. This is why his studies of women; Laetitia, Constantia, Clara, Renee, Rose, Cecilia, the Countess de Saldar, Mrs. Harrington, Rosamund, Mrs. Mountstuart, are great portraits. They may not be real as objective portraits by which you could identify them on the street; Meredith cared little for such identification. But they are real, wholly understood beings from within. If it were possible for us to meet the mentalities and spirits of people walking down the street, we could always say, "Why, there is Clara Middleton. . . . Look, don't you see Constantia?" The people are real because they are so thoroughly understood as thinking beings.

[45]

They act, they react; given an impulse, we know how they will respond to it. The sense of well-rounded knowledge never leaves us in our looking at Meredith's women. Clara Middleton is a tragic person because she is painfully and sensitively known by us. The situation is not emotionally startling in the old sense of a theatrical dilemma, but her feeling made emotionally real to us is exquisite torture. There is the semi-comedy situation; Willoughby is a fool, and his heavy love-making is funny, but here is a real woman who is bound by the conventions of the thing she is about to undertake to accept this overgrown, spoiled youngster as serious. Seeing his faults, she is asked to look up and adore. There is the feminism of Meredith—knowing women and knowing what they dislike, and being able to make that dislike poignant to a reading world that is apt to discount such over-refined cruelty. We have a term now in the divorce courts that shows a Meredithian sympathy—mental cruelty. Meredith knows his men, too, as a woman knows them. He knows their crudeness as it is manifest to women; he understands their ridiculousness in terms of a woman's knowing smile. Vernon is kind and lovable—to women's way of thinking; Willoughby is worthy of reverence and worthy of excoriation—to women, that is, to different kinds of women. There is a world of subtle feeling that is hard to approach, and it has its delicate joy and its keen sorrow. It is the world of women and few there be that find it. This is Meredith's feminism. Feminism as a system of subtle thought makes Meredith a feminist rather than his advocacy of feminine advance, although he does that, too, with force and grace. But his attitude has the repose of women who see into the heart of things and who are not troubled by the ex-

[46]

ternals of situations. This is the pastoral attitude, and it is very
near the courtly, gallant pastoral which gave women the center
of the stage and romance the first place as theme of themes,
except that the Euphuistic stories of the past flattered where
Meredith appreciates.

Within its conventions, such an art as Meredith's has its
own reality. With the exception of a casebook record of
events, every record of things that happen is colored by the
writer to a large or small degree. Every fact observed, every
detail selected, every picture, every word spoken shows the
hand of the writer. One cannot write without self-revelation.
Art is not photography. We see this doctrine rather clearly in
the world of paintings, but we do not commonly see it in the
world of writing. In color art, we believe this truth so much
that our exhibits tend to look like madhouses or like the scrib-
bling of children—all because the artist tells us that his painting is the way the objective reality looked to him. And yet in
the novel, we try to believe the opposite. We aim at recording
minute details; we try to keep the author back out of sight.
Meredith puts the author to the front. He must. He chooses
to talk about life actions as he sees them and as he wants us to
see. He is not interested in teaching his way of looking, but
he evidently believes there is pleasure and understanding if
we watch things his way. Otherwise, he would not write.
Meredith has chosen the conventionalized world of human
experience. The question is not, should any one do this or
applaud it? It is rather, this having been done, has it been
well done? His work may not be great; something else nearer
to the infinite sweep of human feeling may be demanded for

[47]

greatness in the absolute, but, in the scale of the absolute, he stands high.

Meredith stands off and looks at life as it might be and as it is if we take time off from the intense business of living to think through realistic details to what they mean in terms of motives and mental moods and subtle emotion. Realism, with all its virtues as the way to greatness, too often gets lost in itself. A writer has something to say or he should not write. When his technique and his matter get beyond him and make him lose himself, there are dangers. Meredith never runs this risk. Being a realist is not a sure sign of knowledge of life and people; too readily it passes for such. That is why Meredith's classic tendency toward unlocated, unfixed pictures has its charm. It reduces facts to their place—and they are important —but spends most of its time with the human motive and desire back of facts. This can be done to excess, and it is a matter of individual judgment and liking whether or not Meredith errs in this particular. With this neglect of facts is coupled Meredith's tranquility, which seems aesthetically sound. It takes great art to write from repose. Anyone with strong emotions can write powerfully when he is wrought up. It takes a great man to make vivid emotion come to artistic birth when he is emotionally sane. Divine madness is not unnecessary; but it is only a prelude to the best artistic expression. It is easy to say strong things when a man is angry; it is hard to say those things after he is himself again. What remains in repose is important; it is vital because it persists, and its emotional appeal is the stronger because it came out of repose. From quiet the artistic faculty does its best work—it reshapes, it orders, it selects in clear judgment, and it gets beauty. The flash of inspiration comes to the painter, but it is in purpose and sustained effort that the artistic product is done. The fire of emotion, the concentration upon the flash of beauty cannot endure over a long period. The artist would go crazy and lose his own power to create, if the first fever lasted as a mania. This is why Meredith's books, written consciously with an eye to style and conventional reshaping and interpretation, approach greatness. They are the fine work of a fine man who can handle his tools. They take life seriously, but they show how comic it is at the same time. Indeed, they picture life by comedy, by showing incongruities and absurd actions on the part of grown men and women. They make life worth while, but they lessen the tension by giving proper values. All this Meredith does. Out of quiet is born beauty and we need beauty. Clear minds and keen spirits will always turn to Hardy and Dickens and Thackeray and Fielding and Sterne and Stevenson and James and Meredith, for they can see in these many ways of saying the same true things, and they are willing to give each the honor that is due. The complexity of life needs many explanations. Meredith gives one view, one idea. For that he is worth our knowing. He thinks in quiet and he loves beauty. What he has to give is beautiful, for it is born of his own love for perfection.

FREDERICK P. MAYER
University of Pittsburgh

Edwin L. Peterson

SEARCHER AFTER TRUTH

[A Paper Read Before The Dickens Society]

IN the heart of every artist is a longing for some unattainable quality that lies beyond the farthest hill, that peers from blue eyes seen once and never afterward forgotten. Awake and asleep, the artist searches after his desire. He never finds it. It leads him into strange streets and down but half-remembered valleys; he looks into strange faces, hoping to find there the one thing missing; he follows after voices in the night, follows through drawing rooms and dens, along moonlit alleys and glittering boulevards, behind portieres and curtains, beneath sheets stained by birth and death.

While he searches, the world looks on and wonders. It blames, reproves, condones, excuses. That is because the world sees the mortal man but not that thing immortal for which he searches. At the end, some weary dawn, the artist dies, rich or poor, happy or unhappy, but always unsuccessful in the search. Nevertheless, it is the search that matters. It is the pursuit of a nameless mystery that explains him, that brings pity and love into the hearts of those who hear him stumbling through the night.

II

A coach is travelling the road to Canterbury. It is driven by a jovial man in a black suit and a bright silk cravat. The

[50]

road is smooth and the horses are fresh. Below him the river sparkles in the sunlight, and ships, white-sailed or black-smoked, move out to sea.

By the roadside stands a small boy in a white cap, blue shirt, corduroy trousers. As the coach comes abreast of the boy, the man pulls on the reins.

"Holloa!" says the man to the boy. "Where do you live?"

The boy looks up. His face is pale and eager. "At Chatham," he says.

"What do you do there?" says the man. The man is looking very closely at the boy as though expecting him to vanish.

"I go to school," says the boy.

"Hop in," says the man. "It's better to ride than walk."

But as the boy steps on the lift, there is no sagging of the carriage. Nor is there any sound as the boy's feet stomp on the floor boards.

For a long time neither boy nor man speaks. There is the clop-clopping of the horses' hooves, and from down in the valley comes the husky hoot of a whistle. The boy points ahead.

"This is Gadshill we are coming to, where Falstaff went out to rob those travellers and ran away."

The man takes his eyes from the road and looks at the boy beside him. "You know something about Falstaff, eh?" he says.

"All about him," says the boy. His voice is shadowy, like a voice half-remembered in a dream. "I am old," the boy says. "I am nine, and I read all sorts of books. But *do* let us stop at the top of the hill, and look at the house there, if you please."

"You admire that house?" asks the man.

"Bless you, sir," says the boy, "when I was not more than

half as old as nine, it used to be a treat for me to be brought to look at it. . . . And ever since I can recollect, my father, seeing me so fond of it, has often said to me, *If you were to be very persevering, and were to work hard, you might some-day come to live in it.*"

The boy stares out the coach window and draws a low breath. "Though that's impossible!" he adds.

"Impossible?" says the man, as though thinking of many things that happened many years before. "My lad, if . . ."

He turns, but the boy is not there. The horses have not slowed their pace, the door has not opened, but the queer little boy is not there.

Charles Dickens is the name of either the boy or the man, but it is hard to tell which, for this happened at the very top of Gad's Hill, which is the hill of God.

III

It is the year 1819. In an upstairs room of a house in St. Mary's Square, Chatham, a boy slumps over a book on the table. There are other books on the table, too—*Roderick Random, Peregrine Pickle, Tom Jones,* and *The Vicar of Wakefield.* The boy's face is pinched and his arms frail. He reads rapidly with eyes that are bright and nervous.

He slams the book shut, gets up from the chair, and goes over to the window. There he strikes a posture, his left arm extended before him, his right hand shading his eyes. He is no longer Charles Dickens, aged ten, but Robinson Crusoe standing at the edge of the sea, looking out across troubled waters, looking for a ship, for a sail, for a raft, for any kind of help to ease his loneliness.

Years later, he writes, "These books kept alive my fancy and my hope of something beyond that time and place."

What hope, we wonder, and what something. What *then* was the desire that drove him beyond that place and time? What was the something that he longed for—a ball and bat? but he was always poor at cricket. Was it music lessons like Fanny's?—but music meant less to him than he thought. Or was it the mystery, the thing immortal, glimpsed once, perhaps, and ever afterward remembered?

IV

He is sitting beside the window of the blacking warehouse on Hungerford-stairs. Beside him, at the window, sits Bob Fagin. Before them, on the table, are hundreds of pots of paste-blacking. With deftness borne of long practice, the boys cover the pots first with a piece of oil-paper, then with a piece of blue paper. A string is wound smartly around the gathered edges, then the shears snip. A flick of the wrist, and the jar, wrapped and trimmed, slides over to join the company of finished products.

Outside, through the dirty windows, he can see the river alternately dark and bright in the afternoon sunlight and the coal barges ploughing up the stream. There is an aching in his stomach and a dullness in his heart. Fannie is at the Royal Academy studying music a million miles away, and his father —but no one, least of all Bob Fagin, must know that his father is in prison. No one does know —no one who works at the blacking warehouse.

Without warning, the pain in his stomach doubles him up.

[53]

A pot rolls across the table and the boy falls to the floor. He writhes there, clutching his stomach. Fagin is beside him.

"Charles," he says, "hit's yer stomach agin, hain't it?" He dashes out of the room and returns again with an old paste pot, stoppered and filled with hot water.

"Hold it agin you, me boy. It'll ease yer belly."

Fagin goes back to the table and keeps on wrapping paper and string about the pots and snipping, snipping. When he thinks the paste jar is cold, he gets up and refills it.

All afternoon the boy lies on the rotten old floor. From below come the squeaking and scuffling of the gray rats. The light fades from the window. Fagin lights a stumpy candle and continues wrapping, snipping. Charles is asleep on the floor, Fagin's sweater over his shoulders.

At last, Fagin gets up from the table. He walks over to the boy and shakes him by the shoulder. "Time we was quittin', me boy. Time you was gettin' home. Where d'ya live anyway? Bob Fagin's the man as is takin' yez home tonight."

Through the boy's sleepy brain rings the question, "Where d'ya live anyway?" The question that dare not be answered.

"I'm all right, now," he says. "I'm all right. I can go home alone." Yes, it would have to be alone, down the dark alleys, across the dark streets until the walls of the prison loom ahead, there to sleep away his sickness within the same walls that hold his father. But it would have to be alone.

Fagin has pulled the boy to his feet, is bustling him out the front door. "Where d'ya live, anyway, fer Bob Fagin's takin' yez home tonight if the devil says no."

They are out on the street. Lights gleam on the river, and from the public house across the street come heavy shouts.

[54]

They cross the bridge and turn into Blackfriars-road. They pass the likeness of a golden dog licking a pot of honey.

"Where d'ya live, boy, anyway?" The question comes again.

"We better turn here," says the boy. There is desperation in his voice. They walk on silently, heels ringing in the night. Across Southwark-bridge, on the Surrey side. There is a house on the Surrey side, a house with stone steps. The boy has never seen it before.

"Here," he says, "here's where I live. You didn't need to come, Fagin. I feel all right. Don't come any further. No, I'm all right."

He walks up the stone steps, knocks boldly at the door. Fagin hesitates a moment. "Goodnight, me boy. Ye'll be feelin' trim as a fiddle come tomorrow." He lounges on.

The door opens. A woman bulks huge before him.

"What d'ya want, boy?"

"Want? What do I want? Oh, is this where —is this where Bob Fagin lives, madam?"

"There ain't no Bob Fagin lives here, boy. What's he do? What do you want him for? Mebbe over across the street at Mrs. Malone's. She takes in boarders, too."

"Thank you kindly, mam," the boy says, throwing a glance over his shoulder at Fagin's retreating figure. "Yes, maybe across the street." His shoes scuffle on the stone steps. He is out again into the London night. It is two miles to Marshalseaprison, two miles to Mother, to Father, to prison, to bed.

V

It is the morning of April second, 1836. Around the breakfast table sit the Hogarth family and the Dickens family.

Thomas Beard is there, too. They have just come from St. Luke's, Chelsea. There is a confused chatter of voices. Charles Dickens sits beside his bride, Catherine Hogarth, a pretty girl with high, full forehead, brown hair, violet eyes. Perhaps it is because he is sitting next to her that he looks at her seldom. Perhaps it is because of the merriment that ripples across the table. Perhaps it is because he is thinking, thinking of a time not yet long past and of a letter written to another girl —"I never have loved and I never can love any human creature breathing but yourself." Perhaps . . . perhaps . . . but toasts are being drunk, and a groom must hear the toasts.

Across the table sits Mary Hogarth and near her Georgina. Are there shadows across Mary's eyes? Is her laughter less gay than Catherine's? Is it because she sits across from him, that her eyes find his? And what does he see there, as he sits beside his bride, finding the eyes of Mary Hogarth, the gray-blue eyes that hint of death and things ineffable? What is it that he seeks in the eyes of Mary? For the search goes on forever, down the dark alleys, into the sunlight and April mornings, and the touch of hidden fingers, and the look on the face of a girl. The search is endless and hopeless, but it leads to strange places, strange faces, to the gayety of Maria, the loveliness of Catherine, the stillness of Mary, the loyalty of Georgina, and beyond them, at last, into the valley of the shadow.

VI

It is an April evening in 1842. The *Messenger* steams down the Mississippi, paddle wheel swishing steadily, engine grumbling. The air is cool and fresh.

Inside the cabin, Catherine Dickens stares out the window at the slowly changing line of darkness across the river. The moon is up, and ripples dance with gleams of light. If there is a lonely longing in her heart, she gives no sign of it, but back home, in England, in April, back home are the children, her children, attended by her sister, Georgina. She keeps on staring out the window.

Sitting on a straight-backed chair, Charles Dickens is writing a letter to John Forster. There is a book on his knee and a paper on the book. "It is well for society," his pen writes, "that this Mississippi, the renowned father of waters, had no children who take after him. It is the beastliest river in the world. . . . While I have been writing this account, we have shot out of that hideous river, thanks be to God; never to see it again, I hope, but in a nightmare."

Charles Dickens does not know that only a few miles away lives a small boy who sees the Mississippi not as a nightmare but as a dream of all things beautiful, who sees the river moving through the forests and swamps to the sea, who watches at night as the great boats churn the river, spouting clouds of sparks and smoke, who sees the stars above him flashing in the steady currents, and where the stars are, there may God be also. But the dream is where men seek it. Samuel Clemens seeks his dream where the Mississippi swirls through the night between dim banks. Charles Dickens seeks his dream where street lamps burn, where prison lamps smoke, where women's eyes tell hints of many mysteries, and where the stage lights promise more than the emptiness they give.

[57]

VII

In Genoa, Charles and Catherine Dickens lie in loneliness in the great bed. It is almost dawn. The convent bells are ringing. In the dimness, the altar at the foot of the bed bulks huge. She is sleeping soundly, he restlessly. Eight years have passed since the wedding breakfast, when Mary and Georgina sat across from him—and Mary has been dead a long time. There are children, now, and many books; and for Catherine, contentment, wealth, a growing waistline. But for him. . . .

He stirs sharply. Tears roll down his face. He sits upright. "Kate," he calls in bewilderment. Then more firmly, "Kate!"

She rouses heavily. "What's the matter?" she says, "What's wrong?"

"Kate," he says, "I've had a dream, a strange dream. I mustn't forget it. I have to tell it to you."

"Oh," she says, "just a dream. I thought. . . ."

"In an indistinct place," he says, "which was sublime in its indistinctness, I was visited by a Spirit. . . . It wore a blue drapery, as the Madonna might in a picture by Raphael. . . . I think (but I am not sure) that I recognized the voice. Anyway, I knew it was poor Mary's spirit."

He rubs the tears from his face with the back of his hand, and so he cannot notice the sudden drooping of Catherine's lips nor the way her heavy hand pulls at the covers.

"I was not at all afraid," he continues, "but in a great delight, so that I wept very much, and stretching out my arms to it called it 'Dear.' At this I thought it recoiled; and I felt immediately, that not being of my gross nature, I ought not to have addressed it so familiarly. 'Forgive me,' I said. 'Yes.'

'But answer me one question,' I said in an agony lest it should leave me. 'What is the True religion? . . . perhaps the Roman Catholic is the best? Perhaps it makes one think of God oftener, and believe in Him more steadily?' 'For you,' said the Spirit, full of such heavenly tenderness for me, that I felt as if my heart would break; 'for *you*, it is the best!' Then I awoke with the tears running down my face."

He pauses. The curtains are swaying in the breeze before morning, and through the window comes the sound of a cart rumbling down the street. The convent bells have stopped ringing.

"Is it not—remarkable?" he says. "It was Mary, your sister."

"Yes," she says slowly. "Quite remarkable."

"I wanted to tell you, now while it is fresh in my mind. By morning, it might not have been clear. You will remember? for me?"

Her fingers tighten on the covers. Her throat is taut. "Yes," she says, "I shall remember."

But what will Catherine Hogarth Dickens remember, and what Charles Dickens? In his waking hours and in his sleeping dreams, the artist searches after his desire. While he searches, the world looks on and wonders. It sees the mortal man but not the thing immortal for which he searches.

VIII

It is fourteen years later. In the *New York Herald Tribune* appears the "violated letter."

"Mrs. Dickens and I lived unhappily together for many years. Hardly anyone who has known us intimately can fail to have known that we are in all respects of character and temperament wonderfully unsuited to each other. . . . Nothing has, on many occasions, stood between us and a separation but Mrs. Dickens' sister, Georgina Hogarth. . . . Both my girls, and all my children but my eldest son (are) to live with me, in the continued companionship of their aunt Georgina . . . who has a higher claim upon my affection, respect, and gratitude than anybody in the world. . . . They are perfectly certain that I would not deceive them, and the confidence among us is without a fear." C.D.

May 29th, 1858

But what, the cynic asks, do children think, when there are ten of them, about the father who found his wife "wonderfully unsuited"?

Strange unsuitability that produces ten children. Strange unsuitability, except that the thing immortal leads men beyond the home and out into the night of discontent, seeking the dream in the eyes of dead but long remembered women, in a house on a hill called Gads Hill, in the sight of strange faces wandering through London fog.

IX

It is December 23, 1867. Charles Dickens is back in America. He is a worn and haggard man, re-creating to a huge audience the characters he has written in the past. He is not Charles Dickens at all, but, by turns, Bill Sikes, Mr. Weller, Tiny Tim.

Wiser and sadder, he has not steamed down the Mississippi, "the beastliest river in the world." Nor has he met the six-year-old Mark Twain, who, in those early days, may well have watched the *Messenger* plough through the night and the stern April currents. But the six-year-old is a man now, sitting in the audience. He should be dreaming of his own Mississippi, seeking God in the reflection of stars, but instead he is dreaming of the girl beside him, sweet-faced, gentle, fragile, seen once in a miniature picture and loved forever after. Her name is Olivia Langdon, though it might just as well have been Maria Beadnell, Mary Hogarth, Georgina Hogarth, or Ellen Ternan.

Two searchers after truth, Samuel Clemens and Charles Dickens, brush shoulders in a December night but there is no handclasp, no call through the darkness. Has either learned the truth, Clemens with Olivia, Dickens without his wife, that the journey can never be made by twos but only singly and silently, searching for something that is never found? Oh, strange, wise, foolish men!

X

It is late in the afternoon of June eighth, 1870. In the lonely old house on Gads Hill, Georgina and he sit at the long table. The twenty-third chapter of *Edwin Drood* has been finished, and the end is near of the fifty-eighth chapter of another unfinished book.

Georgina looks up at him. Her face is puzzled. "You're, you're ill?" she says.

For a moment he does not answer. There is the clicking of a fork on a plate, and from the kitchen, indeterminable noises.

"Yes," he says quietly, "very ill. I have been very ill for the last hour."

She speaks of a physician, but he does not hear her. He is mumbling incoherently —"A sale at . . . but Macready's son, at Cheltenham . . . London, I must go at once —to London."

He rises feebly. She is at his side trying to support him. "Here," she says, "you must lie down, on the sofa."

"Lie down," he mumbles. "Lie down, on the ground." He falls to the floor, falls heavily upon his left side.

So it is with all who would soar heavenward. It is the ground, at last, that claims its own. It is the ground that ends the search. Georgina struggles to lift the broken body, but where are the others who might have helped? Where are Charles and Mamie, Kate and Alfred, Sidney and Henry and Edward? Yes, and where are Maria Beadnell and Mary Hogarth? Is there only Georgina?

But there are those who never die, and he it was who made them, he who now lies stricken on the ground. They come to him with gentle words: Macawber and Barkis, hopeful and willing; and little Dorrit, too, and a child whose name was Nell; Fagin and Oliver. They come through the dark to him who sought them, and a cool hand touches his forehead. If he whispers a name, then, is it Dora? or Agnes? But she stands there in a blue drapery, as the Madonna might in a picture by Raphael, and her hand is cool against his forehead, and somewhere in the darkness there is singing and the smell of plum pudding and a vision glimpsed once and ever afterward remembered.

The stumbling search is over. It has failed. The mystery is nameless still, and the world is already wondering, condoning, and reproving. Charles Dickens, searcher after truth, is dead.

XI

Through the chill austerity of Westminster Abbey comes a sober voice. It is the voice of Dean Stanley, he, too, a searcher after truth, he, too, wearied by the long pursuit. Out of his weariness comes wisdom.

"He whom we mourn was the friend of mankind. . . . I am not going to attempt to draw a portrait of him. Men of genius are different from what we suppose them to be. They have greater pleasures and greater pains, greater affections and greater temptations, than the generality of mankind, and they can never be altogether understood by their fellow men. . . . But we feel that a light has gone out, that the world is darker to us, when they depart. . . ."

This is the benediction over the dead man and the dead dream. Fortunate the man privileged to speak it!

EDWIN L. PETERSON
University of Pittsburgh

Emily G. Irvine

A WAR FOR THE ARTS

FOR several years I have been jotting down notes which I intended to use when on some theme-less day I wrote to the editors who have been publishing articles predicting the death of the liberal arts. I am not especially an optimist, but even during the war, I felt less pessimistic about the future of the arts than many of my colleagues in the teaching profession. Perhaps one reason for my optimism is that I am not a statistician. I have never known—or cared for that matter—just how many students were studying cultural subjects in 1793, in 1895, in 1924, or in 1947. For twenty years, however, I have been watching college students matriculate and graduate. During that time a goodly percentage of them has registered in the colleges of liberal arts—as large a percentage as could be expected if the world is to progress in science and business and ditchdigging as well as in culture; occasionally, I thought, a larger percentage than was really capable of becoming cultured. There were times during the war, to be sure, when the elective courses in English averaged only thirty students to a section instead of fifty or seventy-five and when German departments had to drop advanced courses in Hauptmann or Hebel, but I could never feel that the decreased number of courses would be permanent, and I could not really worry about the smaller sections.

My optimism reached its crest in 1943 and 1944 when it should have been at its ebb. The reason for this upside-down

[64]

thinking was a very personal one in no way substantiated by figures or research and, consequently, perhaps subject to criticism. I had been receiving letters from the South Pacific, from India, from the European theatre—letters written by students and former colleagues who were trying to save the world for a nebulous something. They admittedly did not know quite what, although some of them were wondering why they were willing to endure repeated attacks of malaria or to sleep in muddy foxholes. One thing they did know, all of them. They were waiting for the day when they could come back to college to resume their interrupted courses. Vaguely they considered these courses part of what they were trying to save.

But these men might have returned to study medicine or engineering or atomic physics. Some of them did, but enough of them came back to the arts to keep the courses more than alive. Furthermore they were continuing their education in the service.

A navigator in the South Pacific repeatedly mentioned his diaries, "four closely written books," in which he had described the people he had met, the places he had lived, the non-military things he had done. Parts of these diaries, I feel sure, came to me in his letters when he wrote of a "swimming hole in a clear, cold stream bordered by lush jungle," or of the "cockatoos, parakeets, and small monkeys that clutter up the trees," or of the banyan trees that "drip their branches everywhere." In every letter he mentioned the writing he intended to do after the war—an article about military blunders, a non-reportorial story of Guadalcanal, sketches of the men who had seen action. He felt the change in these men was a serious thing, for "one can't give a man a gun, tell him

[65]

to go out and kill, and afterwards turn him loose at home."
Whatever effect the war was having on this particular man, he
was determined to re-enter the University, "hit the English
course," and write.

In the letters of a pilot were frequent bits of verse, like this
one, which described the moon as the

> . . . beams dance along the fuselage of the plane
> In and out among the props and down the long, cold pieces of steel
> That move occasionally as the gunner changes his position.

Sometimes a young man enclosed a sonnet which expressed
his conversion from an isolationist stand of pre-Pearl Harbor
days, or another, who had discovered in his crew a man from
Asheville, North Carolina, wrote of the Thomas Wolfe characters his fellow crew member could identify. No amount of
bombing or strafing or machine-gunning would kill the interest of these men in literature. They all planned on returning to college to study after the war, and most of them have.

As I have said, many of the letters came from men who
were interested in writing, but I did get occasional letters
from students in fields other than English. Some of these led
me to believe that the war might strengthen the liberal arts
by showing that they have a practical (iconoclast!) as well as
a cultural value. From my own experience I know that although I had had four years of German before I spent a summer in Germany, not until after I had been there did I en-
roll in German classes with the intention of learning to speak
the language fluently as well as read it easily. That experience
must have been duplicated many times. A nurse in North
Africa wrote that she wished she had had time to study French

while she was taking her nursing course. Another student told of interviewing the commander of the submarine which brought General Giraud to North Africa, and he thanked his college French professors for that opportunity.

Even during the sparse years of '42, '43, and '44, the effect of the war on the liberal arts was evident. One group of students who felt that knowing a language well might help them to understand a people organized a class in Chinese. They studied it intensively with the hope that they might be able to help in the post-war reconstruction in China. One afternoon during these years, I found three students of Greek descent writing Greek sentences on the board before class. When I asked whether they spoke Greek at home, they said, "Oh, yes," and one of them added, "All the time. We want to study classical Greek to get a better understanding of the culture of Greece. Maybe we can help over there some day." This possibility of working in the countries of occupation had already stimulated an interest in the language among students who were thinking of the future. So it seemed to me that the very war which had turned many to the sciences might save the languages. It had in reality helped them even then in the program which was training officers for foreign diplomatic service. As a matter of fact, I can think of no logical reason for a war's weakening an interest in languages or in any other of the liberal arts. Both the men in the colleges and those in the services were aware of the need of a healthy reconstruction program. Surely no part of a university can do more toward a sane training for that period than a college of liberal arts.

The ideas I have been expressing, however, are all speculation from the past. The real proof of a theory that the arts will live lies in the present. Again I admit freely a lack of statistics. I admit, too, that courses in chemistry, physics, premedicine, and business administration are overcrowded. But so are courses in the colleges of liberal arts; they are overcrowded with students who want to be there, not with students who are there because they cannot get into a pre-professional school. Perhaps the story of a man who stopped in my office after his discharge will explain why ex-service men are registering in liberal arts courses. After talking enthusiastically of the work he had taken at the American University of Biarritz, he said, "I am going to take as much French and Russian as I possibly can." When I remarked that I remembered him as a pre-medical student, he said, "Oh, yes, I was, but I became so interested in languages while I was in Europe that I've given up the idea of medicine." Then he added very seriously, "Do you realize that most Europeans speak at least two languages?" I did and was glad he had found that out.

Further proof of the continued interest in the arts lies in the number of students who are entering the writing courses in the universities. These are the veterans who have seen many parts of the world and who want to share their experiences with others. Some of them really have something to say, though many of them will never be able to write professionally. Are they wasting their time? I think not. They will always have the satisfaction of being able to express themselves adequately, and in no profession or business is that ability a disadvantage. The engineer or accountant who reaches the top of his profession is the one who not only can do the job but who can explain clearly to someone else what he has done.

The effect on courses other than writing is no less evident.

History means far more now to a veteran student than it did in the past. England is no longer just "a tight little isle across the sea"; it is the place where American bombers were based, where American men danced with British girls, where American soldiers saw the scarred dome of St. Paul's Cathedral and the Houses of Parliament half in ruin. And these students know the continent, too. "All Gaul is divided into three parts." They may not know the names Caesar used, but they will recognize the rivers which formed the boundaries because they have crossed them under fire or have flown above them. History is no longer a study of the very distant past; it is a study of a recent experience with a distant perspective. Geography—the ex-pilot knows where Regensburg is, what the weather conditions are in the German mountains. Music— "Why even children in Italy sing snatches of operas. There must be something to them. I'm going to take a course in music appreciation," says the veteran. Art—"The Cathedral of Cologne? We weren't allowed to bomb it. I understood why after we occupied Germany." And so it continues. The liberal arts mean something to veterans now in the colleges and universities. These veterans are serious students; they will keep the liberal arts alive.

But after 1950 the veteran peak will have passed. What about the liberal arts courses then? I sometimes wonder if people in the liberal arts colleges are a little greedy. Never has the world tried to educate every one in the arts. I am sure that compiled statistics of all the colleges and universities in the world would show that a very small percentage of the people has sought culture in any given period. The colleges of liberal arts are centuries old; the business and professional

[69]

schools are comparatively young. They are still growing rapidly. The percentage of people in the cultural courses is as high, I suspect, as it ever has been. The business and professional schools are not crowding out the liberal arts; they are educating a different class of young people. The world needs all these educated people and, for the ditch-digging, a few who are not. The college of liberal arts can ask only for its share.

Here in part is what one soldier wrote about an article he had read concerning the creeping death of the liberal arts:

You need not worry about the liberal arts. We did not like what the Nazis did to music and art and books in Europe. If I remember correctly that is part of what we are fighting for—to keep our colleges, our books, our music, our art.

If even a few of the American youth of this generation feel that they fought to save these things, people in future generations will not change so much that the colleges of liberal arts will lose their just percentage of the population—not even in the distant future.

EMILY G. IRVINE
University of Pittsburgh

Philip Sauers

WISDOM IS A NUT; OR, THE IDOLS OF JONATHAN SWIFT

> Thus, like a captive in an isle confined,
> Man walks at large, a prisoner of the mind.

FEW men have endeared themselves more to succeeding generations than Jonathan Swift. Like Chaucer and like Shakespeare, Swift knew human nature; he studied it and felt himself a part of it. We all bow before his inimitable wit and his keen, analytic mind with admiration, somewhat overfilled with awe, yet at the same time we feel the attraction of the pathetic in him. Our feeling for him is somewhat the one he had for his friends. He is a great prose master, seldom equalled, a great satirist, perhaps never equalled; yet he had his little weaknesses, and he had his deep sorrows. He was disappointed in his ambitions, and he had to accept the surety of a lamentable and terrible end. All these things place him somehow in an intimate relationship that is not usually felt with great men. He has a bond with common humanity that we can all feel, for we can see that even in his harshest satires, he has a note (implied but surely there) of sympathy for the sad lot of man, whose hopes must lie at the mercy of an arbitrary fortune and whose fate it is to accept worthily the disappointment of his defeated endeavors. There is in Swift a sense of the *lachrymae rerum,* strongly felt, without sentimentality. Like Shakespeare and like Chaucer, he was a sympathetic spectator of the Triumph of Life.

But what Swift saw there did not raise bootless inquiries and never brought forth a smile. Swift and Chaucer (I leave Shakespeare to his own pre-eminence) were indeed very different. Chaucer deals with the concrete example before him; Swift deals with the abstraction of the concrete example before him. Chaucer is good natured and tolerant; Swift is not. The one tickles the world; the other vexes the world. But what does not appear at first sight, the two men are really fundamentally in agreement, for both intended that the world should be forced to look inward, and examine what it found there, and the two men were also fundamentally in agreement that what it found there would probably not be entirely to its liking. Chaucer implies slyly that the old proverb may have something in it, "that the Devil sometimes sleeps," and Swift between a layer of *Dulce* and a layer of *Utile* pushes home his theme that "mankind is the most pernicious race of little odious vermin that nature ever suffered to crawl upon the surface of the earth."

The agreement between Swift and Chaucer is, I think (and here I surprise myself by my own conclusion), probably greater than it is between Swift and our own age. A Swiftian might imagine what Swift would have to say about things that our world seems to accept without much thought. Look over the last ten years: we have seen hogs burned and farmers paid for not planting in order to prevent abundance; we have seen Stalin deliberately starve millions of people (3 to 11,000,000— the figures differ) in order to assert a political doctrine; we have seen the Nazis develop a science of starvation diets; we have seen the Czechs democratize their country by confiscating and driving out the Sudetan Germans; we have seen academic politicians make plans for maintaining an economically dependent Germany; we have seen victorious nations judging in a court, with 250 seats alloted to pressmen, their defeated enemies; and we have seen developed what has been called "an important advance in the science of Destruction," the atomic bomb, and what is more we have seen it used against the Japanese; the Sunday supplements have popularized artificial insemination. There is something Swiftian in all these things I have just mentioned. But we, and here is the great difference between Swift and us—that is, at least the vocal part of us—, we do not find these things odd.

Here is the point: deviations from the normal do not seem any longer to appear monstrous. Why? Because there is no norm. Ours is an age of relativity. We seem to accept without questioning that the end justifies the means. Swift saw similar things happening in his day; he saw the workings of government; he saw the carrying on of War; he saw the double-dealing of Allies. But he inquired into the hidden springs of man's actions and set side by side those things which men do and those things which they ought to do, and then he passed judgment. Without judgment there cannot be satire. Without a norm, there cannot be the monstrous. Swift's point of view towards mankind is not, therefore, our point of view. Swift judged man as a moral being; we judge him, as far as I can see, as a political being, as a social being, as an economic being, according to our individual point of view. Ours is not an age of satire, and even the few that we have, such as those of C. S. Lewis's or Aldous Huxley's, have fallen into the class of MacFlecknoe's, whose, as it will be remembered, are "inoffensive satires that never bite."

Swift's are very bitter. He places man in the scales and finds him wanting in the very quality that he prizes most in himself—his reason. He looks at him curiously from a detached point of view, and puts down objectively, as objectively as one could who has a bond of sympathy with his own kind, what he sees before him. His point of view is from "the vantage ground of Truth (a hill not to be commanded, and where the air is always clear and serene)," and he sees "the errors and wanderings, and mists and tempests, in the vale below," always, be it remembered, not as the angels in Heaven, whose supreme joy was the contemplation of the tortured souls in hell, but a mortal being "full of pity, and without swelling and pride." There he rests in a glory of effulgent wit that offers to the beholder a vision too bright for ordinary eyes. I myself have been dazzled, but I shall nevertheless attempt to approach that high ground and tell what I see. I expect to treat primarily Swift's second masterpiece, *Gulliver's Travels,* and to expatiate (to use one of his favorite words) on the Third Part, which is usually entitled "The Voyage to Laputa, etc."

Before I can begin with *Gulliver's Travels,* however, I must say a few words about the manner in which Swift's extraordinarily original mind worked. Swift's approach to his subject is always roundabout and deliberately puzzling. He enjoys inventing symbols for his ideas that are as clear-cut and detailed as any allegorical figure of the Middle Ages. These symbols he sometimes call hieroglyphs, or sometimes when they become extended allegory, fables, myths, or parables. He dares you to find out what they mean, for, as he put it, such vehicles of thought meet "the usual fate of coaches over-finely painted and gilt, that the transitory Gazers have so dazzled their eyes, and filled their imaginations with the outward lustre, as neither to regard or consider the person or the parts of the owner within."

Perhaps the easiest way to make clear what I mean is to take a passage from *A Tale of a Tub*. I take a typical one, the passage on the True Critics. It is, somewhat cut, as follows:

It well deserves considering, that these Ancient Writers in treating enigmatically upon the subject, having generally fixed upon the very same hieroglyph, varying only the story according to their affections or their wit. For first; Pausanias is of opinion that the perfection of writing correct was entirely owing to the Institution of Critics; and, that he can possibly mean no other than the True Critic is, I think, manifest enough from the following description. He says, "they were a race of men, who delighted to nibble at the superfluities, and excrescencies of books; which the learned at length, observing, took warning of their own accord, to lop the luxuriant, the rotten, the dead, the sapless, and the overgrown branches from their works." But now, all this he cunningly shades under the following allegory; "that the Nauplians in Argia, learned the art of pruning their vines, by observing, that when an ass had browsed upon one of them it thrived the better, and bore fairer fruit." But Herodotus holding the very same hieroglyph, speaks much plainer, and almost *in terminis*. He hath been so bold as to tax the True Critics, of ignorance and malice; telling us openly, for I think nothing can be plainer, that "in the Western part of Libya, there were asses with horns": upon which relation Ctesias yet refines, mentioning the very same animal in India, adding, "that whereas all other asses wanted a gall, these horned ones were so redundant in that part, that their flesh was not to be eaten because of its extreme bitterness."

Then Swift changes his hieroglyph and quotes:

[75]

so Diodorus [not really Diodorus, but perhaps Dicaearches] speaking to the same purpose, ventures no farther than to say, "that in the mountains of Helicon there grows a certain weed, which bears a flower of so damned a scent, as to poison those who offer to smell it."

And again from Ctesias, who speaks of strange animals in India:

"Amongst the rest there is a serpent that wants teeth, and consequently cannot bite, but if its vomit (to which it is much addicted) happens to fall upon any thing, a certain rottenness or corruption ensues. These serpents are generally found among the mountains where jewels grow, and they frequently emit a poisonous juice whereof, whoever drinks, that person's brains fly out of his nostrils."

All of these mean the True Critics. What Swift is saying is really this, that critics are envious, ill-natured, superficial, maliferous parasites. They have nothing to say themselves and therefore snuggle up to the fame of a great name. Woe to the man who listens to them.

When these symbols are put into action, or you have what Spenser calls a "continued allegory," you run into a kind of myth. This method is an adaptation of the renaissance mythologers, who saw in the ancient myths the teachings of wise men covering their abstractions in parable. Bacon's ingenious interpretations in *The Wisdom of the Ancients* must have delighted Swift.

In this passage I have just quoted Swift gives you the key to unlock the meaning. But such is not always his fashion; he often, with "the sort of smile that ariseth from pity to the ignorant," deliberately holds back the key in order to vex his reader the more. This is what he does in *Gulliver's Travels*, with the result that, if he were alive today, he would doubtless be most happy to see the True Critics at work "nibbling at the superfluities and excrescencies" of his work.

In *Gulliver's Travels* Swift is "treating enigmatically upon the subject" of human nature. He presents an analysis of man. The only statements he makes about it are two (both of them well known) written to his friend Pope in 1725 (September 29 and November 26). He says in one:

> The chief end I propose to myself in all my labors is to vex the world rather than to divert it; and if I could compass that design without hurting my own person or fortune, I would be the most indefatigable writer you have ever seen.

The other letter is more precise. Here is what he says:

> When you think of the world give it one lash the more at my request. I have ever hated all nations, professions, and communities, and all my love is towards individuals: for instance, I hate the tribe of lawyers, but I love Counsellor Such-a-one, and Judge Such-a-one. . . . But principally I hate and detest that animal called man, although I heartily love John, Peter, Thomas, and so forth. . . . I have got materials towards a treatise, proving the falsity of that definition *animal rationale,* and to show it would be only *rationis capax.* Upon this great foundation of misanthropy, though not in Timon's manner, the whole building of my Travels is erected; and I never will have peace of mind till all honest men are of my opinion.

Swift's purpose, then, grows out of the philosophical bias to rationalism in the eighteenth century. He grants that man is an animal, but he does not grant he is a rational animal. He proposes that he is an animal only capable of reason. Swift's point of view, therefore, leads him perforce into an analysis of those things that prevent man from using his reason. Here is the true theme of *Gulliver's Travels.*

These things that prevent man from using his reason I can find no better term for than *idols,* a term that everyone recognizes at once as coming from Francis Bacon. This is what Bacon says of *idols:*

> Idols are the deepest fallacies of the human mind. For they do not deceive in particulars, as the other [fallacies] do, by clouding and snaring the judgment, but by a corrupt and ill-ordered predisposition of mind, which, as it were, perverts and infects all the anticipations of the intellect. For the mind of man (dimmed and clouded as it is by the covering of the body), far from being a smooth, clear, and equal glass (wherein the beams of things reflect according to their true incidence) is rather like an enchanted glass, full of superstition and imposture. Now idols are imposed upon the mind, either by the nature of man in general, or by the individual nature of each man, or by words, or nature communicative.

Then Bacon elaborates on his four types of idols, which he calls the Idols of the Tribe, the Cave, the Market Place, and the Theatre.

Swift, since he is analyzing mankind in general, is interested almost exclusively in what Bacon calls the Idols of the Tribe.

The idea of a minute examination of man's thralldom to Idols, or false appearances, seems to have come to Swift at an early date, for here is a remarkable passage in *A Tale of a Tub,* which seems to point directly to it and even to indicate that he had established three general types of idols. This was written in 1696 or 1697.

> To this end [the general good of mankind], I have some time since, with a world of pains and art, dissected the carcass of Human Nature, and read many useful lectures upon the several parts, both containing and contained; till at last it smelt so strong, I could preserve it no longer. Upon which I have been at a great expense to fit up all the

bones with exact contexture, and in due symmetry; so that I am ready to show a very complete anatomy thereof to all curious gentlemen and others. But not to digress farther, in the midst of a digression . . . , I do affirm that having carefully cut up human nature, I have found a very strange, new, and important discovery; that the public good of mankind is performed in two ways, instruction and diversion. And I have further proved . . . that, as mankind is now disposed, he receives much greater advantage by being diverted than instructed; his epidemical diseases being fastidiosity, amorphy, and oscitation.

Note well the three epidemic diseases of mankind: fastidiosity, amorphy, and oscitation. They are the three main groups of idols, those things which predispose man to act contrary to reason. *Fastidiosity* means "thinking too well of one's self," or the Vice of Pride. *Amorphy* means "having no sense of form, order, harmony, proportion." *Oscitation* means "yawning," or as Swift undoubtedly intended it, "vacuity of mind." Of these three amorphy is the most general. It might, I should think, include the other two, but Swift apparently considered man's overweening pride and his thoughtless bestiality at opposite poles and therefore emphasizes them. Amorphy seems not to be connected so much with man's animal nature as the other two. I point this out now because it will be the most important when I come to analyze the Third Part of *Gulliver*.

In this passage from *A Tale of a Tub,* it seems to me, is the kernel of *Gulliver's Travels.* The later book is merely the anatomy presented in another form. The idea seems to have taken shape slowly if we are right in our dating of the various parts of *Gulliver's Travels.* The First Part, that of the Voyage to Lilliput, seems to have been thought of at the time of the

Scriblerus Club in 1714, though it was revised in 1721–1722. Swift, we know, was fascinated and shocked by the travel books of his day, most of which, written by sea captains in a plain matter-of-fact style, he considered "less consulted truth than [their author's] own vanity, or interest, or the diversion of ignorant readers." No doubt, as he read some of these improbable tales with his mind ever looking for myths and hieroglyphs, he hit upon his symbol of man overcome by the disease of fastidiosity. It was little man. The rest was easy for him.

The Second Part is a natural development of the First Part. In the Land of Brobdingnag the situation of the little man is reversed. Gulliver, instead of being amused at the swaggerings of the little beings around him, becomes the little being, who, with a full sense of the dignity of man, amuses the great ones by his pretentions. He tries to instruct the Brobdingnagians, who are admirable people, in the polite ways and advanced thought of European civilization. One of the finest examples of Swift's use of satiric irony in the whole book occurs when Gulliver explains the use of gunpowder and cannon, and offers to let the King in on the secret:

The King was struck with horror at the description I had given of those terrible engines, and the proposal I had made. He was amazed how so impotent and grovelling an insect as I (these were his expressions) could entertain such inhuman ideas, and in so familiar a manner as to appear wholly unmoved at all the scenes of blood and desolation which I had painted as the common effects of those destructive machines, whereof, he said, some evil genius, enemy to mankind, must have been the first contriver. As for himself, he protested that, although few things delighted him so much as new discoveries in art or in Nature, yet he would rather lose half his kingdom than be privy to such a secret, which he commanded me, as I valued my life, never to mention any more.

A strange effect of narrow principles and short views: that a prince possessed of every quality which procures veneration, love, and esteem; of strong parts, great wisdom, and profound learning, endued with admirable talents for government, and almost adored by his subjects, should, from a nice unnecessary scruple, whereof in Europe we can have no conception, let slip an opportunity put into his hands, that would have made him absolute master of the lives, the liberties, and the fortunes of his people. . . . I take this defect among them to have risen from their ignorance, by not having hitherto reduced politics into a science, as the more acute wits of Europe have done.

After such a passage as this the reader can have little satisfaction in the place he holds in the group, and he must retain his self-respect by refusing to accept responsibility as an individual. This is exactly what Swift was aiming at. It is a purge of fastidiosity.

The next part of *Gulliver's Travels* to be written seems to have been Part IV (1723), which deals with the Voyage to the land of the Houyhnhnms. In this Swift treats the disease of oscitation. Man without reason is pictured in the Yahoo, a detestable, filthy creature that resembles a man but acts like an animal without reason, and is set over against the animal with reason, the Houyhnhnm, which is a horse.[1] Gulliver stands in between; he is here the ordinary, normal person who is capable of reason, and, as a matter of fact, seems to have an almost Platonic longing to attain it; but, on account of his resemblance to the Yahoos, or, in other words, on account of his

---

[1] It is pleasant to imagine that the Houyhnhnm and the Yahoo derived from the centaur. Chiron, part human, part animal, represented wisdom. Swift separated the two parts and presents a paradox.

humanity itself, he is forced to forego the terrestrial paradise of the Houyhnhnms and make of his life the best he can among his own kind in England. Throughout this part the symbols are clear, and it is difficult to understand how often this part has been misinterpreted. The Yahoos do not, as the Victorian authorities asserted, stand for mankind, but only mankind giving himself up to his bestiality, mankind as he can sometimes be seen in history—in, for example, the Albigensian Crusade, or in the Sicilian Vespers, or in the Bloody Terror.

The part to be put together last is the one I wish to analyze more in detail, the Third Part, which deals with the Voyages to Laputa, Balnibarbi, Luggnagg, Glubbdubdrib, and Japan. It is indeed the most mystifying of all the travels, and perhaps for the reason that it has not been understood, it has sometimes been considered less interesting than the other parts. It has even been declared to be "of marked inferiority," and without any "unifying scheme." "Written in a mood of relaxation," it is "a catch-all for fragments not used in other places," where Swift threw together "a satire on the misuse of the intellect, satire on the desire for long life, and satirical allusions to the Anglo-Irish situation." Now all this is certainly nibbling on the superfluities and excrescencies. These voyages are as much a part of the whole anatomy as any of the other voyages.

Swift himself has given us a hint of their content. In Part I (Lilliput) and Part II (Brobdingnag), he treated *Fastidiosity;* in Part IV, *Oscitation*. There is left only one other disease of Human Nature, and that is *Amorphy*. Amorphy is the subject of these voyages.

The part is not a "catch-all for fragments not used in other places." It is a presentation of symptoms (not systematically) of Amorphy, or in other words, it is a list of idols, those things that predispose man to act in an unreasonable manner. The animal nature of man Swift treated in Parts I, II, and IV; here he treats almost entirely the mind. This Part, therefore, seems set apart from the others in its content. Its manner, too, is different, for Swift, while he at times goes in for extended allegory, works almost entirely through symbols. Man, Swift seems to be saying, can be led away from the paths of reason not only by his overweening estimation of himself, or by his fundamentally bestial nature, but by his mind itself. The exercise of the mind, the accumulation of learning,—yes, even greatness itself—none of these things, unless accompanied by wisdom, avail. This is what is implied but never said.

Let us look first at the Laputans. They live in a flying island, suspended in mid-air, like Mahomet's coffin, by a system of magnets. Here is Swift's description of them.

Their heads were all reclined either to the right or the left; one of their eyes turned inward, and the other directly up to the zenith. Their outward garments were adorned with the figures of sun, moons, and stars, interwoven with those of fiddles, flutes, harps, trumpets, guitars, harpsichords, and many other musical instruments of music, unknown to us in Europe. These strange creatures were attended by "flappers," or servants who touched their lips and ears with a blown bladder full of dried peas to remind them to pay attention to the affairs of life, for, it seems, the minds of these people are so taken up with intense speculations that they neither can speak, nor attend to the discourses of others, without being roused by some external taction upon the organs of speech and hearing.

Their favorite study was the mathematical, and their favorite avocation music. Even their food was cut into geometric shapes.

Here, obviously, is a hieroglyph. The flying island represents a removal from earth; its inhabitants are all up in the air. Their heads are inclined right or left; that is, these people deviate from the vertical, or the rational (the normal). Their eyes, one looking upward, show that they are interested only in themselves (introspection) and in useless speculation (unreality). Their clothes bear symbols and their food is cut into symbolic shapes that give the key to their nature—music. But this is not a satire on mathematics or on music, and the reader is kept dangling over a precipice until he comes to a concert that all the Laputans take part in, which, Gulliver said, "quite stunned [me] with the noise; neither could I possibly guess the meaning, till my tutor informed me. He said that the people of their island had their ears adapted to hear the music of the spheres, which always played at certain periods, and the court was now prepared to bear their part, in whatever instrument they most excelled." The music of the spheres is a time-honored symbol of the harmony of the universe. It is a favorite with Milton, who uses it to show that before the Fall of Man, man could take part in the universal harmony; since the Fall, only the Elect, through their greatest efforts, can ever hope to hear it. Swift seems to say that his people of Laputa intend to gain a place in the universal harmony through study, or, we might say, attain a throne in Heaven through the exercise of the intellect. This is not merely a satire on the "misuse of the intellect," nor is it a satire on the study of mathematics, or the study of music. It presents an idol, or a false appear-

ance that predisposes man to act in an unreasonable manner.
Swift aims directly at the process of ratiocination. Man tends,
he implies, to place too much faith in this activity of the
mind. If he is not careful, in attempting to find a place in the
harmony of the spheres, he will lose his place in the harmony
of his own world. And he will suffer from that disease known
as Amorphy. It is no wonder, Swift adds, that the women of
Laputa run away from their husbands. Why, even the wife of
the Prime Minister preferred to live in poverty with an old
deformed footman, who beat her every day, than return to
the inhuman society of the Flying Island.

From their superior knowledge and position, however, the
Laputans control a large territory. As far as their island can
cruise, all underneath is under their subjection. If a rebellion should arise, they can crush it immediately merely by letting the Island drop upon the troublous spot. Such extreme
action, however, they do not like to take, because most of the
courtiers have property on the islands below and because they
fear that unless they hit just right, they might break the
adamantine bottom of their island. Their usual practice is
merely "to descend with great gentleness, out of pretence of
tenderness to the people," and hover above threateningly.
Here the satire becomes political, and I think it needs no
comment from me.

Gulliver, having become "heartily weary of those people,"
asked leave, and attained it, to depart from the island. He
went accompanied by a friend of his, a "great lord who was
universally reckoned the most ignorant and stupid person
among them," because he had such an "ill ear for music." In
Logado, the capitol of Balnibari, a country ruled by the Fly-

ing Island, he was at first glad to be once more on firm ground, but he soon found that all things were not right there either. There was no grain or grass, though the soil appeared good; the houses were in a general state of unrepair; the people's faces expressed "misery and want." He soon discovered the reason for all this: "about forty years ago, certain persons went up to Laputa, and after five months' continuance, came back with a very little smattering in mathematics, but full of volatile spirits, acquired in that airy region. . . . These persons, upon their return, began to dislike the management of everything below, and fell into schemes of putting all arts, sciences, languages, and mechanics upon a new foot." And so there came about the Academy of Projectors. Projects, as they were called in Swift's day, were schemes of all sorts for the making of money or for the bettering of mankind. Those who are curious should look into Defoe's *Essay on Projects*.

Gulliver visits the Academy of Projectors and reports what he sees there. One man is trying to extract sunbeams out of cucumbers to be let out in the air in bad summers; another, to calcine ice into gunpowder; another, an architect, "to contrive a new method for building houses, by beginning at the roof"; another, a blind man, to mix colors for painters. A very ingenious projector had invented a way of plowing ground with hogs. "The method is this: in an acre of ground you bury, at six inches distance, and eight deep, a quantity of acorns, dates, chestnuts, and other mast, or vegetables, whereof these animals are fondest: then you drive six hundred, or more of them, into the field, where, in few days they will root up the whole ground in search of their food, and make it fit for sowing." Another professor has developed a writing machine.

All you need to do is to turn a crank and a word is formed without the labor of having to think. And others work on language in an attempt to do away with language entirely. The School of Political Projectors was particularly mad to Gulliver. In it he saw "unhappy people proposing schemes for persuading monarchs to choose favorites upon the score of their wisdom, capacity, and virtue; of teaching ministers to consult the public good; of rewarding merit, great abilities, and eminent services; of instructing princes to know their true interest, by placing it on the same foundation with that of their people; of choosing for employment persons qualified to exercise them; with many other wild impossible chimaeras, that never entered before into the heart of man to conceive; and confirmed in me the old observation, that there is nothing so extravagant and irrational which some philosophers have not maintained for truth."

All this is not disconnected. It all points in one way. Here, in a "continued allegory," is presented another idol, another of those false appearances that predispose the mind to unreasonable action. Swift seems to be aiming at the power of novelty. Man tends, he implies, to consider anything new, even though it may go contrary to experience, better than what already is. As we might put it today—and we always give it a favorable turn—"It is an interesting experiment."

The third island that Gulliver visits in this voyage is that with the resounding name of Glubbdubdrib, an island of sorcerers or magicians. The Governor of this land (so called, by the way, from the practice of nonsensical magic formulas) has the power of calling up spectres from the dead, whom he uses as servants to wait upon him. Gulliver is at first very much

frightened to see them about him, but as he becomes used to
them he asks the Governor to satisfy his curiosity of the past.
The Governor grants his request and evokes for him the great
men of history. First a group of great conquerors appear:
Alexander the Great, Julius Caesar, Hannibal, Pompey. Upon
questioning, Alexander informs Gulliver that he died, not of
poisoning, but of excessive drinking; Hannibal confides that,
when he crossed the Alps, he had not a drop of vinegar in his
camp; and Caesar confesses that "the greatest actions of his
own life were not equal by many degrees, to the glory of taking it away." None of this group, obviously, does Swift approve of. Theirs is a false greatness. A second group is more
to his liking. This group consists of Brutus, his ancestor Ju-
nius, Socrates, Epaminondas, Cato the Younger, and Sir
Thomas More—each of them, it will be noted, a man who
put the cause of Truth or Liberty before his own life, each
of them,

> The only son of light
> In a dark age, against example good,
> Against allurement, custom, and a world
> Offended,

and each met with the condemnation of his times and each
ended miserably.

The great rulers of modern history pass also in review.
With them Gulliver is particularly disgusted. He gives his
final conclusion thus:

. . . Having strictly examined all the persons of greatest name in
the courts of princes for an hundred years past, I found how the world
has been misled by prostitute writers, to ascribe the greatest exploits

[88]

in wars to cowards, the wisest counsel to fools, sincerity to flatterers, Roman virtue to betrayers of their country, piety to atheists, truth to informers: how many innocent and excellent persons had been condemned to death or banishment by the practising of great ministers upon the corruption of judges and the malice of factions: how many villains had been exalted to the highest places of trust, power, dignity, and profit: how great a share in the motions and events of courts, councils, and senates might be challenged by parasites and buffoons. How low an opinion I had of human wisdom and integrity, when I was truly informed of the springs and motives of great enterprises and revolutions in the world, and of the contemptible accidents to which they owed their success.

Swift's meaning, it seems to me, is here recognizable beyond much question of doubt. He is pointing out another idol, or false appearance: it is one form of tradition. History, he says, records with honor the wrong men, those who attained worldly power at the expense of Justice, Liberty, and Truth, and the memory of their example still leads man to give worth where it should not be. The essence of the true heroic lies in moral greatness. The historians, a group of "prostitute writers" on the whole, preserve these traditions to the bane of mankind. That there was little difference between a Prime Minister and a pickpocket was a favorite idea of Swift's. It was at Swift's suggestion that John Gay wrote the *Beggar's Opera,* and it was to amplify this idea of False Greatness that Fielding wrote *Jonathan Wyld.* Swift lays the blame for Fame's vagaries on the perverted nature of man, not as Chaucer does, in accordance with a comfortable doctrine, on the arbitrary nature of the Goddess Fame herself. That Swift enjoyed passing ethical judgments on historic characters may be seen in notes he has left which contain lists of worthy and despicable actions.

The fourth land to which Gulliver goes in this voyage is the land of Traldragdubb, or Trildrogdrib, "for it is pronounced both ways." Only one important episode is related. Gulliver requests "The honor to lick the dust before the footstool of the King" and finds that though he is using a "court style, it was more than a matter of form." He had to do it literally. But he came out pretty well, for that since he was a newcomer, the floor had been pretty well swept. Some persons, he heard, had met with a floor purposely dirty, and had come up "with their mouths so crammed they could not speak a word," and some, whom the king wanted to get rid of, had had a poison scattered about that killed them in a day.

In this fable, Swift, with a sidelong jeer at the extravagance of the Oriental style of flattery then in vogue, seems to be expounding another idol that is closely related to the one preceding. It is the stultifying power of established authority and the hocus pocus with which authority invests itself. Man, unreasonable man, takes pleasure in the debasing ceremonies of solemn, and hollow greatness.

The fifth and last adventure of Gulliver on this voyage takes place in the Island of Luggnagg, the land of the Struldbrugs, or immortals. And so this Part of the *Travels* ends as it began with a hieroglyph. The symbol that Swift here presents is one of the most striking in all his works. It is indeed unforgettable. Even the most casual reader will find it haunting his imagination years after the rest of the book has passed into an oblivious mist. The Struldbrugs are people, who, by an accident of birth, are fated not to die. As children, they have a "red circular spot in the forehead, directly over the left eyebrow," the mark of its immortality. "This spot," Gulliver is informed, "was about the compass of a silver three-pence, but in course of time grew larger, and changed its color; for at twelve years old it became green, so continued till five and twenty, then turned to a deep blue; at five and forty it grew coal black, and as large as an English shilling."

The thought of immortality sends Gulliver into a rapture. "Happy Nation," he cries out, "where every child hath at least a chance of being immortal! Happy people who enjoy so many living examples of ancient virtue, and have masters ready to instruct them in the wisdom of former ages!" And then he formulates a way of life that he would lead if he were a Struldbrug: he would spend perhaps the first 200 years becoming wealthy, then he would learn all the arts and sciences; he would record all the actions of consequence taking place in the world and mark down his observations upon them; he would entertain himself in forming and directing the minds of hopeful young men, by convincing them from his own remembrance, experience, and observation, fortified by numerous examples, of the usefulness of virtue in public and private life; he would, in short, work ever for the good of mankind, "opposing the corruption that steals into the world," and bring about by a steady progress a final state of perfection.

His listeners hear him in amazement, and finally feel they must set him right on the mistakes that he has fallen into "through the common imbecility of human nature." They tell him the Struldbrugs are quite different from the beings he has imagined. First of all, he has foolishly supposed that these immortal beings enjoyed a "perpetuity of youth, health, and vigour." As a matter of fact they were subject, like everyone else, to the laws of nature, and were "compelled to pass a perpetual life under all the disadvantages which old age brings along with it." Then they gave him a precise account of the truth. The Struldbrugs "commonly acted like mortals, till about thirty years old. After which, by degrees, they grew melancholy and dejected, increasing in both till they came to be fourscore." At this age they were full of "follies and infirmities" that were made all the worse because of their "dreadful prospects of never dying." "Envy and impotent desires are their prevailing passions." And they live on and on, their bodies becoming feebler, their minds becoming weaker, and their evil passions becoming stronger, until they become, horrible to behold, public charges, hated and despised.

Here is Swift's *memento mori,* a symbol of universal meaning and awful force. There is a folk quality about it, and the mind surrounds it with memories of futility and satiety:—the myth of Tithonus, who was given immortality but not perpetual youth, the fountain of life, whose waters gave immortality but were in some way always fouled, the Apples of Sodom, which turned to ashes in the mouth, the bargain of Dr. Faustus, who gained riches and wisdom, but also death, the dice play between Death and Life-in-Death in the *Ancient Mariner,* the fable of the Wandering Jew.

We can see now the symbolism of some of the details: the spot above the left eye—red in childhood, green in youth, blue in early manhood, and black in middle age, always, be it remembered, increasing in size. The brightness and innocence of childhood gives way slowly to the melancholy and evil of the world (green, blue, and black are all words commonly ap-

plied to melancholy). Swift is on the same track as Wordsworth, "The world is too much with us," but he has no mystic
corrective to offer. The opposition of youth and age is implied
throughout. The horror of youth at age and the envy of age
at youth. They are mutually repulsive. But yet, in spite of all
this, man has set as his highest desire the possession of immortality. Man, unreasonable man, never learns; he is perpetually
showing, as Johnson said a second marriage did, the triumph
of Hope over Experience. And he cannot help it. The idol
to which I should relate this hieroglyph is instinct.

This hieroglyph Swift means also to be applied to his own
age. He shows the target he is aiming at in those speeches of
Gulliver, which I have already quoted: "Happy nation where
every child has a chance of being immortal! Happy people
who enjoy so many living examples of ancient virtue, and
have masters ready to instruct them in the wisdom of former
ages!" Also in his choice of life. In these speeches he satirizes
the optimism and the faith in progress that characterized his
time. The sad truth, he says, or seems to say, is that age does
not bring wisdom, nor does youth have a desire to learn from
age. Generation after generation goes through the experience
of life; each thinks itself superior to the preceding; new age
follows new age. Man acts, powerless before his idols, but acts
on the whole unreasonably. The Struldbrugs do not, as Gulliver thought they might, have wisdom. Instead, there is a time-
lessness about wisdom, and because the world is older than it
was does not mean that it has more of it.

His own age, which looked upon itself complacently as considerably in advance of former ages, he considered Struld-

brugish, to have fallen into the sear and yellow leaf, and he had no patience with those, including his favorite butt, Bentley, who thought that *they* were the Ancients and that those Ancients of classical times were what we might now call primitives. Wisdom is not the possession of age; it is the possession of reason; and can belong to any age.

Wisdom is the theme of all Swift's works. Injustice, Hypocrisy, Cant, the externals of things—all these he never made peace with. It was a passion with him to speak from his vantage ground of Truth. It was a passion with him to point out the weaknesses of man, to enumerate the idols that kept him under subjection. But he cannot, or will not, give a definition to Wisdom. Wisdom, to him, seems to be the true judgment of the essence, and not the surfaces, of things, which calls for not only man's reason but man's whole moral nature, for it comes in the end to the separation of the good from the evil. *Gulliver's Travels* is his great anatomy of mankind. When man can cease to bow before his idols, can learn that even those things he accepts most for granted—intellect, the fascination of innovation, the example of the past, respect for false authority, and the instinct to control the forces of nature, with a full understanding too, be it remembered, of his own overweening pride and of his unavoidable bestiality, then perhaps he will not suffer from his three epidemic diseases—fastidiosity, emorphy, oscitation,—then perhaps he will have wisdom.

Wisdom, therefore, is hard to come by. As Swift puts it:

Wisdom is a fox, who after long hunting, will at last cost you the pains to dig it out; 'tis a cheese, which by how much the richer, has the thicker, the homelier, and the coarser coat; and whereof to a judicious palate, the maggots are the best. 'Tis a sack-posset, wherein the deeper you go, you will find it the sweeter. Wisdom is a hen, whose cackling we must value and consider, because it is attended with an egg; but then, lastly, 'tis a nut, which unless you choose with judgment, it may cost you a tooth, and pay you with nothing but a worm.

PHILIP SAUERS
University of Oregon

J. Welfred Holmes

STANDPOINT OF A REPUBLICAN RADICAL

. . . occupying, as I have, the standpoint of a republican radical, desirous that all men, of all creeds, should enjoy the civil liberty which I prized so highly for myself.—From "Letter on Italian Unity," Whittier's Collected Works.

FULLY aware throughout a long life of his limited abilities as a poet, Whittier always displayed quiet pride in his achievements as a man. To Whittier, the ideal human being was the man vitally concerned in helping others get civil and religious liberty and in guaranteeing for all people freedom from oppression and exploitation. This rather quaint conception of human conduct was the man's deepest conviction. It was the basis for his humanitarianism, the ideal for his course of action. Such critical opinion that disregards what Whittier the man accomplished presents an interpretation of him that needs to be examined carefully.

The section "John G. Whittier, Puritan Quaker" in Parrington's *The Romantic Revolution in America,* though primarily concerned with Whittier the poet, contains generalizations and arrives at conclusions that this writer feels are untenable. Similarly, Albert Mordell's stimulating and controversial biography, *Quaker Militant: John Greenleaf Whittier,* contains a chapter "The Reactionary" that, upon the evidence presented, seems entirely unjustified. Parrington, and especially Mordell, harshly berate Whittier for a supposedly in-

[96]

different, even reactionary, attitude in later life toward labor and social problems. Parrington bluntly states that Whittier never understood even in his more vigorous days the multiple economic forces at work in nineteenth-century American society that made clashes between economic and social groups inevitable and wholly disastrous for the weaker ones. Mordell's charge is more serious. He asserts and attempts to prove that Whittier, like Wordsworth, deserts his early liberal principles and in his later years becomes a reactionary. Both writers, beginning with somewhat different premises, arrive at the same conclusion: Whittier's attitude toward labor and the swiftly changing social pattern of his day must be severely condemned.

In so condemning him neither writer has given full credit for Whittier's contributions to the cause of labor. Unless they were unaware of the existence, both have ignored, and in some instances even suppressed, certain of Whittier's prose writings the better to support their contentions and render their sweeping judgments. Parrington refers casually to Whittier's early prose writings, but nowhere mentions specifically any early Whittier articles on labor. A number of these articles appeared in newspapers, not readily accessible but available, between 1829 and 1836. Whittier's later stand on labor, unchanged from his earlier position and even more detailed, is found in the statements of several biographers, in editorial contributions to various newspapers, and in numerous letters. Though Mordell gives a somewhat detailed account of Whittier's youthful editorship of one newspaper, the *American Manufacturer,* he fails to mention either a series of five articles or the editorials in this same paper that give in detail Whittier's liberal views on labor and industry. In making grave charges, the serious biographer examines his subject's writings and actions with great care and thoroughness, documenting fully his damaging assertions. In a number of instances Mordell has not followed this elementary procedure. The very nature of Parrington's tremendous survey makes some generalities inevitable. But generalizing with complete assurance and finality upon incomplete or questionable evidence is scarcely the sign of the discriminating critic.

Mordell's procedure in arriving at Whittier's supposed defection is best illustrated through his curious omissions in summarizing a phase of Whittier's editorial career and his suppression of facts in stating Whittier's part in a strike.

While editor of the *Middlesex Standard* published at Lowell, Massachusetts, Whittier wrote for the paper a series of eighteen articles called "The Stranger in Lowell." In 1845 these articles were published under the same title in book form. Mordell mentions this book and some of the pieces it contains, but he neglects to mention one, "The Lighting Up." This piece is important in any discussion of Whittier and labor, for it shows specifically the man's reaction to the fourteen-hour work day, then standard practice in Massachusetts mills and factories. Mordell's neglect of this piece is strange because he censures Whittier for remaining silent about the long work day at Lowell and at the mills in his home town of Amesbury. Even stranger is his neglect when one realizes that the biographer refers several times to the original series in the *Middlesex Standard* where "The Lighting Up" was No. 11, to the book *The Stranger in Lowell* in which it appeared, and even to a second book of prose, *Literary Recollections and Miscel-*

lanies, published in 1854, that also contained this piece. True enough, only one file of the *Middlesex Standard* has been preserved and these two little books are quite rare now; but their availability is unimportant, for "The Lighting Up" is in all six issues of Whittier's collected writings printed from the plates of the Riverside Edition of his works. These six editions were published at various times between 1888 and 1910. Nor was a persual of "The Lighting Up" the only means of learning Whittier's stand on labor.

Enamored by his thesis that in later life Whittier turned reactionary, Mordell flays the temporizing attitude Whittier supposedly took in connection with the Amesbury-Salisbury strike of 1852. The complete story of the affair has been ably told in Mr. T. Franklin Currier's article, "Whittier and the Amesbury-Salisbury Strike," that appeared in *The New England Quarterly* after Mordell's biography was published. Still, some facts about Whittier's part in the strike were available when Mordell was at work on his biography, enough to show that his account is questionable. First of all Whittier is accused of saying nothing about the long work day, the low wages, or the general treatment of the workers. In his account of conditions that precipitated the trouble and of the strike itself, Mordell accomplishes two things: he successfully minimizes Whittier's part and suppresses facts that show Whittier's efforts to secure a shorter working day. His charge of reaction is thereby effectively substantiated.

Since Currier's article giving Whittier's full participation in the strike appeared two years after *Quaker Militant,* what sources of information were available to the biographer? At least two: Thomas Wentworth Higginson's *John Greenleaf*

Whittier and George E. McNeill's *The Labor Movement: The Problem of Today* (1887). Higginson was closely associated with Whittier in the antislavery effort and in labor reform; the author of the second volume was an Amesbury man and should reasonably be expected to know the facts about a local happening. In general outline Mordell's account is somewhat similar to the one given by Higginson, but certain pertinent facts that Higginson gives Mordell omits. These omissions too conveniently compromise Whittier. Such an omission is a letter from Whittier Higginson quotes; it is about the former's efforts in behalf of a proposed law to limit the working day for mill and factory laborers to ten hours. Higginson, taking pains to verify the date of the letter—it was sent undated—places it in 1848. If this date is correct, here is proof that some years before the strike in 1852 Whittier was interested in the passing of a ten-hour law. And there is the article, "The Lighting Up," showing his concern about the long hours of mill workers as early as 1844.

More pertinent to this discussion than the date is the letter's substance. The very thing the later biographer, Mordell, refuses to credit Whittier with doing is plainly stated in his brief letter to Higginson: he and others in Amesbury are agitating for a ten-hour law, the passage of such a law must be a part of the fall elections, and there is hope of final passage through the legislature. As Higginson's little book on Whittier is listed in the bibliography of *Quaker Militant,* the author must be held accountable for ignoring this letter as well as for overlooking the significance of Higginson's comment immediately preceding it. Here Higginson has given his considered opinion that interest in bettering conditions for the working class was a part of Whittier's religious and spiritual inheritance. Higginson testifies that he had aided Whittier in such efforts and is at pains to specify that several times in letters to him Whittier had referred to a ten-hour bill and expressed his happiness in helping bring such a bill before the Massachusetts legislature. Higginson troubles himself to confirm his statement of Whittier's position in the Amesbury-Salisbury strike by quoting a letter from an Amesbury resident, G. W. Cate, who knew definitely of the part Whittier played. Higginson's assertion that Whittier was in full sympathy with the strikers is corroborated by Judge Cate's letter. Mordell's version condemns Whittier by implication and direct statement until the final sentence, which at best is a grudging admission that Whittier sympathized with the workers and wrote a poem in their behalf. Nevertheless, the full account by Mordell places Whittier in a totally false light.

That this is true is seen only too well in Mordell's summary of the causes of the strike. First, he gives the impression the workers went on strike because of dissatisfaction with the fourteen-hour work day. Next, he says the workers struck because the new mill manager withdrew the male worker's long-standing privilege to stop work for a few minutes in the morning for lunch. The facts brought out in the Currier article and the McNeill account show that *before* the strike occurred a number of men *had been discharged*. These men had been discharged because they had ignored the order of the new manager, Derby by name, that the fifteen-minute intermission at ten o'clock had been abolished. In defiance of the new order many of the men left the mill at ten o'clock anyway— some, as local tradition has it, to drink beer. Upon their return, "agent" Derby immediately discharged them. *Because* they were summarily discharged, the other workers protested by staging what is called nowadays a sympathy strike. Even the "female operatives" of the mill joined the sympathy strike. The entire village of Amesbury became involved, for a large number of the inhabitants depended upon the mills as a source of livelihood. Mass meetings were held; resolutions explaining the workers' position and the community's vital concern were drawn up. The Currier article shows conclusively that Whittier wrote the resolutions almost in their entirety and was a leading member of the several citizens' committees that were organized. Perhaps the only part of the entire affair with which Whittier was not directly connected was the "social levee" given by the "female operatives," at which some thirteen toasts were offered. If these were genuine toasts, Whittier's absence—he was prominent in the temperance movement during this time—is understandable. Now Mordell could not have known all of this, but the facts he should have had—those related by Higginson and McNeill—are distorted so that Whittier's part dwindles to insignificance.

In commenting upon working conditions in the Lowell mills, Mordell admits that Whittier did not approve of the long working hours. But the biographer's colorless phrase contrasts significantly with Whittier's actual words. In the article neglected by Mordell, Whittier, speaking about the fourteen-hour work day in Lowell, had said: "This is a serious evil, demanding the earnest consideration of the humane and philanthropic." This, and even stronger statements, were made in a mill town, entirely dominated by the manufacturing interests, where the writer was literally a stranger. If Whittier said this about the Lowell girls' (and men's) long day, is it not conceivable that he would be equally concerned about the identical long day of the mill workers in his home town? From the letters in Higginson's biography and from the account given by McNeill one knows, as Mordell should have known, that Whittier was actually doing something about this "serious evil."

Such distortions make one wonder if Mordell's account of Whittier's "reactionary" attitude in the Chicago anarchist trials can be wholly accepted. With very little documentation Mordell states that William Dean Howells had asked Whittier to write Governor Atgeld urging clemency for the condemned men. Mordell's verdict is that Whittier peremptorily refused to write, but nowhere does he state how he arrives at this categorical assumption. Nor does the biographer mention that Howells had approached another man about the clemency plea, George William Curtis, who, like Whittier, had suggested that Howells write the letter himself. Brand Whitlock's letter, reproduced in *Life in Letters of William Dean Howells,* gives a rather different version of Howells's actual approach to Whittier than Mordell's; it refers, also, to something else that Mordell might have considered: Whittier's age. He was eighty years old at the time of the anarchist trials.

Though avoiding Mordell's direct charge of reaction, Parrington's complete disparagement of Whittier's grasp of contemporary social and economic patterns becomes unconvincing when all the evidence is weighed. Immediately after commenting upon the numerous excellent poems of Whittier's later years, Parrington sums up patronizingly enough that it was well indeed that Whittier could turn to the past for po-

etic themes as he had never understood the new age of exploitation characterized by manufacturing towns like Lowell
and Lawrence. The critic emphasizes his theme by asserting
that the poet understood black slavery, but not wage slavery,
and by nature was totally unequipped to understand the ruth-
less industrial exploitation of his day. The critic dismisses
Songs of Labor as pathetic, and as for the Friend with his reliance on the Inner Light, there is little place for him in such
a world as this.

From such comment it is obvious that Parrington pays as
little attention as Mordell to Whittier's collected prose and
none at all to the uncollected material. It is unfortunate for
the critic that he overlooked Whittier's letters and ignored
his acts. To the very end of life Whittier, among other similar
acts, gave money to several of the newly developed schools for
the freedmen. He defended one by denouncing the action of
a state legislature in an open letter written at eighty-one. His
keen interest in world affairs in later life is shown by his enthusiastic "Letter on Italian Unity" (1871) and his letter of
sympathy for the Cuban masses (1873). His lifelong interest in
the fate of the Indian is attested by several references in letters written when he was past eighty. "Rum-selling ruffians"
is the un-Quakerlike phrase he uses to describe rascals who
interrupted the work of the Friends' mission in Alaska. He
was eighty-four at the time. Since the critic asserts how well
it was Whittier turned to the past, it is just as well that apparently he knew nothing of Whittier's part in the Amesbury-
Salisbury strike, of articles like "The Lighting Up" and "The
Factory Girls," or the efforts for shorter working hours. It is
not well in so asserting that he overlooked an editorial of

Whittier's youth denouncing a judge for sentencing journey-men tailors who joined in an effort to raise their wages. It seems apparent that Parrington has overlooked letters like "Hours of Labor," written in 1871, commenting upon the recent action of the Massachusetts legislature in regulating working hours.

However poorly prepared Whittier may have been to understand the new industrialism, he seems to have understood well enough, for instance, that our war with Mexico was essentially an imperialistic venture. A casual reading of "Dancing and Sabbath Breaking," "The Guerilla," and "Piety and Justice," editorials which appeared in May and June exactly a century ago in *The National Era,* will show how well he comprehended. Let the reader note that these editorials come just two years after *Songs of Labor,* peremptorily dismissed by the critic. Perhaps Whittier's ideas about economics were pathetically outmoded, as Parrington charges, yet some of his editorials show that he had at least heard of a new and disturbing political theory: communism. Since Parrington and Mordell assert repeatedly Whittier's ignorance of nineteenth-century American capitalism, both might at least have acknowledged that he was aware of the elementary principles of communistic theory—and once actually defended some communistic principles and practices against the denunciations of a coreligionist. Mordell, in fact, quotes a part of the editorial, "Labor—The French Revolution," published in *The National Era* for April 27, 1848, that best shows Whittier's grasp of communistic principles—and an equally thorough comprehension of some fallacies in democratic theory and practice. But Mordell quotes an excerpt merely to help prove his thesis, contenting himself in pointing out here that Whittier, at one time a radical, had dared to attack the democratic form of government. The biographer ignores the true import of the editorial: the defense of some communistic principles and their application to daily affairs. He refuses, like Parrington, to state how well this piece shows Whittier's complete understanding of men's motives and actions in time of economic stress and change.

Not only have both men neglected the writings that give a complete portrait of Whittier the man, but each critic in his own way has condemned his subject without first fully examining his basic beliefs and ideas. Parrington comes closer to a thorough examination than Mordell, but neither gives full consideration to what Whittier felt and believed. Call it primitive Christianity, Quaker Inner Light, or simply a naive faith in the brotherhood of all men; this was the basis of the man's beliefs, reiterated at times with a wearying monotony. He inveighed against class differences in his youth just as he fought slavery in his prime and all forms of oppression and injustice continuously. Not with mere words, but with acts. Because of this very belief in the brotherhood of man he denied the Marxian theory of the class struggle, opposed strikes in principle, and enthusiastically praised the newly organized co-operatives of the working classes. A juster approach to any criticism of his attitude on labor would include a sound examination of his principles and an evaluation of his total effort in terms of these principles. Neither critic takes into account another first principle that Harry Haydn Clark has pointed out: Whittier's belief that conflicts between social groups are to be solved best by self-reform.

Why have Parrington and Mordell made so many contradictory statements and expressed such confusing generalities
about the Quaker poet? For one thing, Parrington, preoccu-
pied with the entire range of American thought, has adjudged
Whittier solely on the basis of his collected verse. The letters
to correspondents and to the press, the generous amount of
collected prose, and the mass of uncollected prose have been
ignored. Relying too much upon the earlier biographers—
even the "official" biographer, Pickard, by no means tells all—
Parrington has presented an outline of the man that but su-
perficially adheres to the facts. Mordell, who has probably investigated Whittier's uncollected writings and original sources
more thoroughly than any previous biographer, commits two
serious mistakes in his appraisal. His portrait lacks adequate
"emotional engagement" with his subject, and even worse, a
main portion of his treatment is the attempt to prove a thesis:
that Whittier's later life is a parallel to the later reactionary
attitude of Wordsworth. What both men failed to perceive is
the close emotional and intellectual relationship between
Whittier's prose and verse. Forty years ago Bliss Perry, in his
centenary article "Whittier for Today," pointed out that
Whittier's anti-slavery rhymes were often but a verse arrangement of the substance of an anti-slavery orator's impassioned
speech or an abolitionist editor's fulmination. This observation can be applied with even greater force to the similarity
between Whittier's verse and his own frequently emotional
prose. Any attempt to judge Whittier solely on the basis of
his verse is certain to present a mutilated portrait, a grotesque
that can only show the man in a distorted pose.

Whittier's prose writings contain the same basic ideas found

in his verse. His faith in the fundamental Christian virtues
was unwavering. This faith, reinforced by his ultra-liberal
interpretation of the Quaker doctrines, was transformed into
social action, into practical Christianity. This concern for society, based upon Christian ethics and inherent in Quaker-
dom's humane and democratic tenets, permeates equally the
verse and the prose. What is especially important here, the
prose often gives a clearer and more explicit picture than the
verse of the man's profound humanitarianism. Hence, those
critics who would dismiss Whittier's economic and social
thought as beneath contempt should examine his prose more
carefully. The writings on labor show that he thought much
more clearly and more liberally on the social problems of his
day than he is usually credited with doing. The prose fur-
nishes clues to his activities in various labor reforms and presents a more genuinely liberal attitude toward social thought
than his verse would indicate. For example, his verse dealing
with Indian life and character leans strongly to the romantic
and the sentimental; it is concerned almost exclusively with
the "Noble Savage." Though it is true that traces of this romantic approach to the Indian are in the prose, the articles in
the twenties and thirties and the letters in the eighties and
nineties portray in the main clear, hard-headed estimates of a
government policy that was indifferent and often vicious in
dealing with its uncivilized wards. The sane, concrete pro-
posals these articles and letters offer for helping the surviving
Indian tribes to become properly integrated into American
life and culture have been neglected by Parrington and Mordell—and others. Sufficient examples can be adduced to show
that in the prose one finds the complete development and ex-

position of the few ideas upon which Whittier's poetic reputation chiefly rests.

It is only when the forgotten prose is examined that the true outlines of Whittier's full stature begin to emerge. Then he appears as no fanatical reformer obsessed by the righting of one single wrong, or as a mere sweet singer of a faded rural New England. The forgotten prose actually reveals the man as the "republican radical" he once characterized himself as being. The prose writings recount in detail his deep interest and his personal efforts to insure civil liberty for all men, to alleviate human suffering "at home and abroad," and to stamp out injustice and oppression everywhere. Without doubt these are also the themes of much of his verse. But the prose amplifies and develops them to reveal the poet, far more than is usually imagined, as the man of action in the cause of all humanity. Even though the bulk of the prose is so closely bound to dead issues and events as to be largely "worthless," the labor of searching through it is amply rewarded. Here and there a phrase or a sentence focuses for an instant on a rare spirit, one which tempered the moral rectitude of the Puritan with the compassion of the Quaker and, hating only the wrong which men in their greed and blindness did to other men, had complete charity for the wrongdoer.

J. Welfred Holmes
Morgan State College

Theressa Wilson Brown

FROUDE'S *LIFE OF THOMAS CARLYLE*

THE revived interest in the writings of Carlyle justifies a brief comment on Froude's biography of the Sage of Chelsea. Written at the expressed wish of Carlyle, the volumes belong to that well-known nineteenth century biographical category known as the "official life." Any similarity to Victorian life-writing ends here, for Froude's work has nothing in common with the traditional Victorian "life."

The convincing reality of Froude's portrait is partly the result of the writer's intimate association with the subject. For many years Froude was a frequent visitor at 5 Cheyne Row. Writing of the closeness of their association he said, "For twenty years, up to his own death, except when either or both were out of town, I never ceased to see him two or three times a week and to have two or three hours conversation with him." When Carlyle realized, therefore, that despite his desire his life would be written, he attempted to guard against its being a "ghost of a biography, white stainless; without feature or shadow" by giving the materials for the work to his disciple whom he knew would follow the master's wishes. In 1874, at the request of Carlyle, Froude resigned as editor of *Fraser's Magazine* in order to devote all his time to the materials in his hands. When Carlyle died in 1881, his biographer had been at work on the manuscripts for more than six years.

Within three years of Carlyle's death all the volumes dealing with the Carlyles had been completed. *Thomas Carlyle: A History of the First Forty Years* appeared in 1882, the *Letters and Memorials of Jane Walsh Carlyle* followed in 1883, and *Thomas Carlyle: A History of His Life in London* closed the series in 1884. The volumes were met by an overwhelming avalanche of adverse criticism. Froude had definite theories regarding the duties of the life-writer, however, and he refused to sacrifice them to satisfy false contemporary standards. He believed that the public had a right to know the truth about its servants. "In writing the biography of a great man," he said, "you are to tell the truth so far as you know it. You are not to trouble yourself with the impression you may produce on the rank and file of immediate readers." And with utter disregard for the Victorian *de mortuis nil nisi bonum* he turned the searchlight upon every aspect of Carlyle's life and character.

For almost a half century Froude's biography of Carlyle was a storm center of controversy. Led by two members of Carlyle's own family, critics accused Froude of distortion, inaccuracy, and maliciousness. Their objections centered around the delineation of Carlyle and the picture of the domestic life at Cheyne Row. The Carlyle whom these volumes reveal is a "strange mixture of good and ill together." Generous to a fault with his immediate family, yet he was close to the point of miserliness when it came to household expenses; a preacher of the doctrine of silence, yet he "loved silence only platonically"; courageous in the face of a great disaster like the burning of the manuscript of the *French Revolution,* yet he was weak, irritable, and unreasonable when facing the trivial annoyances of daily life; tender and sympathetic at heart, yet he was brusque and sarcastic in social intercourse. Added to a naturally gloomy and pessimistic temper was a preoccupation with his own sufferings that made him see his ailments "through the lens of his imagination, so magnified by the metaphors in which he described them as to seem to him to be something supernatural; and if he was a torment to himself, he distracted everyone with whom he came in contact." Yet if Carlyle was inconsiderate and negligent in small things, he was, said Froude, in great things "the noblest, most considerate and generous of men." With keen psychological insight he explains, too, some of the reasons for Carlyle's limitations. To chronic dyspepsia, for example, is attributed his irritability and nervousness. Likewise, to the effect of his profession upon a temperament already egocentric is traced his selfishness. When such interpretations are added to the multitude of details concerning Carlyle's life and character the resulting portrait is convincing and unforgettable.

The Victorians objected not only to the Carlyle whom Froude's volumes revealed, but they also protested against the picture of the domestic life at Cheyne Row. Since Froude's day the married life of the Carlyle's has become a literary problem, and enough nonsense has been written about it to fill a closet. Froude attributed their unhappiness to several things—one of which he kept for a posthumous *apologia,* but all of which make a good story. So excellent is the autobiographical method, however, that without the explanation of Jane's disappointment in love or the Ashburton-Carlyle infatuation we know that two individuals of the temperament of Jane and Carlyle would find it difficult to live together.

Although Froude is Jane's champion and speaks of her "drawn white face haunting" him, it is impossible after reading her letters to think of her as a worn-out household drudge who suffered in silence from the agony of neuralgia and the selfishness of her husband. "Gey ill to live wi" Carlyle was, according to his mother, but Jane did not fail to let him and everyone else know she lived in a madhouse; and certainly her sarcastic tongue and quick temper were responsible for much of the tension. But this is not the place to discuss the question of who was to blame for what. The fact that we find ourselves adding more nonsense on the Carlyle marriage to a pile already too large is an excellent indication of the reality of the personalities. It is enough to say that as in his portrait of Carlyle so in his account of the domestic life Froude is honest. With the letters and the journals of both Carlyles before him he could only write that "the married life of Carlyle and Jane was not happy in the roseate sense of happiness. . . . She never flattered anyone, least of all her husband; and when she saw cause for it the sarcasms flashed out from her as the sparks from lacerated steel. Carlyle himself did not find his marriage the miraculous transformation of nature he had promised himself. He remained lonely and dyspeptic, possessed by thoughts and convictions which struggled for utterance, and which could be fused and cast into form only . . . when his whole mind was like a furnace at white heat." We have only to compare this statement with that of a contemporary writer who said "it would be difficult to name another equally eminent man of letters, in any land, who was so perfectly happy in his marriage" to realize what the public expected Carlyle's chosen biographer to reveal. That in an age which placed a premium upon idealization and the suppression of unfortunate details Froude wrote with no other than the fear of God before him is added tribute to his accomplishment.

The score upon which Froude's work has been most constantly criticised has been its inaccuracy. Since truth is the first requisite of biography, the question immediately arises— is the delineation true? There are errors in the biography which greater care in proofreading could have prevented. In *My Relations with Carlyle* Froude admits to some mistakes and explains the difficulties he faced in deciphering much of the material Carlyle gave him. Analysis of the errors, however, shows that they are not vital enough to alter the outline of the portrait. It is difficult, indeed, to read the volumes without being convinced of the truth of Froude's delineation. His love of the graphic might have misled him in some directions, but the errors are those of proportion rather than fact. Desiring to be accurate, he made two trips, in 1876 and 1880, to visit the scenes of Carlyle's early life, and where he was uncertain of the facts he tried to verify them. There were those among Froude's contemporaries who commended the work, but the public in general was unwilling to admit that "an angular and somewhat disordered soul was more interesting, more valuable, and more impressive than the popular conception of a prophet, the romantic conception of an ideal husband."

Froude had an abundance of material with which to work. Froude used the materials skillfully to give a full length portrait of his subject. The canvas is large and the details are many. We follow Carlyle from the peasant's cottage at Ecclefechan through the student days at Edinburgh, the teaching experience at Annandale, the tutorship with the Bullers, the marriage to Jane Walsh and the six dreary years at Craigenputtock, to London and the success of maturity and the honors of old age. By means of the journals and letters we know his thoughts and activities almost from day to day; we see the world through his eyes; we see him through the eyes of others. Innumerable descriptions of domestic life at Cheyne Row, Ecclefechan, the Grange, and elsewhere give color and life to the narrative. The movement is slow, solemn, stately; and the story that is unfolded is one that Carlyle would have approved—a noble character struggling heroically against the disappointments, sorrows, and difficulties of life to achieve the high purpose for which the Maker destined it. Froude's biography is a complete soul portrait in which all the "inward springs and relations" of character are revealed.

Enhancing the excellence of the materials is Froude's matchless style. It is simple, clear, unaffected. In fact, it is so in accord with the subject that we are unaware of the medium. Skilled in narrative, graphic in description, restrained in emotion, he is one of the masters of English prose. Like Carlyle's ideal biographer, he not only had the "loving heart" that opened his eyes to reality, but he also had the ability to "utter forth" what his insight revealed.

A collection of the reviews of Froude's volumes from 1881 to the present reveals the change that has taken place in the conception of what constitutes adequacy in life-writing. It is a far cry from the statement of an anonymous reviewer in the *Athenaeum* that "Mr. Froude's books are crude compilations, and he has inflicted a blow on the reputation of Carlyle from which it is unlikely that it will ever recover" to Mr. Oscare

Brudett's "Froude has written a very fine biography on a most interesting human being; rich in contrast, alive with light and shade. . . . [It] is a fine piece of living portraiture." Between the two extremes there is a story of changing ethical, social, and moral attitudes and their corresponding effect upon life-writing. By refusing to depart from what he knew to be his duties as a biographer, Froude struck the death note to the "incredible" Victorial panegyric. Aware that "the sharpest scrutiny is the condition of enduring fame" he left no blank spaces to be filled in by rumor or conjecture. In so doing he "anticipated (present day) microfiers and scandal mongers" and thus took the "wind out of the sails of later biographers."

Froude made no contribution to biographical method but in using the "Boswell formula" he produced a work worthy to stand beside the *Life of Johnson*. His manner, however, was new. At a time that the public demanded subjective and emotional delineations he dared to write what he knew would be condemned. But he had learned his lesson from a master, and the biography the disciple wrote was what the master would have approved. Judged not only by Carlyle's criteria but also by the general laws of biographic art, Froude wrote a great biography. With something of the prophet's vision he said in his *apologia*, "My book, if it is still to be condemned at present, will be of use hereafter." He was right.

THERESSA WILSON BROWN
Miner Teachers College

Frank D. Curtin

ARNOLD BENNETT, AND AFTER

VIRGINIA WOOLF in commenting on "Modern Fiction" (1919) in *The Common Reader* singled out Arnold Bennett for especial dispraise; and in her *Mr. Bennett and Mrs. Brown* (1924) she devoted herself to the limitations of his books and of his methods. Bennett, more than Galsworthy or Wells, is the betrayer of the younger novelists; it is of the technique which he exemplifies that she warns her contemporaries. The Edwardians, she declares, "have made tools and established conventions which do their business. But those tools are not our tools, and that business is not our business. For us those conventions are ruin, those tools are death."

Mrs. Woolf, as well as the other experimentalists who were to lead the English novelists in the twenties, rejected the tradition which Bennett carried to an extreme: the realistic tradition of massed details and objectivity. Bennett failed, in Mrs. Woolf's opinion, to capture the essence of life; giving undue emphasis to background, he lost his characters among the furniture. "I have formed my own opinion of what Mr. Bennett is about—he is trying to make us imagine for him; he is trying to hypnotize us into the belief that, because he has made a house, there must be a person living there."

Like James Joyce, Mrs. Woolf shifted her focus; her concern was the moods of character: not the world observed but the impressions of the observer. Externals became relevant

[117]

when they afforded opportunity to display a response, a state of mind or feeling. Not only indeed did Mrs. Woolf subordinate setting, but she also discarded story. The characteristic pattern of her novel is a kind of jigsaw puzzle, though the pieces are rare and precious, with the last piece completing the revelation of the central character: Mrs. Dalloway or Mrs. Ramsay. Through these methods as through the exquisite discriminations of her style, Mrs. Woolf accomplished a good deal that was beyond Arnold Bennett. It is little wonder that she rejected him and the realistic tradition he followed. One can understand the harshness of her judgment more readily when one remembers that during the twenties, when she was establishing herself, Bennett was continuing to provide prolific illustrations of his faults and was failing, in spite of his repeated efforts, to duplicate his earlier masterpieces.

Yet those masterpieces remain; his methods had succeeded, however temporarily. Deficient though he was in the sensitive perceptions which characterize Virginia Woolf—as in Lawrence's sensory and emotional intensity, Joyce's controlled complexity, Forster's and Huxley's intelligence—Bennett had great abilities of his own, the abilities which reached their fullest expression in *The Old Wives' Tale* and *Clayhanger*. He observed widely and closely; he could create characters, against backgrounds which helped to make them real; he could tell an absorbing story. And what he accomplished with these talents—in scope, in characterization, in progression— were the very qualities notably lacking in the work of Virginia Woolf, as they have been in fact in most of the distinguished English novels of the past generation. In detecting Bennett's limitations and in repudiating his weaknesses, the more eminent of his successors may have rejected the sources of his strength. They have, whatever their achievement, lost some of the traditional values which Bennett at his best shared with the great English novelists of the past.

II

On December 31, 1928, Bennett wrote in his *Journal:* "This year I have written 304,000 words; 1 play, 2 films, 1 small book on religion, and about 80 or 81 articles." To the end of his life, in 1931, he drove himself, until the bulk of his writing seems prodigious. He had earned his way up from the meager existence and income of a middle-class family in the Midlands; he had succeeded as a journalist; and when wealth began to come, he adopted a manner of life which demanded the continuance of a tremendous income. Writing was his trade; he never ceased to be a journalist. "As a *man,*" he said, "I should be disgusted if I could not earn plenty of money. . . ." [1] The great mass of his writing serves that purpose. Bennett knew how to be popular, in his essays which his publishers euphemistically entitle "Belles-lettres," in his plays, in most of his short stories. Of his novels many were written primarily to maintain him in the luxury he required; his *Journal* bears witness to this. Among such novels were the "fantasias," melodramas, as listed on the flyleaves of his English editions. Since of the score of novels which remain there are several which cannot be accepted as seriously as the author intended, one may wonder whether any other English writer with pretensions to rank has ever published such a huge bulk of negligible work.

---

[1] *Journal* (New York, 1932), I, 32.

If anyone can doubt the selective value of criticism, let him examine the writings about Arnold Bennett and see with what discrimination the paste is sorted out from the gems. *Sacred and Profane Love* (1905), *The Lion's Share* (1916), *The Pretty Lady* (1918), *Lillian* (1922) are thrown aside. On the other hand, *Clayhanger* (1910), with sometimes the rest of the trilogy, *Hilda Lessways* (1911) and *These Twain* (1916), and above all *The Old Wives' Tale* (1908) are set apart for the warmest praise. Though about ten or twelve other novels there has been less uniformity of judgment, all of them have had a measure of critical esteem. They are the comedies *Denry the Audacious* (1911), *Mr. Prohack* (1922), and—best of these —*Buried Alive* (1908); some of the early novels set in the Five Towns, *Anna of the Five Towns* (1902), *Leonora* (1903), and *Whom God Hath Joined* (1906); *The Roll-Call* (1918), pendant to the Clayhanger trilogy; and the later novels *Riceyman Steps* (1923), *Lord Raingo* (1926), and *Imperial Palace* (1930).[2] Quite apart from the fantasias and the failures, there remain a group of ten to fifteen novels on which Arnold Bennett's reputation must rest. In these his way of handling a novel can be judged, with its weaknesses and its success.

III

Opposition to Arnold Bennett's novels centers on two characteristics which they share with the realistic tradition: the massing of details and the minimizing of interpretation. In

---

[2] Frank Swinnerton makes an admirable survey of Bennett's writings in *The Georgian Scene;* Georges Lafourcade's full-length study: *Arnold Bennett,* though informative and illuminating, gives an indefensibly high estimate of the later novels, including *The Pretty Lady.*

both respects the criticism is often justified, but by no means is it always justified.

"What makes a novel important enough," Bennett asks, "to impress itself upon both the discriminating few and the less discriminating many? . . . The first thing is . . . that the novel should seem to be true. It cannot seem true, if the characters do not seem to be real." [3] For Bennett the aim of a novel is its picture of human experience; and his use of details may be judged according to that aim. By such a test long passages throughout his novels are found to be superfluous— for example, the description of pottery-making in *Anna of the Five Towns* and the dissertation on English divorce in *Whom God Hath Joined. Imperial Palace,* Bennett's last considerable novel, is a monument to his mistaken notion that his own fascination for the machinery under a grand hotel and for the masterly organization of its services can give life to the automatons which move through the great lobby and along the carpeted corridors. And even in his best novels Bennett may pile up two or three details about a party at Edwin Clayhanger's or the reconstruction of the Baines shop where one would serve. Judged even according to his own purposes, Bennett may be criticized for excessive detail. He records a conversation with Henry James: "When I told him that sometimes I lay awake at night, thinking of the things I had forgotten to put in my novels, he said that my novels were 'crammed,' and that when something was 'crammed,' nothing else could be put in it, and so it was all right."

But the term *excessive* implies a standard of selection, no matter what kind of novel is being considered. When Jane

[3] *Things that Have Interested Me* (London, 1921), p. 317.

Austen writes a humorous satire on the relationships of a group of gentlefolk in southern England, she need not mention the revolution in France or the growing industrialism of England. When Dickens pictures the more varied activities of the Victorians and attempts more varied moods, he is justified in more detailed description. Rex Warner may, in *The Wild-Goose Chase,* suppress references to the commonplaces of everyday experience in order to abstract the elements of a social conflict he wants to stress. Joyce and Dorothy Richardson require more details to show the complex mental lives of Leopold Bloom or Miriam Henderson, more details for a given episode than even Arnold Bennett will use.

Since for Virginia Woolf "life is a luminous halo," "not a series of gig lamps symmetrically arranged," she does well to eschew consecutive narrative and details of environment which seem irrelevant to her purpose. She is, however, hardly just in condemning Bennett because he finds environment more significant than she in picturing human experience. Many aspects of commonplace life which attract Bennett seem unrewarding to Mrs. Woolf. Her observations are largely limited to the impressions of a sensitive, well-to-do, and somewhat snobbish spectator. Bennett often chooses to depict the lives of more ordinary people, who must devote their days to more productive interests than the savoring of their own impressions. Details which would be excessive in Mrs. Woolf are helpful to Bennett—details of costume, speech, interiors, and even those which specify the sources of income of his characters and the maladies which afflict them, though use of these latter can become the obtrusive mannerism that Max Beerbohm makes fun of in *A Christmas Garland.* When, as he regularly does, Bennett employs environment to depict his characters, he is using the realistic technique to advantage.

The achievement vindicates the means. Bennett produces a picture of the industrial Midlands in the late-Victorian age and over the turn of the century, where a whole society, from the Countess of Snell in *Denry the Audacious* to Auntie Hamps' servant in *These Twain,* is shown in its constant interaction. Without the complex patterns of Dos Passos or Jules Romains, Bennett succeeds in six or eight novels, with help from a few short stories like "The Matador of the Five Towns," in depicting a society. The panorama of the area, presented with some fullness in *Anna,* is added to in successive views from Toft End and the Bursley Park; and with Leonora Stanway and Samuel Povey and Edwin and Hilda, the reader descends into the streets and squares of the towns. There he sees the people at work in the potteries or the print shop or their kitchens; he sees them along the streets shopping, visiting, coming from school and work, gaping at the house where Daniel Povey has murdered his wife. With the Fearnses and the Swetnams he sees them at evening parties at the Orgreaves' and the Clayhangers'. He sees them concerned with religion—at the Wesleyan revival in *Anna,* at the Sunday-school anniversary in *Clayhanger* and *Hilda Lessways,* and, with Mrs. Baines and her daughters, leaving the New Year's watch night:

Then the aisles were suddenly crowded, and there was a good-humoured, optimistic pushing towards the door. In the Corinthian porch occurred a great putting-on of cloaks, ulsters, goloshes, and even pattens, and a great putting-up of umbrellas. And the congregation went out into the whirling snow, dividing into several black, silent-footed processions, down Trafalgar Road, up towards the playground, along the market-place, and across Duck Square in the direction of St. Luke's Square.

Here is the world Bennett knew from boyhood; and this world, through his wealth of details, he recreates for his readers.

When, after the First World War, Bennett turned his back on the Five Towns, his method became less successful, not because he used greater masses of details but because the materials he used were less evocative, and often rather the careful collection of conscious observations, as evidenced by the *Journal,* than a selection from a rich experience.[4] Even so, as Rebecca West points out in *The Strange Necessity,* there are vividly created episodes in the later books. The crowded streets of London, the boarding-houses, and the studios surround George Cannon as he moves through his first love affair, which with the brief epilogue of the book does much to offset the formlessness of *The Roll-Call.* Counterbalancing the tedium of the Paris department store in *Imperial Palace* is the picture of Smithfield Market in the dawn. As earlier there had been the Putney of *Buried Alive,* so there are, in that best of the post-war books, *Riceyman Steps,* Earlforward's second-hand book shop and the populous environs of Clerkenwell.

Scope has different definitions for different novelists. Huxley's scope is intellectual, the grasp of modern thought which he displays from *Antic Hay* to *Time Must Have a Stop.* Ben-

---

[4] This explanation of the weakening effectiveness of Bennett's later novels seems more tenable than the suggestion that he sacrificed everything else for money; he worked with great earnestness on *Riceyman Steps, Lord Raingo,* and *Imperial Palace.* Frank Swinnerton attributes the decline to the exhaustion of Bennett's creative vitality in his activities during the war.

nett's scope is creative, the transfer to the reader of the whole environment—human, natural, and industrial—of the Five Towns, as well as certain aspects of London; and always the portrayal, in the foreground of these general pictures, of his leading characters.

The chief function of this created world is to bring the characters to fuller life. Though they typify characteristics of their environments, as Anna Tellwright's father the miserliness and Constance the provinciality of the Five Towns, Bennett does not select his characters to display the leading tendencies of their time and place, as H. G. Wells does in his thesis-novels or Aldous Huxley in his satires. Edwin Clayhanger's Auntie Hamps shows, it is true, the uncharitable bigotry of many late-Victorian Evangelicals; she is a symbol of the pretentious hypocrisy of Midlands Wesleyanism. But she is much more: she is a rounded character displayed in a multitude of relationships, from the time she first appears, to the admiration of Darius, as an ample and becurled widow of forty-two, till the night a generation later when she lies dying, revealed in all her tawdriness in her threadbare room, and demands that her servant, lapsing from virtue, be sent penniless into the midnight streets.

Nor does Bennett, like Dreiser and Dos Passos, show his characters as subordinate to the fatal forces of environment. Bursley helps to explain Constance and Sophia Baines, but it does not determine their careers. When Sophia elopes, she carries with her the middle-class standards of the Five Towns to London, where they impel Gerald Scales to marry her, and to Paris, where they stiffen her resistance to Chirac after Gerald's desertion. But inborn differences between the two girls have been revealed from the opening scenes. Sophia will risk comfort for adventure, for her dreams of romance; Constance, quieter, less imaginative, will live out her years at home.

For Bennett the center of interest is his characters, even in the farcical *Buried Alive* and *Denry* and in the comic *Mr. Prohack*. He shows his leading figures in innumerable relationships, each requiring detailed development—reacting to their environment, seeking to work out their desires, falling in love, adjusting themselves to marriage, moving through the changes of the passing years. Regularly it is in the relations of parents and children that Bennett displays his characters most vividly. As Sophia defies her mother, Mrs. Baines dimly foresees the day when, "encumbered with trunks and parcels," she will get into the waggonette for Axe, "leaving the scene of her struggles and her defeat, whither she had once come as slim as a wand, to return stout and heavy, and heavy-hearted, to her childhood. . . ." Much later, Constance's son, neglecting to write as he begins his life in London, leaves her lonely in the empty rooms at home. Edwin, first dominated by his father, has his pitying revenge as Darius weakens into senility. So may be summarized relationships which Bennett displays in many episodes; by means of these as well as background a whole gallery of memorable characters is portrayed.

Yet "gallery" is hardly the term. For his people are not static; they move constantly through the scenes, providing the immediacy of drama by their actions and their speech. How skilfully Bennett concentrates his interest J. W. Beach points out in his *Twentieth-Century Novel*. The curtain rises when an episode is under way, and in a moment the new situation is explained and the new action is begun. Thus Bennett can avoid generalized narrative, and illuminate even the minor crises of his characters' lives. And yet he avoids too the spottiness, the incomplete development, which Mr. Beach finds in Galsworthy. Bennett follows one character or set of characters through successive scenes: Constance and Sophia separately in the middle books of *The Old Wives' Tale* and Edwin and Hilda through the separate volumes of *Clayhanger* and *Hilda Lessways*. In this way Bennett can take advantage of the special effects of both drama and narrative.

For, a third feature of Bennett's novels, in addition to ample scope and effective characterization, is absorbing narrative. Unlike E. M. Forster, who minimized story telling both in his own novels and in his *Aspects of the Novel,* Bennett provides a story. But his stories are not, in his serious novels, based upon artificial mysteries or climactic revelations or even upon extraordinary events. Usually in fact he plays down events which in themselves might seem sensational, as for example the siege of Paris in *The Old Wives' Tale*.[5] When Leonora detects her husband's attempt to hasten the death of his ailing old uncle, she thinks in surprise: "So that is murder, that little thing, that thing over in a minute!" Though recalling the events of *The Old Wives' Tale* reveals an unexpected number of extraordinary happenings, their effect is simply to give variety to the everyday occurrences. It is through such more ordinary scenes that Bennett gives the sense of cumulating experience which means life to his characters and suggests life to his readers. Seen in the almost imperceptible changes that the passing years bring to them, the

[5] M. Lafourcade in an appendix to his study shows how artfully Bennett used his sources.

leading figures, and many of the minor ones, take on the familiarity of old and intimate acquaintances. One becomes concerned with their welfare, enjoying their triumphs, interested in their more trivial affairs, distressed as they grow old. There is a suspense here independent of melodrama and factitious plot. With what anxiety one anticipates the meeting of Constance and Sophia in the Knype station! *Hilda Lessways,* less substantial than *Clayhanger,* has the strong attraction of its new revelations about people already well known.

Bennett's characters, seen against their backgrounds, move through time, carrying their readers' interest with them. Such a source of interest deserves no disparagement; it is the kind of interest one has in people as individuals and not as representatives of sociological problems or even as exemplars of special theories of perception. One pays tribute by such interest to the creative achievement of Bennett, throughout *The Old Wives' Tale,* and in many of the other novels as well. Here are the worlds he has portrayed through the use of his many details.

IV

The second of the objections to Arnold Bennett is that the picture of life he provides is not interpreted. Mrs. Woolf again attacks him (in *The Common Reader*):

He can make a book so well constructed and solid in its craftsmanship that it is difficult for the most exacting of critics to see through what chink or crevice decay can creep in. There is not so much as a draught between the frames of the windows, or a crack in the boards. And yet— if life should refuse to live there! That is a risk which the creator of *The Old Wives' Tale,* George Cannon, Edwin Clayhanger, and hosts of other figures, may well claim to have surmounted. His characters live abundantly, even unexpectedly, but it remains to ask how did they live, and what do they live for?

This is Henry James's major charge against Bennett (*Notes on Novelists*, "The New Novel, 1914"), Bennett's failure to interpret. James has praise for the documentation, what he calls the "saturation." Of *The Old Wives' Tale* he remarks:

. . . the canvas is covered, ever so closely and vividly covered, by the exhibition of innumerable small facts and aspects, at which we assist with the most comfortable sense of their substantial truth. The sisters, and more particularly the less adventurous, are at home in their author's mind, they sit and move at their ease in the square chamber of his attention, to a degree beyond which the production of that ideal harmony between creature and creator could scarcely go.

This is a generous tribute; James speaks as well of *Clayhanger*. And yet he is constantly disturbed by the implication:

Nothing is further from our thought than to undervalue saturation or possession . . . for it represents on the part of the novelist, as on the part of any painter of things seen, felt or imagined, just one half of his authority—the other half being represented of course by the application he is inspired to make of them.

The question he asks of Bennett is: "Yes, yes—but is this all?" What is the center of interest, the application? *Clayhanger* and *Hilda Lessways* are a monument, he says, "not to an idea, a pursued and captured meaning, or in short *to* anything whatever, but just simply *of* the quarried and gathered material they happen to contain. . . ."

And surely no one would care to take Bennett as a guide to the experience he pictures. His ideas are few and often super-

ficial. Miserliness, for example, is a topic he often returns to—
in *Anna, Clayhanger* (with Darius), *Helen with the High
Hand,* and *Riceyman Steps;* he shows it as a trait of his characters which causes distress for their intimates, but he fails to
indicate its implications for society or even, except in *Riceyman Steps,* for the miser himself. His closest approach to the
problem-novel, *Whom God Hath Joined,* is more concerned
with the sensational publicity which attends divorce than with
its effect upon the persons involved. Bennett praises the efficiency of the modern world, especially in providing luxurious
services, in *Mr. Prohack, Lord Raingo,* and *Imperial Palace;*
but he never questions the aim of such efficiency, or, though
he more than once notices the exploitation of domestic servants, the great contrast between the human cost and the human value. In *Denry* he pokes fun at the snobbish worldliness
of the international set; in *Imperial Palace* he admires that
very quality in Gracie Savott and his hero Orcham. The great
rewards of modern life, he seems to say, are money and the
luxuries it can pay for.

Arnold Bennett, and most of his characters, can be used as
horrible and unconscious examples of the spiritual barren-
ness which characterizes the Five Towns and late-Victorian
industrialism. Like Edwin, whose early life parallels his own,
he reacts bitterly against the Wesleyanism represented by the
Sunday-school centenary, where under the torrid sun of St.
Luke's Square crowds of children sing of the blood of the
Lamb. "It only wants the Ganges," Edwin remarks, "at the
bottom of the Square—!" This is the religion of Auntie Hamps
and of Ephraim Tellwright, "who reduced the cost per head
of souls saved, and so widened the frontiers of the Kingdom of

Heaven." Bennett has little more to do with religion, except to record the wistful imaginings of the dying Lord Raingo. And for a religious ideal of life he has no substitute. His characters have moral qualities—independence, honesty, industry, sometimes kindliness; but their concerns are selfish, limited to the satisfactions of their own desires, even within their own families, even in marriage, where Hilda and Edwin, George and Lois spar constantly each for his own advantage. Altruism is beyond them, and apparently outside Bennett's interest, in his fiction. When Mr. Prohack, suddenly wealthy, is at a loss to fill his days, the only solution is a new business, where he can occupy himself in details of organization and money-making. Not only does Mr. Prohack ignore the altruism which gives satisfaction to, say, Squire Allworthy and John Jarndyce; he, like Bennett's other characters—despite Edwin's musical evenings—largely ignores the possibilities of culture—learning, science, the arts. G. M. Hoape in *The Pretty Lady* shows an interest in furnishing his apartment tastefully, but otherwise aesthetic interests are limited. Only George Cannon of *The Roll-Call* realizes in his role of architect the rewards of artistic creation. As one reads Bennett, one asks himself with Henry James: "Yes, yes—but is this all?" What do these people live for? What is the result of all their activities?

But Bennett does have certain leading themes. One implication which pervades his early novels, and weakens later, is that details of ordinary life are fascinating in themselves. This is the old Dickens theme, the romance of the commonplace. Without Dickens' gusto, the early Bennett has nevertheless a contagious interest in the minutiae of his characters' daily experience, an interest which his leading characters share. Meals

[131]

and costume, neighbors and family—there is so much to absorb them that sensational events, like the murder in *The Old Wives' Tale,* soon lose emphasis among what Bennett calls, in *Literary Taste,* "the marvellous interestingness" of the world.

Another theme is related to this. The characters who live most successfully are those who perceive most clearly that fascination, who live most intensely, presumably with Pater's gemlike flame. Hilda Lessways had, Bennett comments, "the most precious of all faculties, the power to feel intensely." Even "in her unhappiness," he says, "she was blest. She savoured her unhappiness. She drank it down passionately, as though it were the very water of life—which it was. She lived to the utmost in every moment." The statement is commonplace, as are most of Bennett's generalizations, but the idea rises more forcefully from the episodes of Hilda's experience, and again from those of Sophia's.

Yet even this intensity, with its rewards, is apparently temporary, in a life where all things pass. The major theme of Bennett—and it is hard to think of anyone who gives it more compelling expression—is the theme of the ravages of time, the slow and then surprisingly rapid fretting away by age of all beauty, strength, capacity for thought and feeling. Mr. Shushions, who had been the guardian angel of Edwin's father when Darius was a boy, had grown senile . . . "the old man had lived too long; he had survived his dignity; he was now nothing but a bundle of capricious and obstinate instincts set in motion by ancient souvenirs remembered at hazard. . . . He was a horrible and offensive old man. . . . He was Time's obscene victim." The motif thus introduced receives more and more emphasis. Seven years later, it is Mr. Shushions' death in the workhouse which overwhelms Darius and begins his own disintegration. From month to month he lingers, his mind uncertain; then comes slow and painful death. "It seemed intolerably tragic that the enfeebled wreck should have had to bear so much, and yet intolerably tragic also that death should have relieved him." It is this theme, more than any other, which gives dignity to *The Old Wives' Tale.* Here Bennett has taken a theme of universal importance and given it substantial, and powerful, and moving form.

But again Bennett's point of view is limited. Not in Bennett do the years bring the philosophic mind, of mellow wisdom and calm content, nor the prizes of reverence or rich reminiscence, even to Lord Raingo among his luxuries or to Sophia from her adventurous past. "Our daily life in time," says E. M. Forster in *Aspects of the Novel,* "is exactly this business of getting old which clogs the arteries of Sophia and Constance. . . . Of course we grow old. But a great book must rest on something more than an 'of course,' and *The Old Wives' Tale* is very strong, sincere and sad,—it misses greatness."

In that comment is a key to what Forster, as contrasted with Bennett, requires in a novel and seeks to achieve in his own— an illuminating interpretation of experience. Lionel Trilling's brilliant analysis of Forster's work shows how well Forster has succeeded. In Forster, for example, death plays a far different role from the one it has in Bennett. "Death destroys a man," Forster says, "but the idea of death saves him—that is the best account of it that has yet been given." The idea of death shows how trivial are the values of the money-civilization which Bennett seems to accept. And the other themes of Forster, with their subtle interrelations and complications, these are far beyond Bennett. "E. M. Forster," says Mr. Trilling, "is for me the only living novelist who can be read again and again and who, after each reading, gives me what few writers can give us after our first days of novel-reading, the sensation of having learned something." Such intellectual stimulation one cannot find in Bennett; but there is something else, a creation, such a picture of reality as Forster does not provide. For Forster the story is unimportant, and even some of the most suggestive characters—Mrs. Moore in *A Passage to India,* Mrs. Wilcox in *Howard's End*—fade into symbols. His career as a novelist implies his real interest: five novels by 1910, *A Passage to India* in 1924; no novel since, instead largely essays. "I believe," remarks E. K. Brown, "that Mr. Forster appreciated that his ideas were not only agonizingly difficult to incarnate, but inappropriate to the novel, and that he elected to retain the ideas . . . and to abandon the novel." [6] When, in an earlier article, Mr. Brown had written about Forster's ideas, Forster had written in comment: "I have been praised for my character drawing, sense of social distinctions, etc., but seldom for the things which really interest me, and which I have tried to express through the medium of fiction." [7] Forster's concern is for ideas; he is fundamentally an essayist, an interpreter. Arnold Bennett's concern is with character and background and story; he is primarily a creator. Though one does not reread his books for his comments on life, one revisits in them a familiar world and lives again with people intimately known.

[6] "The Revival of E. M. Forster," *Yale Review,* XXXIII (Summer, 1944), p. 681.
[7] *Ibid.*

v

One of the great distinctions of the novel is its versatility. It has had Sterne as well as Fielding, Dickens as well as James, Turgeniev as well as Tolstoi. Each of the leading novelists of the past generation in England—since 1920—has made his special contribution to the novel: Forster, Virginia Woolf, Dorothy Richardson, Joyce, D. H. Lawrence, Huxley; each has had his meed of praise. They have in their various respects been experimentalists. They have reacted against the realistic tradition, almost inevitably, for the weaknesses of the Edwardians and especially of Bennett were increasingly obvious. On the other hand, traditionalists like Walpole and Priestley lacked the creative vitality of their predecessors; and Somerset Maugham has apparently been unable to recapture the vividness and force of *Of Human Bondage.* Perhaps only Elizabeth Bowen, employing new means of characterization like Virginia Woolf, has had notable success with the full-bodied characterization and the consecutive narrative of the older novel. Yet the tradition cannot be outworn, for it has been used with continued effectiveness in America, by for example Hemingway and Steinbeck, and on the Continent by Silone and Malraux.

The question rises: Did the experimentalists react too far? Did they give up too readily the rewards, even in readability, of story, of rounded characterization, and of background? As Poe declared, ". . . it is an obvious rule of Art that effects should be made to spring from direct causes—that objects should be attained through means best adapted for their attainment. . . ." Surely a unique achievement of the novel has

been its spacious picture of human experience, of memorable
characters in their interrelations, moving against their backgrounds and through time. This is what the past generation
in England seldom attempted; and yet this is what Arnold
Bennett at his best managed to do.

FRANK D. CURTIN
Washington and Jefferson College

Walter L. Myers

AGAIN THAT DEAR COUNTY

FOR every indefatigable turner of the printed page there are books to be forgotten, books to be remembered, and books to be reread. Clever and competent enough time-passers are often of no further value once their beguilement has been exercised; and it may well be that certain volumes capable of much use, if read long since, perhaps in some enchanted vale of youth, and unopened thereafter, should remain the undisturbed treasures of recollection. Fortunately, however, most writings of high excellence are not thus conditioned for us; and though the years and their vicissitudes see to it that no book in all the world, granted a measurable interval between its perusals, is ever read twice by the same man, yet there are for all of us unchanging needs, and to that which has once met them we will come again, confidently or hopefully or questioningly or, because we know what is good for us, at least dutifully.

The more these returnings are instinctive and unforced the more solidly they demonstrate literary worth and justify literary perpetuity. Yet nothing is more difficult to determine than the extent to which a man has been or is being reread rather than "first-read" or not read at all but studied, for toward such distinctions much of the evidence concerning an author's vogue gives slight or untrustworthy aid. Until there are more authoritative studies in this connection we must satisfy ourselves with probabilities substantiated by self-questionings. We can reread experimentally; or better yet we can report upon what we find in someone to whom we have returned recently and voluntarily—Anthony Trollope, for example, in those novels so conveniently representative of him, where the folk of Barsetshire, his "dear county," are most at home.

Whatever its incentive, a pondered rereading of these books strengthens the opinion that statistics upon the sale of reprints, records of a steadily increasing demand at public libraries, and a more and more favorable evaluation by critics during the last thirty or forty years all signify one thing; there is a need and Trollope meets it.

The most obvious historical explanation of Trollope's progress among readers and rereaders of the past three or four decades will, of course, refer to wars beyond all wars, the very roots of life turned up—and in any turmoil no saner refuge than that heart-land of Trollope's domain, the Barset novels. To this may be added a more conjectural, but in the end more fruitful, explanation that connects him with the very twentieth-century developments in fiction most foreign to him, namely, the all-telling minute objectivism, the equally unblushing and detailed subjectivism pursued into the unknowable of the subconscious, and the resort to signs and symbols, huge and cloudy, of which only poets are masters. Possibly all the questings and searchings represented by these developments demanded certain well-fixed points of departure, or as it were, rafts back to which winded swimmers could flounder between attempts to get somewhere in sorely troubled waters; and the platform offered by Trollope was gradually seen to be most safe and stable. In one way or another the extreme of anything will always call attention to its opposite.

Whatever the soundness of this suggestion, to its placing of Trollope as a most conservative elder-day realist his confirmed rereaders will not object; indeed they will be ready to consider him as such frankly and in some detail because that manner of thought about him can lead to the definition of his true value. They will agree, for example, that he was strictly governed by his avowed determination to write nothing that would bring the blush to the maiden cheek—in a day when that phrase had wide meaning. In all the Barset novels the most cheek-suffusing words are those of Lucy Robarts in *Framley Parsonage* when, in a tone half tragic and half jeering, she justifies her unhappy love for Lord Lufton because he has "fine straight legs." Equally limiting is Trollope's avoidance of all shock whatsoever. The nearest approach to it in the Barset books occurs at the moment when the Reverend Thumble looks into the staring eyes of Mrs. Proudie, bolt upright, dead on her feet, a thing, however, too incredible to be very startling.

Concerning the round of daily life to which he restricted himself in the Barset chronicles Trollope is not detailed. Because he was interested only in what he called the social life of his clergymen, he offers nothing like a full account of any clerical routine. As for his landed gentlemen, his Lily Dale once remarked teasingly and with justice that they never had much to do. Farm and shop people and professional men appear when needed, but information on their activities is meager. Trollope does not make his reader an authority on the ways of Barsetshire.

In the depiction of scene he is more helpful, though not distinguished or even very conscientious. He doubtless knew each region of his imagined Barsetshire as well as though, to use his own words, he had "lived and wandered there"; but he rather takes it for granted that, once the whole area has been mapped in *Framley Parsonage,* the countryside of that "pleasant green tree-becrowded county," will be sufficiently in mind. He makes some dutiful attempts to utilize the moods of its seasons, but little comes of them. There are some excellent blocks of description but their effects do not carry far. A girl named Lily Dale perforce is courted out of doors, but most of the important scenes are interior. Certain rooms are excellently identified, but what happens at Greshambury could very well happen at Framley. There is no Mill on the Floss in the Barset novels, the nearest approach to it being the cathedral close in Barchester and muddy, meager Hogglestock of *The Last Chronicle of Barset.*

And finally, to this familiar enough arraignment, should be added a word about Trollope's account of what goes on in the minds of his characters. The shrewdness and aptness of this element in the later volumes of the series become more evident with rereading, though for the detailed record of a character's actual experience nothing elsewhere in the books surpasses that chapter in *The Warden* recounting poor Septimus Harding's "Long Day in London." The latter, however, is exceptional. Perceptions, thoughts, and emotions are usually named and summed up in Trollope's language rather than that of the character who has them, and there are few flashes of vivid immediacy, nor is there any true inner monologue. Thus a character's subjectivism, as Trollope shapes it, though it conveys traits and significance in the world, does not make us feel personality, and is not, as so frequently in present-day novels, a powerful agent of objective actuality.

This listing of obvious features in the Barset novels undeniably marks out a limitation in scope and vividness; yet it is not a fault which impairs the larger value of the books. Indeed one may stoutly assert that with too much detail and vividness Trollope would cease to be Trollope and would lose his unique quality. Being what he is, he satisfies capably certain large needs; writers of an opposite persuasion, being what they are, satisfy other needs.

This distinction merits a clarifying. English fiction most unlike Trollope's differs in something toward which minuteness and vividness in actualities are but agents. Narrative of this sort is virtually a product of the last three or four decades and was not possible until certain powers of language native to poetry and romance had been adapted to prose realism and science had sharpened self-conscience and observation. To produce the value which most distinguishes this fictional mode, achievements in both subjective and objective, both inner and outer actualism have united to draw the reader nearer and nearer to the strongest immediacy of which words are capable, hallucination fortunately being impossible, namely, an experience as absorbing and real as anything that memory can provide from the reader's own recent, all-but-present past. The type and symbol of this development through the immediate into what is at moments almost the vicarious appears in Conrad's story titled so aptly "The Secret Sharer," with its magic, well-nigh hypnotic fusing of personalities. It represents something that has become as recognizable as those hard-to-define but unmistakable mastermodes of fiction called realism and romance. Where this quality is sufficiently dominant it has produced the Novel of Things to be Experienced, a few notably interesting examples of which emerged from the excellent reporting of World War II.

The important nearer progenitors of this fictional mode reached maturity long before it became a discernible tendency. They are drama on the stage, which reproduces life for the witnessing and the traditional English novel, first given form by Fielding, which has remained essentially a Novel of Things to be Observed. Of it, all the Barset series except *The Warden* are mature, full-bodied instances. Though this sort of fiction owes much to the drama, the most identifying fact of its history is that it evolved from the reciting, the chanting, the telling of tales and retained its *narrated* quality. Being narrative rather than acted drama it relates what happened aforetime; it recalls a past for observation rather than creates a present for experience, and its reader is not to fancy that he had a place in its events. He is to sympathize with fictional characters, but he is not to confuse himself with them. In all, he is to keep a certain aloofness, even though he may be at moments "enfisted," as Meredith puts it, with fictional immediacies. He receives from the page before him, as do all readers of fiction, something akin to actual memories, but they resemble the less detailed, more fused and assimilated recollections of the long-gone past rather than the sharply detailed awareness of that which, by the closing of a door or the mere turning of the head, has just ceased to be the bewildering present. Obviously this more retrospective mode suits well the novel of many characters, whether in the manner of Dickens or of Thackeray, particularly of the latter, in that style which Percy Lubbock's *The Craft of Fiction* designates as the panoramic. The Victorians, however, have no monopoly on this novel of life observed, and it will persist in competition with its rival offspring for the same reason that staged drama coexists with both of them, and that neither prose literature nor poetry obliterates the other.

With reference to the sharpness of imagery it produces in the reader's mind, the novel of life observed occupies a middle ground between staged drama and the novel of vicarious experience or secret-sharing; and this middle ground is the realm of narrative proper, where we gather when we want someone who knows whereof he speaks to tell us about persons distinctly not ourselves even in disguise. And so in the appropriate mood we come back to our Barset novels.

Straightway Trollope once more shows himself the wise narrator—whose very wisdom seems to beguile him into moments of foolishness. He knows that not uncertainty and surprise but an expectancy which is based on decisive characterization and which is ever being satisfied yet ever maintained is the essence of durable realistic narrative. All too sure of this in the earlier Barset novels, he tells us what is to be expected and reminds us bluntly that what we are reading is fiction. Unhappy sessions with fictionized biography have convinced us that the mood in which we accept fact is not that in which we accept fiction. We could not for a moment believe Trollope's story if we thought that he quite literally wanted us to do so. Yet there are pages in *Barset Towers* where we all but lose our acquiescence to make-believe; and we are grateful that his give-aways subside finally into half-serious grumblings about the requirements of storytelling. Fortunately nothing can halt a reader's progress through novels whose action is not what happened to the people but what the people do because it is what they must do to be their significant selves.

Trollope is at his worst when he defies his readers to take him seriously, and his transgression seems even worse than it is because it brings to mind Thackeray's ease and grace in commenting on his characters. Yet viewing the Barset novels as a whole and judging them according to their type, one cannot say that there Trollope takes undue advantage of his narratorship save in *The Warden* and *Barchester Towers;* and the element of comic intention in these novels lessens the offense of larded-on facetiousness. There are never any interpolated essays in the *Tom Jones* tradition, no chapter "In Which the Story Pauses a Little" à la George Eliot. Usually Trollope does what we expect and welcome from a man whose observations constitute a novel: he comments on the characters, summing up their thought and defining their motives. Indeed this feature of the novels offers an interest that grows with re-readings, a sense of Trollope in the book, kindly, amused, discerning, vigorously plain-prose Trollope. We are willing to grant him such extraneous passages as he desires because we like him. Also we will remember that he has a greater freedom, after all, than that to be accorded the novelist who would have us, through the medium of his consciousness, participate in what he presents. Such an author must be chary about attracting attention to himself. The most serviceable windowpanes are those of which we are all but unaware.

But one does not come back to the Barset novels chiefly for story or for Trollope's personality and the pleasure of recalling with him Barset lanes and of agreeing that Barset fields, though pretty, are a bit "too well-wooded" for an ardent fox hunter. Nor do we return largely because of an interest in Barset ways of life, or the satisfaction of making sure about the terms of tenure in the livings of Crabtree Canonicorum and Puddingdale, or to separate the impression of Childicotes from that of Boxall Hill, or even to measure our growing familiarity with the books by catching Trollope in such minor inadvertencies as his confusing of St. Ewold's with St. Cuthbert. The outstanding truth about Barsetshire is that this dear county is its people. We come back to it as we return to haunts that evoke for us unsurpassably the memory of those with whom we lived there.

Dreams and visions are more vivid than memories, but on the whole less satisfying. In the recollecting of people "believing" is not so much a matter of seeing as of feeling the personalities recalled, and much the same is true of fictional characterization. Mere detailed exactness and vividness of depiction are of no avail unless they make us feel an entity and, at the will of the author, sense a presence as convincingly as we are aware of the existence of the man with whom we have an appointment at ten o'clock tomorrow. All novelists worthy of the name must command this power, whether they would have us be observers or sharers in secret. The importance of this for narrative poets, particularly in the epic style, is a matter for debate.

In any event Trollope possessed it. We scarcely need that familiar passage in the *Autobiography* to convince us that his characters were not fabrications pieced out while he was writing but entities that existed in his mind before he set to work.

I have wandered alone . . . crying at their grief, laughing at their absurdities. . . . I have been impregnated with my own creations until it has been my only excitement to sit with my pen in hand and drive my team before me at as quick a pace as I could make them travel.

Occasionally, indeed, the pace was too rapid, and he did not take time to give a reader all the needed help with a character; but it is probable that not one of his persons was to him a mere name, despite seeming indications to the contrary. For example, Plantagenet Palliser's brief appearance in *The Small House at Allington* is rather bewildering. His stubborn, passionless, all but disastrous pursuit of Lady Dumbello is hard to accept in a young man otherwise sensible and moderate. It is only in later novels, particularly *The Prime Minister,* that his actions in *The Small House* are fully accounted for: he is possessed of a proud, idealizing sort of contrariness, difficult to define but evident enough when he is well known. Trollope felt this in the character from its inception.

With this in mind we can better understand differences in the effectiveness with which Trollope pictured his Barset people. He could offer glimpses and incidental details with the best, but he did not always put them where they were needed or manage them in the conscientious, workmanlike way of such a slower-paced author as George Eliot. Thus Mrs. Proudie's forefinger that semaphores her references to "souls" in *The Last Chronicle* is a perfect mannerism, but Septimus Harding's sawing on an imaginary violincello in *The Warden* and *Barchester Towers* becomes almost psychopathic. There are excellent block descriptions throughout all the books, but even some of the best of these Trollope appears to put out of

mind once they are finished and makes little use of thereafter. In fact he apparently resented all personal descriptions
that cost him effort, and he did not hesitate to say so. His most
frank protest of this sort in the Barset novels is that outburst
over the description of Lucy Robarts in *Framly Parsonage:*
"If one might only go on without those descriptions how pleasant it would all be!"

This is amusing and does not constitute a damaging confes-
sion. His difficulty was not laziness or lack of descriptive skill—
it was rather that he knew his people too well before writing
about them. Instinctively he doubtless preferred to keep them
with him in just the way that old friends are recollected, not
by means of finished portraits but by a rapid sequence of somewhat unorganized images, and with a sense of personality so
strong that the outer evidences of it need not be brought into
sharp focus. This hypothesis is not essentially contradicted by
the assertion in the *Autobiography* that he saw with clarity
the details that identified his people, and it is well supported
by the novels. In his dutiful approach to the depiction of Mary
Thorn, for example, he remarks, "She is my heroine, and, as
such, her mind and inner qualities are more clearly distinct to
my brain than her outward form and features." And there is
that prelude to the account of Francis Arabin in *Barchester
Towers,* where Trollope deplores the impossibility of putting
into a book exactly the man an author has imagined.

The agency that permitted the nearest approach to his desire Trollope found in dialogue, which can convey personality, establish presence, speed action, and do a variety of
things at one and the same time. He understood the art of it,
knowing, as the *Autobiography* declares, that neither bookish-

ness nor the transcript of actual speech will serve. About half of each Barset novel is devoted to conversations and their necessary adjuncts, some long, many very short and scarcely localized. Lightly concerned as he was about background, he could set people conversing nowhere in particular and cut them off with equal ease. Barsetshire is populated with talkers, who come before the mind's eye in pairs or groups, thereby, as it were, combining actualities, the more impressive authenticating the realness of the less. Meeting them thus often and in more than one book, we come to know them by the slow, sure process that makes us familiar with actual associates. Some of them, like their counterparts in actuality, are distinguished eventually by little more than the fact that we have seen and heard them more frequently than we have others of the same type.

Of all the Barset persons concerning whom it may be said, "They talk; therefore they are," none is more an entity than Lily Dale. She is never described completely with identifying exactness, and there are few glimpses of her that are very suggestive. Yet she is a most undeniable presence instinct with whimsical humor and such pretty, vivacious Victorian audacity as permits her to say that an archdeacon has "skedaddled." Her personality is felt before she has come to a sentence-end, and throughout her appearances it never fades save for one or two hints of bookishness when she has to be serious. Equally identifying and lively is the conversation of Mrs. Thorne, the former Miss Dunstable, that unillusioned, uncynical, understander of the Vanity Fair into which her father's highly merchantable ungents have eased her way. The companion of these two as speaking likenesses of actuality is Lucy Robarts, whose frankness and vigor of utterance led Trollope to place her first among his heroines for naturalness. She tries to ridicule herself out of her heart-struck misery at having "refused a live lord," and suppresses all signs of distress that she may not "go about moaning like a sick cow." Many an eyebrow must have been lifted over Lucy—that is, as she is in *Framley Parsonage;* when she reappears in *The Last Chronicle,* Trollope does not contrive to let her be fully herself.

An excellent foil to these vocal personages is Griselda Grantly. Trollope constantly insists upon her statuesquely beautiful silence—which responds so effectively to the inarticulacy of Lord Dumbella. They approach a mating by "dumb signs, such as birds give to each other." Griselda is very blond, and Trollope held that blondness is anything but an evidence of heart and mind. Griselda has enough of the latter, however, to know that as Lady Dumbello and a future marchioness she will need to talk less than as the wife of the mere baron, Lord Lufton. She understands herself, and she knows the world before which she is always consciously and silently on exhibit.

When Griselda did not know what to say she kept silent; but most of Trollope's heroines always know what to say, particularly in crises. One who rises most gratifyingly to the occasion is Grace Crawley by her conquest of Archdeacon Grantly in *The Last Chronicle.* Before this event she is characterized less by what she says than by the fact that people are always telling one another of her rare intelligence and delicate beauty. There is about her an air of starved girlhood, excessive seriousness, and self-abnegation; and the shadows are deepened by the cloud that hangs over all connected with her father. The portrayal culminates with that perfect scene in which Archdeacon Grantly, intent on putting her in her place and separating her from his son, suddenly perceives her strength of spirit and innate gentlewoman's charm and is reduced to tears and fatherly tenderness.

To discuss fully the importance of dialogue in the Barset characterizations would be to consider a majority of them; and to single out certain ones for comment is to risk the implication that they stand forth more boldly than they do while the books are being read. To be sure there are differences. In any fictive account of human kind there will be some unevenness of portrayal; and it takes a variety of persons to make a world or a shire or even its clergy and gentry alone. There is no exaggeration of these natural differences in the novels.

Trollope was essentially the realist, that is, one who dealt with the common denominators of life, perforce, then with the average of it, hence with the well-known rather than the exceptional and the strange. He did not, like the novelists of the Sensation School, put faith in authenticated improbabilities. He was one, however, who would have his "picture of common life enlivened by humor and sweetened by pathos," and his humor often became satiric. Satire calls for exaggeration or the presentation of the exceptionally objectionable, and a deliberate enlivening and sweetening of fiction may accentuate the comical and the pathetic beyond the normal. In his characterizations Trollope kept the realist's faith against these temptations, even throughout the gratuitous satire of the *Times* which appears in *The Warden* and the Fieldingesque mock-heroic passages designed to enliven both that book and *Barchester Towers*.

Neither of these exuberances distorts character; indeed they serve to make certain of the satiric and comic stressings of portrayal appear less marked than they would in the later and more preponderantly realistic books of the series. Thus Mrs. Proudie, Trollope's masterpiece of comicality, satire, and realism, is at her best in *Barchester Towers*. Her characterization is in rather delicate balance for all its vigor, and "One shade the more, one ray the less" could make her either a cartooned impossibility or an overstressed improbability. She is almost too much the former when she interrupts Harold Smith's lecture in *Framley Parsonage* with her clarion demand for Christianity in the South Seas; and she is almost too much the latter in the circumstances of her death. Otherwise she is all that heart could wish to the very end, for nothing could surpass the ironic probability of her epitaph, with its *"Requiescat in Pace."*

Barchester Towers includes also a triumph in the hard-to-believe, the portrayal of the Signora Neroni, that invalided siren of the sofas, with her untellable Italian past, her diabolical cleverness, and the eyes of a beautiful "she devil," which are equally effective on the susceptible Slope and the presumably unassailable Arabin. A summary of her characterization suggests something possible, perhaps, but not realistically probable in the very shadow of sanctified walls. Yet Trollope guides her sweepingly past our incredulity, away from our pity or detestation, carries her with dignity through that scene of all but slapstick humor in which her sofa's castors ravage Mrs. Proudie's train, and maintains her steadily as chief agent of the very acceptable high comedy that brightens the realism of the novel.

[151]

The over-insistent Pecksniffian variety of satire was not for Trollope despite what seems indicated of him by his fondness for such names as Dr. Fillgrave, Scratcherd, Supplehouse, and Omnium of Gatherum Castle. *Barchester Towers* contains what appears to be an attempt at it, but one that did not carry through. Rev. Slope comes into the book with sweaty Dickensian hands and trailing clouds of ancestral unreality, being none other than the grandson of Sterne's Dr. Slop. He triumphs over these artificialities, however, to become a credible enough villain, though never so realistic a creation as the evil-doing Crosbie of *The Small House* or Sowerby of *Framley Parsonage*. More characteristic of Trollope is his use of the comic and the pleasantly satiric in the portrayal of Archdeacon Grantly. This robust, single-minded cleric charms us amusingly with his very lack of spirituality and affords us something of a satirist's gratification when, in *The Warden,* his domineering efficiency is powerless against the mild, distressed but unwavering impracticality of Septimus Harding. Our chuckles over Grantly have varied implications, just as his own favorite exclamation "Good Heavens!" rings so delightfully all the changes of archidiaconal mood.

In humor entirely for the fun of it, Trollope is moderate, and there are few characters in the Barset novels that attract attention because they are dedicated to comic relief. Trollope was on guard against the danger, ever enticing to the older English realists, of devising minor characters that are more effective than the principals, a transgression of which Dickens is accused when he is satirized as Mr. Sentiment in *The Warden*. For a time during a first reading of *The Last Chronicle* one may feel that the seeming minors with whom John

Eames is enmeshed in London are getting out of hand, but it soon develops that they are principals satirically touched up. A rereader's chief complaint about them is not that they are improperly drawn but that they appear to have strayed in from another and more sharply sarcastic novel and so deprive *The Last Chronicle* of the blending and interlocking of narratives to be expected from the author of *Barchester Towers*.

Trollope's judicious use of minors in a conventionally humorous way appears in such a figure as Old Hopkins of *The Small House* and in sundry groups such as that which assembles for the Ullathorne Sports in *Barchester Towers* or the London boardinghouse persons of *The Small House,* including that pleasant borrowing from Dickens, Miss Spruce, who needs tactful handling because she is "only an old woman." And for a truly distinguished minor depiction in the best Trollopian vein of realism tinct with comedy one should turn to the account of Earl de Guest in *The Small House*. He is at his best in scenes with the never too mature John Eames. The old nobleman in all befriendings of the younger man never seems to be patronizing him but rather to be manifesting a sort of kinship. Something bluffly, naïvely youthful, almost juvenile, about the earl responded to Eames at first meeting. The battle these two wage against the bull that attacks the earl is stout realistic comedy of the best; there is cheerful, unforced absurdity in the methods of the two matadors and the beaddlement of the bull, yet the seriousness of the situation is never lost to sight.

In the management of pathos Trollope is even more restrained than in the use of satire and humor. Mrs. Qiverful and Mrs. Crawley, for example, are both figures of pathos, but neither is permitted to be very saddening. Such an effect is precluded, in part, by an efficiency possessed by both of them, particularly by Mrs. Crawley, who displays it in the guise of steadfastness and loving self-sacrifice. She has a life work in getting on with Josiah Crawley and she performs it nobly. Pathos is rather more insisted on in parts of the Septimus Harding story; but when all is told and he is slipping away into death, no one is asked to lament or pity a man so loved and honored and one so entitled to feel that life had granted him virtually all he had ever demanded of it, and that he had employed well the talents God had given him.

A most circumspect subordination of what, in other hands, might have been the pathetic in the vein of conventional romance Trollope displays in his whole account of Lily Dale. Jilted and humiliated in her ardent, girlish first-love, she is left with little prospect of happiness. Yet Trollope will have no tears shed over her. One might bemoan her wounded sensibility if it were not for her unimpaired and ever quizzical good sense. Both these qualities account for her refusal of the devoted John Eames. That Trollope should appear irked at times by her persistence in this is evidence of the lifelike way in which the elements of her nature are blended. Perhaps he had her in mind when, in the *Autobiography,* he declared that he sometimes argued with his characters. Certainly he must have known better when he called her a prig, and when he implied, in *The Last Chronicle,* that because she no longer cares for Crosbie, stubbornness has much to do with her holding out against Eames. The truth is that though she is fond of him, she knows all too well that what she feels for him is not love. Indeed he is the sort of man for whom a woman like Lily could feel only a maternal or older-sisterly regard, and neither her sense nor her sensibility would let that suffice for a marriage.

If Trollope never allows sentimentalism to distort his portrayal of Barsetshire heroines, it is equally true that no romantic idealization exalts unduly the young men who woo them. He goes out of his way to admit that the narratives are novels, but he refuses to equip them with conventional heroes. The young men are permitted few opportunities for anything more heroic than the defiance of strong-minded mothers and fathers. They are allowed to trounce a rascal or two, but the punitive engagements test nobody's prowess; and it is only an old man who is rescued from a bull, and a rather dull one at that. Trollope, who was slow in reaching maturity, may have seen too much of young manhood to regard it very highly; moreover, in his one complete account of it, the story of Eames' approach to manhood, he could not be very laudatory, because he was writing of himself.

One of the wooers most evenly leveled to strict realistic requirements is Henry Grantly in *The Last Chronicle*. He is old enough to be a major and a widower, and he is very much his father's son in the respect that he pays to worldly position and wealth; hence he is by no means the man to dash forward under the threat of disinheritance if he marry Grace Crawley. His love for her surmounts everything else after he has yielded to it; but he is brought to the yielding-point not entirely by his growing regard for her but also by pride and resentment at parental opposition. Thus he embodies one of Trollope's reiterated and very realistic convictions: "Our motives are

usually mixed." No hero is Henry Grantly, but a respectable
and very credible man of his type.

Indeed the force in his characterization is that of demon-
strable truth or significance rather than of personality. In the
description of his appearance, in his speech, in the form taken
by his thinking, in what others say and think about him, there
is little that compels us not merely to believe in his existence
but to feel it. This is an undeniable fault, but there is a measure of compensation for it in the clarity with which the portrayal speaks the truths that it embodies. In these respects it
is representative of the way in which a considerable group of
Barsetshire's younger men is characterized, including John
Bold, Frank Gresham, Lodovic Lufton, Mark Robarts, Na-
thaniel Sowerby, who may be called young because he knows
when to seem ingenuous, and Adolphus Crosbie, whose significance is so ably supported by Trollope's analysis of his
motives, and whose none too definite personality is vouched
for by the fact that Lily Dale succumbed to it. Trollope was
no amorist, but young women seemed to evoke his personaliz-
ing powers more surely than did young men (could it be that
feminine readers hold an opposite view?); even John Eames,
though well defined in his significance, is, as a presence, just a
bit foggy. No doubt all this dimming was unintentional, due
both to haste and to the perennial difficulty of avoiding the
mediocre presentation of innate mediocrity. The effect of it,
at any rate, was to accentuate Trollope's intentional subordination of heroism, and for that matter, of villainy as well.

The identity of the older Barset men is better attended to,
though Bishop Proudie is more a significance (of petticoat-
smothered insignificance) than a personality. Indeed he is all

but personalized by his nonentity, absurd in *Barchester Tow-ers* and *Framley Parsonage,* and almost pitiable in *The Last Chronicle* when Trollope gradually ceases to treat Mrs. Prou-die satirically and prepares her for death. Most of the Bishop's coevals have personality in very proper balance with the sig-nificance that shows itself as clear-cut traits combined accord-ing to familiar formulas. Dr. Thorne, for example, who is treated without humor or satire, is a character with a plain meaning and a character that has an ever recognizable way with it. Of such as he is the very kingdom of Trollope's real-ism in the novel of life observed.

Dr. Thorne's kind of man offered Trollope no problem; of the more troublesome type among the older men there is but one striking instance, the Rev. Josiah Crawley. The problem, put simply, was to keep him from changing the whole tone of *The Last Chronicle* or from seeming as foreign to the book as a figure out of Elizabethan tragedy. He is the most vividly personalized character in the Barset Series. Almost every ref-erence to him, even (for rereaders) that first nameless one in *Barchester Towers,* evokes a sense of his entity; and so does every detail of his appearance, gesture, speech—his grovelling in desperate prayer, his stalking through the mud with long arm extended, clutching the air, "crushing in his hand the bishop, and the bishop's wife, and the whole diocese—and all the Church of England." The significance of the man is equally to be felt. When we come to know him thoroughly in *The Last Chronicle,* we learn that his nature has been a battle-ground of intensities, Christian zealotry against an innate de-sire for the public recognition of his superior attainments and virtues. The mere consciousness of supremacy cannot satisfy

him. He can play St. Paul, says Trollope, but he must have
the veneration accorded to a saint. He has kept a high resolve
never to seek clerical advancement, but because it has not
come to him, he has fallen into an "antagonism with all the
world," especially with those who would be kind to him. He
loves his family deeply but with bitter self-approach. Before
those who had profited in life whether fairly or unfairly, he
can abase himself with a distressing humility that is both a
luxury of martyrdom and a device to make him master of the
situation. Thus he is above vanity and buried by it; he is in
a constant flux of weakness and strength, of false pride and
true—and when the understanding of what he is comes in
upon him, he battles with himself in unavailing prayer. He
can see the way for others and proclaim it like a prophet, but
he can do nothing for himself.

That Trollope contrived to use Crawley in anything but
violent tragedy is to be accounted for largely by an element
of pettiness in the characterization which, by the Aristotelian
formula, denies it tragic value; also there is a grim, intermit-
tent comicality throughout the portrayal that tends to abate
high seriousness and hold Crawley to the level of prose realism. Desperate things seem imminent now and then; but in
the end and without anticlimax Trollope manages to persuade
Crawley into a new, clean suit, to provide him with a comfortable living, and to avoid speculation about the improbability
of his being able to enjoy anything but misery. Thus Crawley
is not denied his position among Barset folk, there being a
place for him as for Lord Dumbello because they are not extremes of human nature outside the bounds of realism.

Nor does that which is represented by Crawley monopolize

a reader's interest. Barsetshire is its people, and its people are a unit, a group rather than an association of individuals. Hence the unity, the *gestalt* if you will, of these novels is not to be defined entirely by a study that isolates personalities. Such a procedure will serve better for certain modern novels, those that seem peopled with brooding egocentrics advancing upon the reader in thin, close-lipped deployment indeed by contrast with the wide, freely conversing phalanx of the Barset novels. Trollope, in this series at least, is concerned less with the development, and, save for one or two exceptions, with the definition of personalities than with their comings-together, their matings, and their attainment of a recognized place in their world or a dominance in its affairs. This effect is the more evident because that world is a small one of convention-bound country gentlefolk, and of clerics whose way of life in so far as Trollope feels called upon to record it is pretty much that of an ingrown minor officialdom touchy about its rights and apt enough to brew tempests in its teapots.

It is, however, a world in which "the hasty, normal" readers to whom Trollope addressed himself have always been able, in accordance with his wish, to "recognize persons like to themselves," persons who, as Hawthorne described them in his oft-quoted praise of Trollope's novels, were "going about their daily business and not suspecting that they were made a show of." Thus Trollope, though he implements no social theories in the Barset series, does contribute to that "invincible conviction of solidarity" which Conrad finds in all artistic fiction, and without which no society can endure. Trollope's simon-pure, basic realism of common life gives us full measure of something which we seek unconsciously in crowds and gatherings of all sorts, even among the hurried strangers on a city street—a heartening sense of comradeship in the enterprise of daily living. Conferred by Trollope's fiction it comes to us not as the vitalization granted to the actor, whose art enables him to live the lives of others; it is rather the vitalization in the exercise of imagination, that "half-memory," to use Kipling's phrase for it, whereby one can enter into what seems long-standing sympathetic familiarity with lives but an hour before unheard of.

The wider implication and significance of these lives Trollope asserts somewhat by his own comments but more potently by what he records that his people have done because they are themselves. He never achieves what properly may be called revelation, but for that matter few novelists do. Nor does he simulate it by cryptology and bewildering actuality. What he gives us is mnemonic rather than momentary, not so much an experience as an observation of past things brought before us with the clarity of actual recollection, and surpassing it in organization and completeness and in the sense of that mastery of life which comes with years and much remembering—and even then all too faintly.

There is a need. To it Trollope and such as Trollope must minister again and yet again.

WALTER L. MYERS
University of Pittsburgh

Sister M. Thecla, S.C.

S. THOMAS MORE'S "MERYE LAUGHING
HARVEST"

BESIDES *Utopia* and a few other Latin works, S. Thomas
More wrote some long treatises in English. Few are
aware of them; fewer have read them through. What
renown they now enjoy is for their length and dullness. One
historian views them as the uncontested hunting ground of
two or three intrepid scholars (and he is not one of the two or
three!); another pities More for never having seen the advantage of connecting brevity with wit. Furthermore, modern reprints of most of the treatises are still wanting. And the thick
old Rastell edition of 1557 is by now a rare book and inacces-
sible to most. Some, like Saintsbury, are daunted by the very
sight of its double columns of black letter: *"Non legitur,"* said
he, "with my eyes."

But neither this nor the serious religious content of More's
works was any obstacle to his contemporaries—to whom all
printing was rather new and luxurious, and things theological
were of vital importance. Some readers informed More that
they had gone through the tracts three and four times, and
then made outlines to keep.

Oddly, however, where we think More dull (often somewhat *a priori*), his readers' only objection was that he was too
sparkling. There was something unseemly, they felt, in his
habit of mingling the grave and the gay. More relates the

reproof as coming from many. Manifestly he alone among the circumspect Tudor humanists was endowed with literary charm along with learning and piety. This made him something of a pioneer. No *Spectator* had as yet advertised the wisdom of enlivening morality with wit. But More defends himself and continues to leaven the good solid dough of his arguments with "fansies and sportes, & mery tales." He protests that as a layman it is not his function "seriously and solempnely to preach." And Horace, he adds, has observed that one may indeed "saye full soth in game." Later in the century praise finally came to More's appealing manner along with (or in spite of) the orthodoxy that it clothed. Gabriel Harvey dubbed him "a fine and pleasant confuter in English"; Thomas Nash rejoiced in his "comical wit."

True, the major part of More's English writing constitutes his side in the religious debate with Tyndale and Frith and Barnes. But it is by no means all polemical. More had written, earlier, a treatise on the Four Last Things, as well as the life of Richard III that Shakespeare built upon; he left incomplete at his execution a tract upon the Passion of Christ. The great finished work of the Tower year, the "Dialogue of comforte agaynste tribulacyon," is timeless for the beauty and truth with which it assuages a human ill. Cresacre More, S. Thomas' grandson and biographer, preferred it to any other, "heathen or Christian, Greek or Latin," on the subject; and one can still agree.

Not the least characteristic of all More's English writings is the sprinkling, through their seriousness, of the fresh figurative phrase and the whimsical aside that for More were irrepressible. The style and the man were certainly one. The same geniality that endeared him personally put the bright touches of alliteration, of dramatic pencilling, of ringing cadence to his practical and often pedestrian prose. One of the most learned men of his time, More knew beyond erudition the memorable shining of "a mery worde in a right ernest worke."

THE MERRY WORD

So More tempers with casual concreteness both his diffuse reasonings and his fierce penetrating arguments. Having summarized an opponent's point, he pauses to approve its first implication before rejecting its conclusion: "And herein he playeth the good kowe, and geveth us a good galon of mylke. But than shall you see how he playeth the shrewde kow agayn, and turneth over the payle." One whose argument gets nowhere, he writes, "fareth lyke a butterflye fallen on a lime twigge, which the more it striveth and flotereth, ever the faster it hangeth." One proved insincere looks to More "like a puffe rynge of Paris, holowe, light and counterfait in deede." A contention of his own he believes to be as prickly as a bush of thorns that even through a pair of hedging gloves cannot safely be rooted out. The promise to refute a point is phrased as promise to pluck off "the most gloriouse fethers from his gai pecokes taile." To prefer a material good to a spiritual one, he says, is like jeopardizing one's body for fear of losing one's old rainbeaten cloak. He bids a disgruntled opponent go home and be thankful (for no worse) "as a man geatteth him to the fyre & shaketh his hatte after a showre of rain." The young reformers, he says, regard themselves "as lustye freshe & grene" as a bed of leeks after a shower. Further leeks spring into view in a clear reminder of Heywood's *Play of the Wether:* how im-

[163]

possible it is that the Lord shall please with the same weather the husband who wants a fair sky for his corn and the wife who would have rain for her leeks. With an engaging liberty More once produces the testimony of saints and Church fathers "made afore a good notary the good man god himselfe."

This freshness of illustration is doubly happy when it narrowly saves its author from conventional moralizing. To this kind of danger the "Dialogue of comforte" is especially open by its very subject. But its sincerity and soundness, far from trite, march by with extraordinary vigor. Using, for example, the familiar scriptural image of the night-fear, wherein to a man walking in the dark every bush seems a thief, More adds that what at first seemed a lion turns out to be but a "sely rude roryng asse." And what at sea appeared by night a dangerous rock, is indeed nothing but a mist. Those who make a fetish of fame seem, as More puts it, to think the world will do nothing else day or night but sit and sing *sanctus, sanctus, sanctus* upon them. Yet, he observes, if one's finger ache with a hot blain, a great many admirers blowing one's praise will not do half so much good as having one boy blow upon the finger! Most characteristic is the sudden twist by which More skirts an imminent platitude. Beginning once on a homiletic note, "For in the short winter day of worldly wealth and prosperitie," he worthwith points his moral with a whimsical sketch wherein the prosperous sit up on a rainbow and survey their erstwhile companions as "sely poore pissemeres and antes."

A JOLLY COMPANY

"A merye tale," More says, "commith never amisse to me." And in the scraps of anecdote that dot his treatises appears a list of homespuns that, collected, would make a quite Chaucerian set of pilgrims. They would be traveling to Walsingham instead of Canterbury: one of the merry tales begins, as "I rode ones in good company . . . to Walsingham in pilgrimage." Into such a frame might be placed, certainly, "good man Gryme," the Cambridge mustard-maker who prayed for himself and his wife and his child and the grace to make good mustard and no more . . . ; as well the pert "wyfe in the red hoode" who turned the tables on the preacher when he publicly scolded her for talking at sermon time . . . ; the "old sage father fo(o)le" of Sandwich Haven who in his Kentish dialect gravely blamed the disastrous rising sands in the harbor on the new church steeple: "For by God I knew it a good haven til that steple was bylded. And by the mary masse, cha marked it well, it never throve since." . . . ; More's man Cliffe (to whom times seems to have denied the fame of his fellow, Henry Patenson), many years mad but harmless, who calmly broke off the head of a statue on London Bridge and berated the officials for not mending it . . . ; the "lewde galante and the pore frere," each calling the other fool for his profession . . . ; the poor ploughman served with water under the name of wine: "God thanke you maister winer for your good wyne, but in good fayth savyng for the worshipfull name of wyne, iche had as leve a drunken water." . . . ; More's own father remarking slyly that "there is but one shrewde wyfe in the worlde . . . (and) everi man weneth he hath her & that that one is his owne." . . . ; the old nursemaid "Mother Mawde" by the fire with the children telling the long story of the Wolf and the Ass and father-confessor the Fox . . . ; the childish old man as full of words as a woman, who loves to "sitte wel and warme with a cuppe and a rosted crabbe, and drivel, and drinke and talke." He may well be the same old man whom More sees elsewhere, "his hed hanging in his bosom, and his body croked, walk pit pat upon a paire of patens wyth the staffe in the tone hande and the *pater noster* in the tother hande." Incidental and scattered as they are, these people come as much alive as any in fiction. Largely a peasant group, they lack the wide range of Chaucer's; after all, they were not designed to be a group at all. More, brought up on the boisterous comedy of miracle and morality, lending a hand (it is thought) to the making of *Johan Johan* and *The Foure PP,* takes a hearty delight in the rustic's simplicity. How he would have enjoyed the tribe of Dogberry and Old Gobbo and sweet bully Bottom!

Spontaneous bits of dialogue and action (still in the dull treatises) show how readily More might, with opportunity, have developed the taste and talent for fictionizing. Most of such action crops up in the long "Confutacion of Tyndales Aunswere" (1532), almost as though so much argument must be lightened somehow. In this tract More asks if Adam, for example, should have met God's first injunction with a question: "Tell me good lord wherfore, and what thou meanest therby, and why should I more dye for eating thereof, then of another tree? tell me this good lord ere thou go, for els be thy backe tourned once, I will eate thereof whether thou wilt or no." And Moses, he adds, should hardly have retorted to God, "Tell me what it meaneth that thou wilt have the tabernacle made of this maner, or els it shal lye unmade for me." In the same work More suddenly enlivens citations from S. Gregory by calling up a kind of courtroom scene in which the saint appears, listens to the opposition, and begins to reply in person. "Why sirs how can that be?" He bids an officer count off the witnesses by name. "Now whan this officer had comen wyth his sticke and patted them upon the pates, and the criour with him, and as he hit them rehearse them thus: frere Luther one . . ." etcetera, then S. Gregory addresses them directly for the remainder of the argument.

The "Dialogue of comforte" contains delightfully more of this fictionizing than its framework would have demanded. Old Anthony, imprisoned, and the nephew Vincent who visits him are better than mere mouthpieces. Where the exposition grows so long that the speaker is forgotten, More brings him back as though he too realized it. "But see now what age is," apologizes old Anthony. "Loe, I have bene so longe in my tale that I have almoste forgotten for what purpose I tolde it. Oh, nowe I remember me loe. . . ." Or Anthony is himself made to dramatize a little in explaining a point. Any man, he tells Vincent, may say to God upon receiving wealth: "Mary I thanke you sir for this with all my heart, and wyl not fayle to love you well whyle you lette me fare no worse." The "Dialogue of comforte" contains, in fact, one of the most beautifully cadenced passages of More's prose, spoken by no less than a personified terrain! Without the savor of its form the passage does no more than present an old truth. But More lets the earth itself sigh it out to humanity, with epic overtones. If, as Plato says, the world were animated with a reasonable soul, it should surely so address its arrogant possessor:

Ah thou selye poore soule, that wenest thou were halfe a God, and arte amidde thy glorye but a manne in a gay gowne, I that am the ground here over whom thou art so prowde, have hadde an hundred

[167]

suche owners of me as thou calleste thy selfe, mo(r)e than ever thou hast heard the names of. And some of them that proudly went over mine head: lye now low in my bellye, and my syde lyeth over them. And manye one shall as thou doest now, cal hymselfe mine owner after thee, that neyther shall bee sybbe to thy bloude, nor any word heare of thy name.

TUDOR LOOKING GLASS

Of learned references in More there is no end; and they shall not be touched upon here. But as More plays with popular phrases, so he casually displays what were the literary commonplaces of his day. Horace, he reminds an over-exacting reader, observes that even Homer sometimes falls into a little slumber. Twice he speaks of a counterfeit saint's relic "that was happely some time as Chaucer saith a bone of some holy Jewes shepe." The presumptuous, says More, will freely handle Holy Scripture as though it were a song of Robin Hood; they will throw out the Doctors of the Church and lean instead to the authority of Friar Tuck and Maid Marion. Here is no appeal to a child's picture book. The Robin Hood plays, with actors all in Kendal green, were a widely loved entertainment, especially at the May games season. As well known too were the fabulous figures of Prester John, vaguely of Abyssinia, and of the great Cham of Cathay. So, says Anthony, flavoring the "Dialogue of comforte" with old romance, will the great Turk if he be not barred overrun all Europe and Prester John's land and the grand Cham's too.

The fables of Aesop appear throughout More's work with extraordinary frequency. One is hardly prepared for the high favor accorded these tales in the most sophisticated of Tudor circles. But More himself is witness to it. Margaret Roper records his telling her one day in the Tower that Wolsey so often related at court the story of the rain, the fools, and the wise men that he is not likely now to forget it. Aesop had been revived and translated with the general revival of Greek, and the printing press put the fables into wide circulation. Caxton had printed his English version in 1485. In the Reformation controversy the fables were bandied about as homely shots of satire. So, and in other ways as well, More uses them, digressing surprisingly often: "as Isop saith in a fable." To the rapacity he sees in the religious war in Germany More applies the story of the dog who lost the cheese in his mouth, trying to grasp as well the cheese reflected in the water. As warning to the ungracious he tells how for the same fault Jupiter saddled the snail with her shell. To show the unreasonableness of fear, he tells of the harts fleeing despite themselves from the little hunting dog. And once he protests:

Nor I use not to folowe the condicion of Isopes ape, that thought her own babes so beawteous (*sic*), and so farre passyng in all goodlye feature and favour, nor the crowe that accompted her own byrdes the fayrest of allthe fowles that flew.

Here and there occur the familiar stories of the hen with the golden eggs, the man with the double wallet, the contest of the envious and the covetous, the old man who calls on death for release from his burden and hastily, at sight of the spectre, prefers his load!

In and out of the most abstruse argument flash glimpses of Tudor pastime and social custom. Disparaging the new sermons of the reformers, More points to that well known figure, "an abbot of misrule in a christemas game," who having been

tossed in blankets would mount a stool and (says More) even
as the moderns do in earnest "make a mowyng sermon." More
had viewed such a scene many a time—in boyhood at Cardinal
Morton's palace, then at Oxford, now at the Court itself. For
this traditional Lord of Misrule—otherwise Christmas Prince,
King of Beans, *Prince des Sots*—presided over the Yuletide
revels in all great houses and in the universities. Random
glimpses of other entertainments are plentiful: a wrestling at
Clerkenwell, bear-baiting, "halowing out the fox," the stage
play wherein "wering a gay golden gown . . . the lorel playeth the lord." Mention of the card game of "poste" dates a
century earlier the famous Post and Pair praised by Ben Jonson as a "thrifty and right worshipful game." The popular
juggler comes in for several bows. He provides a satisfactory
symbol, of course, for the trickery of More's adversaries. Once
he emerges in striking detail as the perfect progenitor of any
Thurston or Houdini:

. . . as a jugler layeth forth hys trinclets upon the table, and biddeth
men looke on thys and looke on that, & blow in hys hande, and then
wyth certayne straunge words to make men muse, whurleth his jug-
linge stycke aboute hys fyngers to make men loke upon that, while he
playeth a false cast and conveieth with the tother hand some thing
slyly into his purse or sleve or some where out of sight.

Much of the magnificence of Tudor dress and ornament
glints through here as well. The "gay golden gown" already
mentioned has companion in the gay golden shirts of those
who also "goe nowe full freshe, in their garded hosen . . .
and in theyr silken sleves." To the little babes one must give
"fayre wordes and pretye proper geare, ratilles and cokbelles
and gay golden sho(o)ne." (And in the last half of the order

listen to the dactylic jingle of a nursery rhyme!) To the objection that too much gold has gone into church vessels, More retorts by pointing indignantly to the lavish quantities of gold one sees everywhere—in the gilding, he says, of knives and swords and spurs and arras and painted clothes: "And (as though these thinges could not consume golde fast ynoughe) the gyltyng of postes & hole rofes, not onely in the palaces of princes & great prelates, but also many right meane menes houses." And on the other side of the picture lie the beggars who on Fridays put their sore legs out in sight "about saynt saviour and at the Savy gate."

More keeps a sense of wonder at the familiar, a wonder that stems less from romanticism than from keen religious insight. Opposing the current fashion for deriding miracles, he recalls things formerly thought miraculous but which Tudor England is beginning to take for granted. The list of these phenomena is illuminating. He observes that it is not so long ago that one discovered the "straunge truth" that the world is round and can be sailed around in two years. (Columbus and Magellan both died during More's lifetime.) Not long ago people were ignorant that "the earthe hangeth in the ayre, and men walk fote against fote, & shippes saile bottom against bottom." And is it not a marvel, he asks, that glass can be made of fern root? Previously men might well have laughed at this apparent miracle. Less than fifty years ago, he adds, the London goldsmiths thought it incredible that gilt could be parted from silver. Now, through repeated seeing, they no longer spare it a thought. Yet essentially it is still wonderful to one who ponders on realities; and "no more mervailous is a koko than a cock, though the one be sene but in somer & the other al the yere." Imagine that a man born blind should suddenly receive his sight: how he would wonder at the sun and moon and stars, whereas one accustomed to them thinks less of the great planets than of his first sight of a peacock's tail.

So, More concludes, the order of the universe is as inexplicable as these miracles the moderns find amusing. It seems to him no less remarkable that a grown man should originate in infinitesimal seed than that a dead man be restored to life. But "the acquayntance & dayly beholdynge taketh away the wondring." Defending the tradition that Saint Erkenwald pulled out to proper length a piece of timber cut too short for the roof of Barking Abbey, More compares this feat to a now accepted one of apparently equal impossibility. Though the former needed God's special intervention, it is now possible by man's hand alone to draw out any piece of metal into a long thin wire. Illustrating further, More makes one of his best descriptions of the sea. Londoners think nothing of the Thames, nor even of the Channel: "But he that had never sene it, nor herd therof, would at the fyrst sight wonder sore therat, to se(e) that great water come walowing up agaynst the wynde, kepyng a commen course to & fro, no cause perceived that driveth him."

It is indeed understandable that one who wore both sanctity and learning with so much charm should have been one of the most influential in all England . . . so that all noblemen set about educating their children because More did . . . so that Roger Ascham in *The Scholemaster* of the next generation could tell of one, no match for More in wit and wisdom, that yet imitated him by "wearing his gowne awrye upon the one shoulder."

More's redundancy cannot well be denied. Of his subject-matter one not read in theology might be pardoned for saying with Piers Plowman, "The more I muse on it the mistier I think it." But the winsomeness of More's humor runs through it all, and the lucid simplicity of one whose favorite among the Psalms was "Beati immaculati in via." More stated confidently that he hoped to have "a merye laughing harvest for ever." Beforehand flowers his harvest of "merye laughing" words that are not at all misty nor redundant. Neither are they dull.

SISTER M. THECLA, S.C.
Seton Hill College

William Price Albrecht

HAZLITT'S *PRINCIPLES OF HUMAN ACTION* AND THE IMPROVEMENT OF SOCIETY

AS the eighteenth century came to an end and the nineteenth began, the rights of Englishmen were suffering curtailment—both in practice and in theory. The excesses of the French revolution had gone far toward discrediting the doctrine of the rights of man and, together with hard times, had made the ruling class in England and even the lower classes fearful of revolt. With bad harvests at home, high taxes, trade disrupted by the war, and the collapse of markets after 1815, distress among the poor became more than usually severe; and in fear of violence, the rights of the working class were narrowly circumscribed. Pitt suspended the Habeas Corpus in 1794, and in 1795 Parliament passed two bills prohibiting public meetings. Societies of working men were suppressed, and their leaders prosecuted; and by the Combination Laws passed in 1799 and 1800, workmen were prohibited from taking any common action in defense of their interests. When, during the hard times after the war, laborers rioted for bread, the work of suppression was carried on with increasing harshness. An act of 1817 suspended the Habeas Corpus, and in the same year three other coercion acts were passed by great majorities.[1]

---

[1] G. D. H. Cole, *The Life of William Cobbett* (London: W. Collins Sons and Co.,

Acute poverty gave force to the theory that the right to sub-
sistence is not society's responsibility but is "naturally" limited to what a laborer can earn in "free" competition in the
labor market. To political economists, therefore, rational
"self-love" appeared to be a more useful motive than "benevolence"; and if the ruling classes considered benevolence socially useful, it was likely to be in contenting the working
classes with poor-relief.[2] The conception of benevolence as a
moral obligation, revealed by reason, to grant the rights of
others persisted in Godwin, Owen, and other radicals, but
their writings had little practical effect in relieving poverty:
Owen's proposed Villages of Cooperation, although safely
within the laws of property, were rejected by the Committee
of the House of Commons on the Poor Laws, partly because
they ran counter to the theories of political economy and

1927), pp. 195–97; Élie Halévy, *A History of the British People in 1815* (New York:
Harcourt Brace and Co., 1924), pp. 218–19, 229, 245–46; J. L. and Barbara Hammond, *The Village Labourer 1760–1832* . . . (4th ed.; London: Longmans, Green,
and Co. Ltd., 1927), pp. 142–43, 153–54; J. L. and Barbara Hammond, *The Town
Labourer 1760–1832* . . . (London: Longmans, Green and Co., Ltd., 1928), pp. 87–94,
98, 103, 112 ff.; Hansard, *Parliamentary History*, XXXII (1795), 242–554; William
Smart, *Economic Annals of the Nineteenth Century* (London: MacMillan and Co.,
1910), I, 263–65, 271–76, 442–43, 455, 493, 530–31, 548–54, 596–98, and *passim;* Gra-
ham Wallas, *The Life of Francis Place* (4th ed.; London: George Allen and Unwin
Ltd., 1925), pp. 25–26 and *passim.*

2 Arthur Young, *The Question of Scarcity Plainly Stated* . . . (London: W. J. and
J. Richardson, and J. Wright, 1800), pp. 32–33, 68–69, 75; [Samuel Whitbread], *Sub-
stance of a Speech on the Poor Laws* . . . (London: J. Ridgway, 1807), pp. 15–19;
[John Weyland], *A Short Inquiry into the Policy, Humanity, and Past Effects of the
Poor Laws* . . . (London: J. Hatchard [and others], 1807), p. 308; Robert Acklom
Ingram, *Disquisitions on Population* . . . (London: J. Hatchard, 1808), p. 86; [Rob-
ert Southey], "Inquiry into the Poor Laws," *Quarterly Review*, VIII (1812), 327; John
Weyland, *The Principles of Population and Production* . . . (London: Baldwin,
Cradock, and Jay, 1816), pp. 165–66; James Grahame, *An Inquiry into the Principle
of Population* . . . (Edinburgh: Archibald Constable and Co.; London: Longman,
Hurst, Rees, Orme, and Browne, 1816), pp. 182, 238–40.

partly because Owen had criticized the established system of property and wages.[3]

On account of disgust with "wild speculations" of revolutionary thought, Southey wrote in 1803, the "moral and political atmosphere" had become "unnatural and unwholesome"; [4] and, according to Shelley in 1817, "gloom and misanthropy" were still "characteristic of the age. . . ." [5]

Hazlitt shared the current skepticism of a society of "perfectly" rational and moral beings, but he continually defended the rights of man. He objected particularly to what he considered the narrow psychology and the low aims of political economy; for, he believed, the insistence that economic improvement depended on rational self-interest free from governmental interference was, practically, a denial of human rights and was, moreover, inimical to any improvement whatsoever. Hazlitt's explanation of human behavior limits society's approach to "perfection," but even a lesser degree of improvement, Hazlitt thought, could be realized only through increased virtue and benevolence.[6]

---

[3] Robert Owen, *The Life of Robert Owen by Himself* (New York: Alfred A. Knopf, 1920), p. 215; G. D. H. Cole, *The Life of Robert Owen* (2d ed.; London: MacMillan and Company, 1930), pp. 20–30.

[4] [Robert Southey], "Malthus's Essay on Population," *Annual Review*, II (1803), 292.

[5] Preface to *Laon and Cythna, The Complete Works of Percy Bysshe Shelley,* ed. Roger Ingpen and Walter E. Peck (London: Ernest Benn, 1927), I, 241–42.

[6] Crane Brinton in *The Political Ideas of the English Romanticists* (London: Oxford University Press, 1926) stresses Hazlitt's "preoccupation . . . with the problem of bringing down the revolutionary philosophy to the level of human nature" (p. 132) and brings out the anti-rationalism with which Hazlitt attacked Malthus and Bentham; but Professor Brinton has not shown the importance Hazlitt attached to *benevolence,* in opposition to *self-love,* as a factor in improvement.

I

In political literature the opposition of "reason" to "passion" and "benevolence" to "self-love" assumed—in Godwin's *Political Justice* and in Malthus' *Essay on Population*—two contradistinguishing patterns. Combining the doctrines of "utility," "necessity," and the rights of man, Godwin finds promise of rational and moral behavior and, therefore, of complete political and economic equality. Just as experience relates cause and effect in the material world, Godwin argues in *Political Justice*, so does it bind them together by necessity in the mind itself, linking with certain propositions "the notion of preferableness or the contrary" and directing, thereby, one's tendency to action.[7] Now, since "men always act upon their apprehensions of preferableness," their actions will be virtuous and just—that is, making for the general happiness— if by connecting cause and effect they can see the preferableness of such actions. But a higher law than any made by man is on the side of justice. The "immutabl[e] tru[th] that whatever tends to produce a balance of [happiness and pleasure] is to be desired, and whatever tends to a balance of [misery and pain] is to be rejected" is "founded in the nature of things," for "vicious conduct is soon discovered to involve injurious consequences." If, therefore, man is allowed the free use of his reason—the faculty that enables him to foresee consequences—he cannot but act toward increasing the general happiness.[8]

---

[7] William Godwin, *An Enquiry Concerning Political Justice* . . . (London: G. G. and J. Robinson, 1793), I, 286–90, 343–45, and *passim*. Godwin acknowledges his debt to Hume. (*Ibid.*, p. 296, n.)

[8] *Ibid.*, I, 31, 75, 121–22, 346 ff.; II, 830–31, and *passim*.

Therefore men have no "rights" in the sense that they may or may not choose a certain line of conduct, for justice demands that they act always to increase the general happiness; but since it is every man's duty to employ himself to this end as best he may, everyone possesses, as the correlative of his neighbors' duties, certain negative rights.[9] That is to say, as Godwin adds in his second edition, "every man has a right to that, the exclusive possession of which being awarded to him, a greater sum of benefit or pleasure will result, than could have arisen from its being otherwise appropriated." [10] A quantity of food, clothing, and shelter necessary to keep a man alive will obviously contribute more to the general happiness by being awarded to a man who is entirely without food, clothing, or shelter than by being granted to one who is already adequately supplied with such property. Therefore, if the division of both labor and produce were made according to the demands of justice, everyone would have enough material goods at the cost of perhaps only half an hour's work per day.[11] Everyone would have the leisure necessary to further mental development, and consequently greater virtue, and would enjoy to a higher and still higher degree the intellectual pleasures which give man his greatest happiness.

For progress toward such a society, truth must be made known through freedom of inquiry and freedom of expression.[12] Government must not perpetuate vice by preserving the distinction between rich and poor, for if a common stock

[9] *Ibid.*, I, 110–12.
[10] *Enquiry Concerning Political Justice* . . . (2d ed. corrected; London: G. G. and J. Robinson, 1796), II, 415–16.
[11] *Political Justice* (1st ed.), II, 790–92, 823.
[12] *Ibid.*, II, 878–93.

of goods were built up through the labors of every citizen, "temptation would lose its power." [13] Along with private property, Godwin condemns such other "erroneous institutions" as marriage, religious conformity, oaths of fidelity, and laws for the suppression of libel. From all of these, government should withdraw its sanction and confine itself to the suppression of injustice against individuals and defense against invasion. As truths become more general and men more just, even the first of these will become hardly necessary and the latter not a matter of maintaining a regular army but of a virtuous citizenry rallying to defend the common interest.[14]

Thus, according to Godwin, reason may dominate passion and, as it does, concern for the benefit of the whole will replace selfishness in directing action. The rational man, when confronted with two alternatives, will choose that tending to the greater increase of general happiness.

Political economy also relied on the power of reason to connect cause and effect and to determine behavior accordingly; but as far as the production and distribution of goods was concerned, "self-love" rather than "benevolence" was designated as the socially useful motive.[15] Adam Smith assumed a natural or inherent principle whereby the good of

---

[13] *Ibid.*, I, 34.

[14] *Ibid.*, II, 564–67.

[15] "Benevolence," as used by most contemporary writers, seems to denote an emotion, whereas "virtue" in *Political Justice* apparently involves only reason without emotional impetus. Later, however, in a memorandum intended "to correct certain errors" in *Political Justice*, Godwin acknowledges the need for emotion in directing voluntary actions, and limits the province of reason "to adjusting the comparison between different objects of desire, and investigating the most successful mode of attaining these objects. . . ." Virtuous action will spring from "a disposition naturally kind and well tempered," but it will be regulated by "general utility." (Quoted in Ford K. Brown, *The Life of William Godwin* [London: J. M. Dent & Sons Ltd., 1926], pp. 135–36.)

all results from the self-seeking of each and laid down competitive effort for gain as the basis of the economic system, inferring that a wise government should leave prices and wages to the law of supply and demand, and charity to the discrimination of individuals.[16] "Benevolence," narrowed in meaning to the public or even private support of the poor, was deprecated as interfering with free competition and therefore as being "unjust." [17]

Malthus, replying to Godwin by elaborating a proposition from *The Wealth of Nations,* stresses the resistance of passion to reason as well as the social efficacy of self-love. Nature, according to the *Essay on Population,* instead of making for a communistic anarchy of disinterested citizens, insures the division into economic classes, with self-love as the ruling principle. Because the sexual passion is "necessary" and "constant" and because the food supply is limited—ultimately by the earth's productivity and actually by many intervening factors—population will always increase to a point where, regardless of human institutions, a marginal group must suffer want. Malthus, however, does not content himself with finding Godwin's "justice" inconsistent with "nature." Equal distribution achieved through benevolence, he thinks, is unnatural; but self-love may work for the happiness of the group and bring about, if not the equitable distribution that would be

---

[16] Adam Smith, *An Inquiry into the Nature and Causes of the Wealth of Nations,* ed. Edwin Cannan (London: Methuen & Co., 1904), I, 142–44.

[17] Jeremy Bentham, *Observations on the Poor Bill* (London: William Clowes and Sons, 1838), pp. 7–8; Edmund Burke, *Thoughts and Details on Scarcity, The Works of Edmund Burke* (Boston: Little, Brown, and Co., 1866), V, 145–46; Hansard, *Parliamentary History,* XXXIV (1800), 1428.

deemed "just" among disinterested men in a world of plenty, at least the approximation to it that must be considered "just" among selfish beings in a world of limited resources. In a community such as that foreseen in *Political Justice,* where the communal stores were open to all, population would increase so rapidly that food production could not keep pace and scarcity would soon result. ". . . The spirit of benevolence" would be "repressed by the chilling breath of want," and "the mighty law of self-preservation" would soon restore "self-love" to its "wonted empire. . . ." "Vice" as well as "misery" would check population. Depredations from the common store would increase until "the laws of our nature" re-established, as the best remedies for overpopulation, private property and the obligation of every man to support his own children. A division into classes—proprietors and laborers—would then be inevitable, for those "born after the division of property" would have to work for those who had more than enough for themselves.[18] The *Quarterly* took comfort in this "incontrovertible answer to all sweeping reformers," considering it an advantage

to know . . . that the face of civilized society must always . . . be distinguished by the same features which it has hitherto borne; that our business therefore is to lessen or remove its blemishes, and to prevent their growing into deformities; but that we can no more organize a community without poverty, and its consequence, severe labour, than we can organize a body without natural infirmities, or add a limb to the human frame.[19]

---

[18] Thomas Robert Malthus, *First Essay on Population 1798* (London: MacMillan & Co., Ltd., 1926), pp. 11–26, 185–206, and *passim.*
[19] "Malthus on Population," *Quarterly Review,* XVII (July, 1817), 402.

II

Hazlitt objected to the acceptance of poverty as something "natural" and to the selfishness that this acceptance both assumed and encouraged. "Naturally," according to his *Principles of Human Action* (1805), the human mind is "disinterested, or . . . interested in the welfare of others in the same way, and from the same direct motives by which [one is] impelled to the pursuit of [his] own interest." Voluntary actions, unlike involuntary ones, do not arise solely from one's desire to avoid pain and to find pleasure, as Locke and his followers hold, but may be determined by the "idea" of good independent of any reference to one's own pleasure or pain. ". . . The mind is naturally interested in it's own welfare in a particular mechanical manner, only as far as related to it's past, or present impressions"; for, since the sensations a person will experience in the future cannot react mechanically upon his present self, only the imagination can connect the present self with the future self, and therefore it alone can produce ideas to motivate voluntary action.[20] Since a mechanical sympathy with one's future sensations does not exist, there must be "something in the very idea of good or evil which [through the imagination] naturally excites desire or aversion," and there must be, consequently, the same psychological basis for interested and disinterested action. It is true that the "love of my own particular good must precede that of the particular good of others, because I am acquainted with it first . . ."; but this "natural self-love," like "natural benevolence," depends

---

[20] *An Essay on the Principles of Human Action, The Complete Works of William Hazlitt*, ed. P. P. Howe (London: J. M. Dent and Sons, Ltd., 1930–1934), I, 1, 9–10. All references to Hazlitt's *Works* are to this edition.

only on the distinctness of the good. "Independently of habit and association, the strength of the affection excited is in proportion to the strength of the idea, and does not at all depend on the person to whom it relates except indirectly and by implication." [21] On the other hand, one may be motivated not by an idea of particular good but by an idea abstracted from "knowledge of various goods." That is, one may transfer "the feeling of real interest in a number of things conducive to [a] person's welfare to the abstract idea of his good in general." Thus, "refined" or "artificial" self-love or benevolence implies that a person is striving for his own or for others' happiness, not because the idea of his or their good in itself excites his affections, but because with the idea of his own or their happiness he associates the feeling derived from various "particular" or "real" goods. The extension of benevolence beyond the "natural" preference for a particular good without reference to the person to whom it relates, depends, therefore, upon

an habitual cultivation of the natural disposition of the mind to sympathize with the feelings of others by constantly taking an interest in those which we know, and imagining others that we do not know, [whereas] the other feeling of abstract self-interest, that is in the degree in which it generally subsists, must be caused by a long narrowing of the mind to our own particular feelings and interests, and a voluntary insensibility to everything which does not immediately concern ourselves.[22]

Although Hazlitt did not hold man to be naturally selfish, he could not accept Godwin's doctrine of universal benevo-

---

[21] *Ibid.*, p. 12.

[22] *Ibid.*, pp. 13–15. For a thorough and excellent analysis of the *Principles of Human Action*, see Horace Williston, "Hazlitt as a Critic of the 'Modern Philosophy'" (Unpublished Ph.D. dissertation, Dept. of English, University of Chicago, 1938), pp. 205 ff.

lence. Godwin explains the desire to increase the happiness of others as the culmination of the reasoning process; whereas, for Hazlitt, it is at least partly the result of "habit" and "circumstance" acting upon the "imagination." Since one pursues a good, either for himself or another, only from "having an idea of it sufficiently warm and vivid to incite in [him] an emotion of interest, or passion," [23] man's disinterestedness must be limited well short of universality. As Hazlitt points out in several of his essays, the universalizing of benevolence or disinterestedness on the basis of a calculation of consequences is impossible. Since reason can be only a guide to morality, since the moral life must derive its impulse from the affections, truly benevolent actions cannot be extended indefinitely. Godwin "conceived too nobly of his fellows," placing

the human mind on an elevation, from which it commands a view of the whole line of moral consequences; and requir[ing] it to conform its acts to the larger and more enlightened conscience which it has thus acquired. He absolves men from the gross and narrow ties of sense, custom, authority, private and local attachment, in order that he may devote himself to the boundless pursuit of universal benevolence.[24]

Hazlitt, then, did not foresee either the anarchy or the communism of *Political Justice*. Like Godwin, he believed that there must be no "arbitrary power" independent of the people [25] and that the right of government to limit the freedom

---

[23] *Ibid.*, p. 12.
[24] "William Godwin," *The Spirit of the Age, Works*, XI, 18–19. Cf. "A New View of Society," *Political Essays, Works*, VII, 103; "A New View of Society" (concluded), *Literary and Political Criticism, Works*, XIX, 159–61.
[25] "What is the People?" *Political Essays*, p. 262.

of individuals in the pursuit of their inclinations can arise
only "from the necessity of maintaining the equal rights of
every one, and of opposing force to force in case of any violent and unwarrantable infringement of them"; [26] but since
he does not accept the possibility of complete disinterestedness, rights must, practically, be more than the reciprocals of
duties, and to insure them the government must supplement
reason with force. A "right," according to Hazlitt, is simply
"that which is thought [good and useful] by the individual,
and which has the sanction of the will as such," but when the
individual lives "among a number of equally selfish and self-
willed beings," the principle of self-interest limits his "rights"
to those which "he can lay claim, [and simultaneously] allow
. . . the same latitude and allowance to others." Were men
completely reasonable, the limitation of individual rights in
order to preserve equal rights for all could be left, as Godwin
believes, to "moral justice, which implies only an appeal to
reason," but in "a real state of things," "political justice,
which implies an appeal to force" must assign "the limits of
. . . individual rights in society. . . ." [27]

Similarly, although he denied the inevitability of private
property, Hazlitt was more concerned with equalizing distribution under a system of private property than with establishing common ownership. The established administration
of property and the evils attendant upon it "would be no
longer necessary" if "sloth and rapacity . . . could be completely subdued, so that no one would refuse his share in the

[26] "Project for a New Theory of Civil and Criminal Legislation," *Literary and Political Criticism*, p. 305.
[27] *Ibid.*, pp. 303–304.

common labour, or endeavor to take unfair advantage of others either by force or fraud. . . ."

> Such a change [Hazlitt adds in a footnote] would not require the perfect subjugation, or rather annihilation of these passions, or perfect virtue, in the literal sense. . . . It might as well be pretended that no man could ever keep his fingers off bank-notes, or pay his debts, who was not perfectly honest. In neither case is there required any thing more than such a superiority in one set for [of?] motives over another, from pride, habit, example, opinion, &c. as just to incline the balance.

At the end of this footnote, however, Hazlitt confesses that he "meddle[s] with these questions only as things of idle speculation." [28] Elsewhere he lists the functions of property,[29] and is more generally concerned with the abuse of power derived from the possession of property than with abolishing this institution. Replying to Malthus in 1807, Hazlitt argues that as far as *"the principle of population . . . alone"* is involved, not "benevolent and perfect wisdom" but simply "self-love, and a little common sense" will serve as the "moving principles" for a "state of practical equality, admitting neither poverty nor riches." [30] The amount of food kept by the rich and the proportion remaining for the laborers is not, as Malthus says, "unalterable and one of the laws of nature," but "any arbitrary division . . . which the rich find it convenient to make, and which the poor are forced to take up with as better than nothing." [31] It is merely a question of power on one

---

[28] *A Reply to the Essay on Population by the Reverend T. R. Malthus, Works,* I, pp. 251 and 251, n.
[29] "Project for a New Theory of Civil and Criminal Legislation," p. 318.
[30] *Reply to Malthus,* p. 305.
[31] *Ibid.,* pp. 332–33.

side and necessity on the other, and if the share kept by the rich were limited—for instance, by the power of combination among the workers—so that the share remaining for wages could really be increased by industry and prudence, the extremes of wealth and poverty could be avoided.[32]

Hazlitt, however, objected to Malthus' emphasis upon a selfish calculation of consequences as the "moving spirit" of society, disapproving of both selfishness and mere calculation as moving forces. There is, it is true, a certain similarity in Hazlitt's and Malthus' depreciation of the power of calculation to control the passions or affections. The strength of the sexual passion is such, according to Malthus, that the good of society as a whole is too remote to enforce the preventive check when parents are sure of society's supporting their children. In one sense, Hazlitt was even more skeptical of the *unaided* power of reason. Even the prospect of having to support one's own children, he replied, will not enforce the preventive check unless "notions of comfort and decency" have fostered habits of prudence.[33] But, harmonized with habitually cultivated affections, a calculation of consequences may effectively control anti-social passions, including sexual desire, so that the increased control of passion is both cause and effect of moral progress.[34] Just because reason is not "the only infallible or safe rule of conduct," it does not follow "that it is no rule at all. . . ."

----

[32] *Ibid.*, pp. 312–21.
[33] *Reply to Malthus*, pp. 314, 360; "On the Effects of War and Taxes," *Political Essays*, p. 221.
[34] *Reply to Malthus*, pp. 234–41, 282.

On the contrary . . . it is, "the guide, the stay and anchor of our purest thoughts, and soul of all our moral being." In proportion as we strengthen and expand this principle, and bring our affections and subordinate, but perhaps more powerful motives of action into harmany with it, it will not admit of a doubt that we advance to the goal of perfection, and answer the ends of our creation, those ends which not only morality enjoins, but which religion sanctions.[35]

Although limiting "improvement" by the limited "benevolence" of human nature, Hazlitt evidently thought of improvement as an approximation to the "perfect" society of *Political Justice*—involving not only a more equitable or "just" distribution of goods but also, as a means to this end, more virtuous behavior. Man has always secured his rights only "by the *wisdom* and *virtue* of the *enlightened* and *disinterested* part of mankind" combatting the "pride, bigotry, and selfishness" of the others.[36] Whereas, in appealing to self-love alone, Malthus would "effect his improvement in the virtue and happiness of mankind [in a way] in which no such improvement has hitherto been effected." [37] To cultivate selfishness in place of benevolence is to encourage tyranny. Yet, by linking "vice, misery, and madness" with "a state of *unlimited* improvement, of perfect wisdom, virtue and happiness," Malthus represents any wise and disinterested action in behalf of

---

[35] "William Godwin," pp. 21–22.

[36] "What is the People?" p. 270. My italics. When Hazlitt explains the possibility of "practical equality" (p. 13 above), it must be remembered, he is not "enter[ing] into the general structure, foundation, or purpose of civil society"—which presumably depend on more than "self-love, and a little common sense"—but "examin[ing] the question only . . . as it relates to the physical sustenance of mankind. . . ." That is, given security in the possession of certain rights, society can depend on the self-love of its members to prevent a shortage of food for any class, but granting the poor that security would require the disinterestedness of the ruling class.

[37] *Reply to Malthus*, p. 344.

the poor as an invitation to calamity.[38] Furthermore, by attacking the Poor Laws, Malthus has formed "selfishness into a regular code," doing "all that was wanting to increase th[e] indifference and apathy" of the other classes toward the poor, and while such prejudice "subsists in its full force," Hazlitt is "almost convinced," any serious attempt to relieve poverty is likely to bind the poor in even more hopeless slavery.[39]

In Hazlitt's defense of improvement, therefore, the pattern of *Political Justice* is modified but still recognizable. Disinterestedness or benevolence, subordinated by political economy to self-love, becomes again a factor in improvement. Reason, depreciated by Malthus, collaborates with the proper affections to control anti-social passions. Once more nature surrenders the burden of evil to institutions. The psychology is different from Godwin's, in that the "perfect" man does not figure in Hazlitt's predictions, and Godwin's communistic anarchy is curtailed to a "practical equality" with government, marriage, and private property; but this practical equality must be fostered by benevolence, maintained by mastery over passion, and freed from "institutions" that artificially limit the production and distribution of goods and confirm selfish or irrational behavior.

Since Hazlitt's day the working classes have gained both politically and economically. Specific measures advocated by Hazlitt, others suggested by his opponents, and still other influences unforeseen by either, have played a part in this im-

---

[38] *Ibid.*, pp. 206, 213. This criticism, of course, does not make due allowance for Malthus's distinction between methods of trying to lessen poverty—that is, between poor-relief and a "natural wage"—but Malthus' followers sometimes disregarded this same distinction. See my article "Hazlitt and Malthus," *MLN*, LX (April, 1945), 215–26.

[39] *Reply to Malthus*, pp. 181–82, 340, 360.

provement, but so many and so varied are these factors that it would be a rash scholar indeed who weighed the respective contributions of "reason" or "self-love" or "benevolence." After more than a century, "nature" still has a way of "limiting improvement" and has come to employ forms of "vice and misery" that would have horrified Malthus, who although he dispassionately catalogued forms of suffering throughout the world was really a kindhearted man. There is evidence, of which we need feel no less sure just because it cannot be presented scientifically, that self-love has played a considerable part in applying these checks. But it can hardly be said that, in eliminating them or softening them, the possibilities of reason and benevolence have ever been exhausted.

WILLIAM PRICE ALBRECHT
The University of New Mexico

George Carver

"MY DEMON POESY"

THE poet as critic of his own work is seldom successful, apt though he may be—like Coleridge, Dryden, or Phillip Sidney—in judging poetry in general. Among many notable examples, one thinks of Poe and his *Philosophy of Composition,* which not a few hold as nothing more than a *tour de force,* or of Wordsworth's "emotion recollected in tranquillity," which is not applicable to *Laodamia* and subsequent poems and but vaguely applicable to earlier pieces.

Sometimes, however, within his poetry itself a writer may all unwittingly include matter which acts as a clue to the origin of his idea and an understanding of his attitude toward it much better than any direct explanation either he or anyone else might give. John Keats, for instance, never attempted any formal explanation of his work; yet in a possible relationship existing between his *Ode on Indolence* and *Lamia* lies a suggestion that may serve in understanding them better.

In a journal-letter to his brother George, written in March, 1819, Keats included the following:

> This morning I am in a sort of temper indolent and supremely careless: I long after a stanza or two of Thompson's Castle of Indolence. My passions are asleep from my having slumbered till nearly eleven and weakened the animal fibre all over me to a delightful sensation about three degrees this side of faintness—if I had teeth of pearl and the breath of lilies I should call it langour—but as I am I must call it laziness. In this state of effeminacy the fibres of the brain

are relaxed in common with the rest of the body, and to such a happy degree that pleasure has no show of enticement and pain no unbearable frown. Neither Poetry, nor Ambition, nor Love have any alertness of countenance as they pass by me: they seem rather like three figures on a Greek vase—a Man and two women whom no one but myself could distinguish in their disguisement. This is the only happiness, and is a rare instance of advantage in the body overpowering the mind.[1]

In May of the same year he wrote the *Ode on Indolence,* a poetic expression of the same thought and feeling, the third stanza of which brings the figures into focus and sets forth the poet's attitude:

> A third time pass'd they by, and, passing, turn'd
> Each one the face a moment whiles to me:
> Then faded, and to follow them I burn'd
> And ach'd for wings because I knew the three;
> The first was a fair Maid, and Love her name;
> The second was Ambition, pale of check,
> And ever watchful with fatigued eye;
> The last, whom I love more, the more of blame
> Is heaped upon her, maiden most unmeek,—
> I knew to be my demon Poesy.

And during the summer, while with Brown upon the Isle of Wight and feverishly engaged in composition—*Otho* and probably portions of *Hyperion* belong to this period—he wrote *Lamia,* one of the most difficult of his works to understand, because of the various interpretations that are possible. Chief among them is, of course, that which considers Lamia, the serpent-girl, as a symbol of poetry, Lycius as a representative

---

[1] Cited by C. D. W. Thorpe in *John Keats: Complete Poems and Selected Letters* (New York: Doubleday, Doran and Company, 1935), page 347 (note).

of the poet, fascinated by Lamia, and the effect of "cold philosophy" as administered by Apollonius in exposing Lamia and so causing the death of Lycius. It is the linking of poetry and the lamia that seems hard to reconcile.

Critics and commentators have been slow to relate *Lamia* and the *Ode on Indolence,* in which occurs the characterizing phrase "my demon Poesy." In fact, Miss Dorothy Hewlett in *Adonais: A Life of John Keats* seems to be alone in noting any relationship, and she does so in a manner most hesitant, saying

> The weakness of the theory [Mr. Claude L. Finney's well-known analysis of the poem] is admittedly that poetry is symbolized by a demon in the form of a snake; though it has a measure of support in the "demon Poesy" in the *Ode on Indolence.*[2]

None the less, in view of the accumulation of detail concerning Keats' experience during this period of his greatest productivity—the year 1818–19—especially as illuminated by Professor H. W. Garrod's opinion that "In Keats himself, after all, there was that which *Lamia* could not satisfy, *nor the best of his poetry at any time,*[3] there may be reason to believe that *Lamia* and the *Ode on Indolence* are closely related through the "demon Poesy" idea. Not only this, but there may also be reason to believe that the relationship, suggestive as it is, helps to authenticate the opinion that poetry was for Keats—unlike Browning, for instance, for whom it was an unmixed joy—a source of both high ecstasy and deep depression, an opinion in support of which both the *Ode* and *Lamia* bear witness.

---

[2] Dorothy Hewlett, *Adonais: A Life of John Keats* (Indianapolis: The Bobbs-Merrill Company, 1938), page 320.

[3] H. W. Garrod, *Keats* (Oxford: The Clarendon Press, 1926), page 63. Italics added.

"The true Poet," said Charles Lamb, "dreams being awake." Shelley had it that,

> Poetry acts in a divine and unapprehended manner beyond and above consciousness. . . . It is not like reasoning, a power to be exerted according to the determination of the will. A man cannot say, "I will compose poetry." The greatest poets even cannot say it. . . . I appeal to the greatest poets of the present day whether it is not an error to assert that the finest passages of poetry are produced by labour and study. . . . Poetry is the interpenetration of a diviner nature through our own.

But lest the point be labored, poetry and dreams are constantly being associated. Wordsworth wrote, "We are laid asleep in body and become a living soul." Severio Bettinelli, the rhetorician, once said, "The happy moment for the poet may be called a dream—dreamed in the presence of the intellect, which stands by and gazes with open eyes at the performance." According to Jean Paul Richter, "Genius is, in more senses than one, a sleepwalker, and in its bright dream can accomplish what one awake can never do." Likewise, Goethe somewhere records that he wrote *Werther* unconsciously, like a sleepwalker. In short, one can find on almost every hand statements concerned with this association; it is one of the most apparent because it is one of the most natural.

For support which draws more closely towards the present theme, however, one can do little better than quote the Prophet Isaiah. "It shall," he said (XXIX. 8),

> even be as when a hungry man dreameth, and, behold, he eateth; but he awaketh and his soul is empty; or as when a thirsty man dreameth, and, behold, he drinketh; but he awaketh, and, behold, he is faint, and his soul hath appetite.

And just as valuable support is provided by Nietzsche in this:

> Why was last night's dream full of tenderness and tears, that of the night before amusing and gay, and the previous one adventurous and engaged in some continual obscure search? How does it come about that in this dream and in that I soar and fly upwards with the delight of an eagle to the most distant heights?
>
> These inventions in which our instincts of tenderness, merriment, or adventurousness . . . can have free play and scope—and every one can recall striking instances—are interpretations of our nervous irritations during sleep. . . . Nothing contains more of your own work than your dreams! Nothing belongs to you so much! Substance, form, duration, actor, spectator you act as your complete selves.[4]

Somewhat in this manner it may be shown that poetry is not to be considered as an effort of the reason and the will, but rather as impinging upon the dream state, and that its function is that of affording release into the ideal. Or, as Francis Bacon described it in Book II of *The Advancement of Learning,* the function of poetry is "to give some shadow of satisfaction to the mind of man in those things wherein the nature of things doth deny it." Only, in thinking in such fashion one must be guided by two restrictions, pointed out some thirty-five years ago by Professor F. C. Prescott of Cornell:

> First, that the gratification afforded by poetry may extend no further than that derived from idealized expression, which in every case is substituted for the imperfect and inhibited utterances of everyday life. Secondly, that in poetry the poet's desires are not represented openly and literally; they are disguised, conveyed through a medium of fiction.[5]

---

[4] Friedrich Nietzsche, *The Dawn of Day,* trans. by J. M. Kennedy (London: Allen and Unwin, Ltd., 1924), pages 126, 132.

[5] F. C. Prescott, "Poetry and Dreams," *Journal of Abnormal Psychology,* vol. VII (April, 1912), page 22.

In the works of Keats—to approach the theme directly—are to be found evidences of such doctrine in profusion: in *Sleep and Poetry,* in *I Stood Tip-Toe,* in the sonnet *To Sleep,* in the longer of the poems *To My Brother George,* in *Endymion, The Eve of St. Agnes,* with its "dreamy richness," and the *Ode to a Nightingale,* to point up the obvious. But Professor C. D. W. Thorpe of the University of Michigan, in the introduction to his edition of Keats's works, defines the mood quite sharply. "The word *sleep* occurs frequently in the poetry of Keats," he says, and continues:

> He who reads closely will find that sleep seems to have for Keats a close connection with aesthetic experience. It is a fact worth noting that in *Sleep and Poetry,* though sleep is celebrated in affectionate apostrophe, there is in reality no sleep:
>
> the morning light
Surprised me even from a sleepless night
>
> The substance of the poem was generated, one would surmise, in that half-world state between sleeping and waking when the mind, the things of present sense shut out, lives within itself alone in peculiarly bright and intense activity. At such moments the imagination presents to the mind imagery and idea in unusual clarity; thoughts come that never came before; the emotions are excited to a high pitch; creative energy is at flood.[6]

One need go no further, however, for definition than to Keats' own comment, included in the previously quoted passage from the journal letter of March, 1819: "a delightful sensation about three degrees this side of faintness."

To step from the idea that poetry is not merely a matter of intellect and will but is allied in its inspiration with the dream

---

[6] C. D. W. Thorpe, *op. cit.,* page xxii.

state in providing means of release into the realm of ideal fulfillment—to step from this idea to thought of Keats as a case in
point, is but a step from here to there. All this is by no means
to say that in his preoccupation with the "realm of Won-
derment," or under the stress of high ecstasy, he remained
unaware of the necessity of reconciling himself with reality.
One remembers the comment in one of the letters to Haydon:
"An extensive knowledge is necessary to thinking people; it
takes away the heat and fever." And a remark in the journal-
letter to George Keats, written in October, 1818, is equally
revealing: "Then I should be most enviable—with the yearn-
ing Passion I have for the beautiful connected and made one
with the ambition of my intellect." Part and parcel of the
"demon poesy" conception is the awareness of the necessity
for knowing, together with the awareness of his own lack of
knowledge; hence the failure of the dream state completely
to satisfy. He realized fully that though the dream state was
necessary, it must rest upon foundations of the real, a matter
discussed to conviction by Professor Thorpe in his *The Mind
of John Keats*. However, the evidence of Keats' reliance upon
the trance-like state is clear enough in the poems referred to.
If further support is needed, it is to be found in *The Poet,* for
instance:

> To his sight
> The hush of natural objects opens quite
> To the core: and every secret essence there
> Reveals the elements of good and fair;
> Making him see, *where Learning hath no light;* [7]

and in a letter written to J. A. Hessey, October 9, 1818:

[7] *Ibid.,* page 35. Italics added.

The Genius of Poetry must work out its own salvation in a man: it cannot be matured by law and precept, but by sensation and watchfulness in itself. That which is creative must create itself; [8]

both which comments recall, incidentally, George Puttenham's figure, used in describing the imagination of the poet: "God without any travail to his imagination made all the world of naught"; and Byron's lines in the fourth canto of *Childe Harold:*

> The beings of the mind are not of clay;
> Essentially immortal, they create
> And multiply in us a brighter ray
> And more beloved existence; that which Fate
> Prohibits to dull life, in this our state
> Of mortal bondage, by these spirits supplied,
> First exiles, then replaces what we hate.

In keeping with this last quotation and in further support of the "release into the realm of ideal fulfillment" idea, Keats' lines in *Oh How I Love* pertain:

> to take a sweet reprieve
> From little cares; to find, with easy quest,
> A fragrant wild, with Nature's beauty drest,
> And there into delight my soul deceive.
> There warm my breast with patriotic lore,
> Musing on Milton's fate—on Sydney's bier—
> Till their stern forms before my mind arise:
> Perhaps on wings of Poesy upsoar,
> Full often dropping a delicious tear,
> When some melodious sorrow spells mine eyes.

In fact, this wish to escape is apparent in much that he wrote;

---

[8] *Ibid.,* page 83.

and not unnaturally, for the whole of his life experience conditioned him for such wishing. On the basis, therefore, of the *Ode on Indolence* and *Lamia* it is not too much to conclude that, in spite of his realization of "soul deception" in the "poet's trance," poetry alone suffices as "Love and Fame to nothingness do sink."

Both mood and material as established in the journal-letter he proceeded to utilize in the *Ode.* The "delightful sensation about three degrees this side of faintness" which he must call laziness becomes the veil through which, in the first instance, the figures upon the vase are but vaguely distinguishable. In the *Ode,* however, each turns its face for a moment toward him. He recognizes each and burns and aches for wings to follow. Love, the "fair Maid," he does not dwell upon, detaching himself almost completely—is he dismissing love, aware that it is not for him, nor he for it? Ambition, "pale of cheek and ever watchful with fatigued eye," is thus characterized discouragedly. But Poesy, "maiden most unmeek," "whom I love more, the more of blame is heaped upon her," "I know to be my demon Poesy," becomes the most important of the three, not only by reason of actual statement but also by reason of space allotment—three lines to two and to one—and of climactic position. But why demon? Shall we say, because poetry was his transcendent urge, persisting even though lack of success with a public that was paying Byron one thousand pounds for a single canto of *Don Juan* and Tom Moore three thousand pounds for *Lalla Rookh* but ignoring him, was forestalling his marriage with Fanny Brawne, and though his work was failing to justify even to himself his conviction of poetic power?

The reception of the 1817 volume by the critics, although it depressed him, could not dissuade him; the arrogance, growing out of his confidence in his great gift, of his comments in connection with the preface prepared for *Endymion* is unmistakable:

> I have not the slightest feeling of humility towards the Public—or to anything in existence—but the eternal Being, the Principle of Beauty, and the Memory of great Men—When I am writing for myself for the mere sake of the Moment's enjoyment, perhaps nature has its course with me—but a Preface is written to the Public; a thing I cannot help looking upon as an Enemy, and which I cannot address without feelings of Hostility. . . . I never wrote one single Line of Poetry with the least Shadow of public thought.[9]

Furthermore, the reception accorded *Endymion* had small influence upon his attitude. The work pleased the persons whose opinions he most valued and so upheld his confidence, but it brought him no nearer success with the public. Most of the edition remained unbound upon the shelves of Taylor and Hessey, until taken over by Edward Stibbs, the bookseller, who eventually disposed of it at eighteen pence a copy, although originally published at nine shillings—a presentation copy, however, ironically enough, sold in 1933 for twenty-four hundred pounds.[10] Concerning his dissatisfaction, the letter to Hessey, written October 9, 1818, is interesting. In it occurs this passage:

> I cannot but feel indebted to those Gentlemen who have taken my part. As for the rest, I begin to get a little acquainted with my own strength and weaknesses.—Praise or blame has but a momentary effect

---

[9] Cited by Dorothy Hewlett in *Adonais*, page 164.
[10] *Ibid.*, page 193.

upon the man whose love of beauty in the abstract makes him a severe critic of his own Works. My own domestic criticism has given me pain without comparison beyond what Blackwood or the Quarterly could possibly inflict—and also when I feel right, no external praise can give me such a glow as my own solitary reperception and ratification of what is fine. J. S. is perfectly right in regard to the slip-shod Endymion.[11]

The link between the *Ode* and *Lamia* now becomes discernible. Lycius is the poet, fascinated by the serpent-girl, Lamia, as poetry. And Apollonius, at whose "mere touch" "all charms fly," is, not science, as a number of commentators have suggested, and not alone the reviewers who judged Keats' work in accord with fact and reason, but the dull cataloguer of "common things" which must be contended with in the world of every day, the indicator of the fact that "the miseries of the world are misery and will not" admit of rest. Hence, since love and ambition are both thwarted by the need to please the world, the only escape is provided by poetry with the ecstasy of its inspiration and yet the depression resulting from its failure to reach ideal accomplishment—its demonic nature consisting, finally, in its fatal enticement.

GEORGE CARVER
University of Pittsburgh

---

[11] Cited by C. D. W. Thorpe in *John Keats,* page 83.

Nellie Slayton Aurner

AN UNKNOWN CASTIGATOR OF CHRISTOPHER NORTH

WITH the self-confidence of a Chatterton and much of his precocity a youth lived and wrote letters in London during the mid eighteen-hundreds. He described himself as sixteen years old, a poet, and a clerk in the Bank of London. Three of his letters eventually found their way into the Luther Brewer collection now in the possession of the State University of Iowa.

The first of these, dated October 23rd, 1850, begins:

"To

    Professor J. Wilson,

            Edinburgh.

My dear sir:

As I am a person totally unknown to you, as well as writing on topics of considerable importance to both of us, I am, in duty bound, before I commence, both to make myself known, and to explain the subjects of which I shall treat. My name, then, is Borradaile:—(my address the Bank of England, Cheque office; in which establishment I hold a clerkship):— and my occasion of writing to you is to make a series of observations,—some laudatory, but the greater part, unfortunately, otherwise,—on various parts of your literary career."

He proceeds to explain that he will deal specifically with Professor Wilson's contributions to *Blackwood's Magazine*,

"As I have been, from my earliest years, a most warm and enthusiastic admirer of that celebrated periodical, I think I may be allowed to make a few observations on such parts of it as have long appeared to all the impartial part of the literary world, to deserve censure."

Before launching upon his castigation, however, he dwells at length upon his profound sympathy with Professor Wilson's political principles and his great admiration for the "originality, truth, and uprightness of your magazine, which has made it one of the most valuable institutions of conservatism." He also declares himself to be an admirer of the literary qualities of Professor Wilson. "Who, indeed, who has been familiar from his childhood with *Blackwood's* . . . could be otherwise?"

He points out, however, that the Tories had failed to make those gradual improvements which were needed "for the comfort of all social classes" and had put down with too great severity attempts to bring about better conditions. "Now, it cannot be denied that all these things were, in some respect, the causes of the *other extreme* which we so often behold in the present day.—The Ellenboroughs, Kenyons, and Bexleys, for instance, were, in great measure, the causes of the Cobdens, and Brights of these times:—and, I think I may add, the *Quarterly Reviews,* and *Blackwood's* magazines bear the same affinity to the *Daily News, Weekly Dispatches,* and *Leaders* which now so prefusely inundate the Metropolis."

He grants that the political views of Hunt and Hazlitt were "of a very *provoking* description, and I allow, in some degree, it was difficult to avoid attacking them.—But your treatment of the others, whose tenets were perfectly inoffensive,—your never paying the smallest heed to any of their rising merits, (they were mostly young),—your coarseness and personality,—your having contributed, literally, to the *murder* of one of them,—the kindest and gentlest of them,—your continuance of your heartless and brutal ridicule of him, even after his death,—your abominable and unparalleled perseverance in spitefulness and malignity even in *1832!!!* . . . your *keeping at it* as late as *April 1849,* with utterly unheard-of obstinacy and malice,—these are things utterly unpardonable."

His first individual instance is Shelley. "Now, I am glad to be able to say that you treated *him* with some small degree of kindness . . . were able to see some merit in his *writings.*— But that critic was not *yourself,*—you, I think, have never condescended to mention his name.—It was some inferior writer in your magazine.—I am aware of the fact, 1st, by his signature of *L;* and 2ndly, by his exhorting our poet to emu-late Wordsworth, Coleridge, and—*Wilson!!!* But, as I am not in a very bad humour at present, I will not enlarge on that curious classification."

At this point he digresses to comment on "L," to demand his name and the identity of "Archous," "Apollodorous," and other of *Blackwood's* anonymities. Returning to Shelley, he continues:

"Our friend 'L,' also, spoke of but very few of his works.— His 'Prometheus Unbound,' his 'Hellas' (which has always been my own favorite), his 'Alastor,' his 'Epipsychidion,' his 'Cenci,' (the greatest of modern tragedies, as you cannot deny:

—and yet you have never noticed it,) and all his beautiful minor poems,—of these you have never spoken. . . .

"But I now come to far graver charges.—I speak of your treatment of Keats. . . . It is now universally acknowledged all over Europe that his life was shortened by the 2 articles in question;—the one written by the notorious Gifford; and the other by the reviewer signed 'L.' . . . Perhaps, as the *Quarterly Review* was most influential in 1819, Gifford was the principal offender:—and he has certainly not escaped punishment!—His name is now never spoken of but with the bitterest abomination and execration:—and nothing, I confess, gives me more pleasure and delight than to think that his murder of Keats is now *the only thing by which he is known.* Tell me another if you can:—excepting, of course, his various insolencies to Hazlitt, Hunt, and Lamb. And yet this is the person whom, in your 'Noctes Ambrosianae' you used to speak of with such warm eulogies as *the greatest critic of the day!"*

And now the flood of indignation is in full tide. Charging Christopher North with envy, jealousy, cowardice, and meanness, in addition to the insolence, spitefulness, and malignity of "L," he exclaims:

"Who but a mean-dispositioned person would have persisted in maligning and abusing him for years after his death, as you did?—And *above all,* who but a mean and cowardly person would have *persevered and persisted, to this very hour* in endeavouring to persecute and annoy all those whose poetical style or political principles resembled Keats's?—Why, some 10 or 12 years after his death, even the Quarterly Review made a most manly and good-natured apology for its abominable treatment of him:—and yet *you yourself have never made any.* You have never given him the very smallest praise:—and have proved in every respect that, (as Mr. Hunt has observed) you disliked his politics, and did not understand his poetry."

Passing to the "regular monthly attacks" on Leigh Hunt, he admits:

"Though he is certainly inferior to the two writers I have previously mentioned, in poetical *depth* and imagination, at the same time he is superior to both in elegance and fancy. He possesses also the greatest value as a critic;—and it is impossible to read his observations on the various writings of Keats, in his 'Imagination and Fancy' without feeling, every moment, a greater love and admiration for that writer's genius; and a more unmingled detestation of all his savage enemies;—but chiefly of the writers in Blackwood's Magazine, who have never yet retracted any of their abominable malevolence."

Stressing the critic's silence as to the best of Keats:

"You also must either imagine that his 'Endymion' was the only thing he wrote, or must be still more open to my charge. His 'Endymion' differs from his 'Hyperion,' his 'Eve of St. Agnes,' his 'Isabel,' or some of his beautiful minor poems, as widely as it does from your 'Isle of Palms.' Why, then, have you never criticised any of his later works? Though you were to write with the utmost disposition to find fault, (as you almost always do) you would seldom find the smallest fault in any of them."

More briefly he challenges the treatment of other living writers, then proceeds to his "gravest accusation . . . your treatment of *Tennyson*. . . . In the first place, then, you wrote a most insolent and flippant criticism of his first volume, using all the disgusting and spiteful expressions about 'Cockneyism' and so forth, which you had used 10 years back in criticising Hunt and Keats. . . . In the second place, when, a year or two afterwards, he gave his next volume to the world, and had redeemed all his juvenile errors which you had so greedily seized at, you would not,—such was your political malice, (which appears, indeed, to have grown with your growth every year,) take the smallest notice of them:—and when, in 1842 and 1848, he had respectively published his 3rd and 4th volumes, you still persevered in your stubborn silence.—At last, however, in 1849,—all your pent-up malice and hatred of 20 years, found vent in a criticism so redolent of malignity (political and personal also,) . . . that it is utterly sickening to read it,—the whole production breathing such an utter ignorance of all Mr. Tennyson's great and glorious qualities,—and such a perfect knowledge of everything spiteful and mean, that can possibly be said, to wound and annoy the spirit of a great writer,—that I most solemnly assure that if you do not speedily retract all such sentiments in some public manner, it will not be very difficult to prophecy the estimate your critical talents will be esteemed at by posterity. . . . (I have been in a perfect agony, for the last 2 or 3 months, lest you should attack his beautiful 'In Memoriam'; —which I feel confident you would have done, had I not written this letter; as you delight in nothing more than ridiculing the personal misfortunes of those who differ in politics.)"

Again, as at the beginning of his letter, he chides the editor for blind Tory partisanship and for "not keeping up with the age." He points out grievous delinquencies in the contributions of two regular writers, Mr. Alison and Professor Aytoun. On the latter he is particularly severe, branding him as "evidently a very young man"—Professor Aytoun was thirty-seven at this date—"and still more evidently possesses insolence, rashness, and silliness fully commensurate with his juvenility. —Who, for instance, but the most *foaming lunatic* would have written two such articles as he has written the last half-year,— on the *Jew-bill* and the great exhibition of 1851?"

He roundly takes *Blackwood's* to task for praising "absurd and worthless writers" whose sole merit is their politics or their Scotch blood. He rebukes the editor for his "far too insufficient praises of Mr. Dickens," but finally proceeds to his crowning enormity:

"And, after all these various insolencies, committed with impunity for upwards of 30 years,—after you have indulged in every kind of 'envy, hatred, malice, and all uncharitable-bess' to a degree perhaps unknown in any literary history,— after never having in the slightest degree moderated your most rigid and bigoted Toryism, and never made the smallest apology or retractation for your various critical libels on those whose politics differed from yours . . . you have had the consummate assurance, *to claim the poet-laureateship!!!!!!* You will not, I suppose, deny the fact:—and I have heard it rumored,—but for the honour of human nature I have never believed the report,—that you put in your claim for the sole purpose of further annoying and possibly supplanting Mr.

Tennyson. . . . Such, then, has been your litery career.—
You have—but it is useless and tiresome to repeat the catalogue of your crimes.—Suffice it, then, to say, that by your
un-heard-of malignity and spitefulness you have rendered
yourself so utterly obnoxious to the literary public that nothing but the most entire retractation (in *Blackwoods Magazine for November 1850*) of all your offensive critical articles;
—a most entire and perfect apology to all the writers, living
and dead, whom you have abused,—but chiefly to *Keats* and
Mr. Tennyson,—(in the same periodical) and lastly, and by
far the most important of all,—a long course of amendment,
in the shape of a long series of kindly, moderate, and discriminating criticisms on these poets,—and a forbearance of anything disagreeable for the future,—extending, I beg leave to
say, even to the word 'cockney'—will be the only means of
saving your literary reputation from eternal ignominy. . . .
I have, indeed, been so familiar from my childhood, with all
the great and glorious qualities in your writings . . . from
the first of the 'Noctes Ambrosianae' to the last of 'Dies Bore-
ales,' that, in penning this letter, I feel perfectly at home as I
should feel in writing to a brother:—and if, in enumerating
your various faults, I may have overstepped the bounds of politeness (for having been excessively excited and agitated by
my subject, I have hardly known what I said) I most sincerely
apologize.

"I have one more observation to make. . . . It is this. I
aspire to be a poet.—Whether my aspirations will ever be realized as fully as I could wish, (I being between 16 and 17 at
present) I cannot say. . . . But this, however, is the request
I make of you:—viz. that you will do as I have suggested;—

make a perfect apology and retractation . . . in your magazine for November. . . . Think of the idea of a *poet* having
so long, through political prejudices, refused to do justice to
his fellow poets,—and ultimately being requested to do so by
another one . . . think also how, if you *do* thoroughly apologize and retract . . . your character will shine forth with double lustre,—and the popularity of your periodical be greatly
increased. . . . Think, then, of all these things and apologize,
in Blackwood's *Magazine* for November 1850, in the following manner:—1. Write in a genial, kind-hearted, and good-
natured manner; avoiding all disposition to scoff or sneer, or
aim at being humorous,—2. Then make a general retractation
of all your obnoxious tenets:—confessing that you have been
too blinded by political bias:—and that you have in general
only looked upon the dark side of these writers' character:
two faults which you must now apologize for.—3. Then make
a grand apology:—first, to the *dead*,—as Shelley, Keats, Lamb,
and Hazlitt,—then to Mr. Tennyson, intreating his forgive-
ness. . . . 4. You may then make a few general remarks on
their writings . . . but, in every case on their merits:—lay-
ing aside all disposition to find fault!

"But you must study *amendment* as well as repentance,—
chiefly in the following four instances:—1. Never make the
smallest attempt to revive any of your old disagreeable tenets;
and do not suffer Professor Aytoun or any of your other writers to do so.—2. Regard all our *younger* writers, (as I have before remarked) and *keep up with the age* more than you have
hitherto done.—3. I would intreat you to use your influence
with Mr. Lockhart to make a similar kind of *palinode* in his
review, for all his equally injurious and un-apologized-for

critiques, on Shelley's 'Prometheus Unbound,' for instance, in 1820:—and also on that on Mr. Dickens' 'American Notes' in 1842, (Prophecying that his ephemeral popularity will soon be followed by a speedy oblivion.—Has it been so!) and 4. By a long series of kind and generous criticisms on the writings of most of these poets, whom you have injured;—and by being as keen to see their merits as you have previously been to see their faults:—to redeem your somewhat tottering critical reputation. . . .

"I have now done:—and have relieved my mind of a burden which has been weighing it down for many months.—Trusting, Sir, to your generous and considerate temper—and wishing you all prosperity,

I am your servant and well-wisher
R.L.B."

Promptly, on November 1, 1850, after receiving the November number of *Blackwood's,* he wrote again, sternly rebuking the editor for his "sullen and impudent obstinacy." On the chance that his first letter had gone astray he reviewed its contents, stressing his earnest request for an apology. "Yet," he concludes, "so far from having paid the very smallest attention to it,—you appear to have acted in direct opposition to it. So far from having made the least retractation of your hateful libels on the poets above named, you have,—by the abominably insolent tone in which you have spoken of *Mr. Hunt* in your wretched review of *Alton Locke,* in this month's number of your periodical,—shown that you are utterly insensible, —equally to the smallest kindness, moderation, or liberalism,— as to common and decent civility.

"Now, I most solemnly warn you to think better of this:—and, as it is too late to apologize in the November number,—to do so in the December one. If you know anything, you must surely know that *the whole age is for Keats and Tennyson and against you:*—and that (although from your stubborn and obnoxious Toryism your writings have fallen into nearly utter oblivion, excepting in your own petty circle) it yet knows enough of you to brand you to all posterity as a kind of modern Zoilus:—of utterly unparallelled malignity, envy, and meanness:—when the facts are more fully known and observed in the literary world. *This can only be averted by an immediate apology.* Requesting, then, an immediate answer, stating your final determination,

     I am, Sir,

          Your obedient servant,
          Reginald Latham Borradaile.

"I here subjoin an inscription for a monument to Keats in Westminster Abbey,—which, at some future period of my life, I intend to erect. The inscription shall certainly be placed there,—unless you speedily do as I have *requested* you:—

Sacred to the illustrious, immortal, and endeared memory
of
John Keats;
born 1796:—died 1820, aged 24:—
The most splendid, imaginative, and promising *young* poet
Which the British Empire has produced.
In political principles
He invariably held the glorious doctrines of freedom and progress
For which reason he was attacked, libelled, and slandered,

All his errors magnified into faults,—and not one of his beauties noticed
Which, preying on his young and sensitive mind,
Caused his immediate death.
The name of the critic,—(who wrote anonymously) was JOHN WILSON
A 'hungry Scotchman,' full of envy, spitefulness, and prejudice,
He was, also, not content with causing the great poet's death;
But, constantly maligned and abused him after death.
And continued his unprecedented malice
To all those whose poetry—or principles,—resembled Keats's
The *name* of the Miscreant,—together with his works,
Is now totally forgotten:—
And is mentioned here, only for the sake of showing
The glorious change in the public mind:—
Which has caused it to remember the good, noble, and liberal poet
And to forget the evil and malignant critic."

One week later, November 7, he closes this one-sided correspondence.

"To
Professor Wilson
Sir:

For the *third* time I now address you, and, as I have but
very little more to say, and I scarcely expect that, after your
previous obstinate silence you will answer *this,*—although I
certainly *wish* that such might be the case,—it will probably
be the *last* time.—Suffice it then, that I make a general summary of the case, which is as follows:—that, in the year 1817,
you, with several others, established a monthly magazine,
which supported, in the most immoderate, and intemperate
manner, every oppressive and obnoxious measure of the Tory
government and attacked with unparallelled malignity all
authors, especially political ones,—whose politics differed from

those of its writers,—that the principal of these reviewers was yourself, and that above all,—(which is the fact that posterity will notice most) when the party which you supported was driven from power never to regain it again; and *when the most obstinate and ferocious of the other Tory writers recalled, in some measure, their various libellous writings on the poetis aforesaid,—your Magazine was the only one which did not do so:*—that you have continued your spiteful abuse of Mr. Hunt down to the very last month,—*November 1850!!* in your review of 'Alton Locke':—and, that you have always been foremost to attack and annoy the earlier writings of young poets,—as those of Mr. Tennyson *in 1832,*—and, to take late instances,—the author of 'The Strayed Reveller,' in September 1849 . . . in a word, that you have given to this your magazine . . . the character of a hard, ferocious, immoderate, spiteful, and cowardly set of authors; to whom anything in the shape of gentleness, kindness, or moderation is utterly unknown:—ultimately and finally, that when, with the utmost civility and politeness, you have been requested to make some apology, by way of amendment, you have not only taken no notice of the request, but, as if out of very spitefulness and insolence, you have in the very same number of the periodical, in which it was hoped you would make the aforesaid apology,—renewed your abominable insolence.— Such is a plain statement of the case.

"Before, however, I conclude, I may remark that it is still *just possible,*—though certainly not *likely,* that you may not have received my two previous letters. If such was the case (which I can hardly think) I may inform you that I recently (about October 23rd) addressed you a long,—and I trust a civilly and moderately written letter, detailing all the facts I have just spoken of,—and requesting that, in the November number of Blackwood's Magazine, you would make some small apology for them:—However, you certainly did *not* make any;—in consequence of which, I wrote you another shorter letter (written in rather warmer language, in which, I am sure, I was fully justified by the circumstances,) requesting that you would, at least, shortly grant me a reply, stating your final determination. . . . I have received, however, not the shortest reply since then:—which is the cause of my addressing you now, for the *third* time.

"I have but one thing more to say.—If you still continue in your unprecedented malice and obstinacy, you cannot reasonably suppose that I shall *forget it* in my future life,—for you may see from my addressing yo*u three times without any chance of success,* that I am not without *determination.* You must also be aware, that in these times of liberalism and progress, the fact of a person being *advanced in years or in a considerably dignified station,* cannot shield him from hatred and contempt (and their *effects*) if he merits them, *as you most richly do,*—Consequently, I consider myself with regard to *you,* in much the same light as Milton might, when at Cambridge, have considered himself with regard to some venerable (but odious) head of a college, who, in his former life, had distinguished himself by his adulation of James the First's court. The latter might have the advantage for a time:—but when Milton had attained to manhood, (as *I* shall soon do)— with whom would the superiority rest?—Such are our respective positions.

"Whether you will yet, before it is too late, do as I have

now so frequently requested you, I know not. Should you *not* do so, you may rest assured, that I shall not be without ample *retaliation*. Should you yet, however, (in the December number) acknowledge, and apologize for, all your previous faults,—the world, I am sure, will be but too glad to forget them all.

Your obedient servant,

R.L.Borradaile"

Note: In all sections quoted from these letters spelling and punctuation has been carefully preserved as they appear in the manuscript.

NELLIE SLAYTON AURNER

The State University of Iowa

Amanda M. Ellis

WHY CAN'T THEY READ AND WRITE?

PARENTS who are concerned because Johnnie doesn't like to read, or worse yet, doesn't understand what he's read, or who lament the fact that Mary can't write a decent sentence, much less a good letter, should ponder a recent nationwide study [1] of the ability of students in high schools and colleges to express themselves and to read. The three-year nationwide survey of junior and senior high schools, colleges, and universities shows that teachers of English are in agreement that students today do not speak or write fluently or read well. Heavy teaching loads and lack of a program in which there is a steady progression or continuity in the teaching and function of language contributing have left many high school graduates far from literate.

Answers to a questionnaire sent to large and small high schools in 30 states, to 48 superintendents of public instruction, and to 79 colleges and universities showed a deplorable lack of understanding between groups as well as between the philosophy expressed in the courses of study and that practised in the classrooms.

The greatest confusion seems to exist in state departments of public instruction. Only two reported having courses of study in which there was continuity of aims and objectives from kindergarten through high school. Nine reported they

---

[1] This study was made by the Articulation Committee of the National Council of Teachers of English, headed by Amanda M. Ellis.

[217]

knew of no such programs nor had they instigated any; yet articulation programs in language arts are being conducted by universities in those states and have received national recognition. One state superintendent said that his state took no cognizance of the elementary school in making his courses in reading and writing; yet his course of study states "The Language Arts program should be conceived as a continuous articulated whole from kindergarten through the twelfth grade."

Of 165 school systems in 30 states, 80 replied that their high schools did not co-operate with the elementary schools or colleges in planning English courses; 27 reported that they co-operated with university English departments. Only 37 high schools stated that they had articulation in English courses within the high school.

Since most English teachers in high school stated that their students did not read, write, or speak well, they were then asked what they did to aid those students who came to high school with inadequate English training. Three-fifths of the high schools had no special courses or plans to deal with them; one-seventh stated that they had special courses in remedial reading; one "left the matter up to the individual teacher"; eight had "after-school classes." Since the English teachers in many high schools are teaching between 169 and 220 pupils each day and supervising study halls as well as such extra-curricular activities as debate, dramatics, and school publications, one wonders how effective these "after school classes" may be and whether the teacher can have left any time to help students needing individual help. If she is in class or study hall six periods a day, she has one hour in which to correct papers, confer with students needing help, make her preparations for the next day, and assist with such extracurricular activities as debates, school publications, dramatics, or radio programs usually assigned English teachers.

Teachers of English in high schools in the United States report teaching an average of 153 pupils in five classes. Some, it is true, teach 100 students in four classes; others, however, teach from 169 to 220 students in five classes. One suspects that the North Central Association requirement of 150 students as a "normal teaching load" prompted many to state that they taught 150 students, for statements giving the number of students in each class show teaching loads far greater. Teaching loads in foreign languages and in science are lighter.

Critical English problems in the pupils' transition from high school to college, from junior to senior high school, and from elementary school to junior high school, ninety-eight percent of the teachers said were "lack of development of such tool skills as reading, writing, speaking, and listening, lack of development of critical thinking," and "inadequate training in grammar." Some bewailed the fact that there was "no uniformity of subject matter taught in the elementary schools"; others recommended that more students "learn to use the dictionary."

Special commendation for articulation work should go to Baltimore, Maryland; La Crosse, Wisconsin; Minneapolis, Minnesota; New Haven, Connecticut; Nutley, New Jersey; Rockford, Illinois; Seattle, Washington; St. Louis, Missouri, and Wichita, Kansas.

Though there are some splendid courses and excellent teaching in high school English courses, the three year study shows that often vagueness and lack of purpose characterize much of the planning.

Teaching, moreover, is more often *correction* rather than *instruction*. The aims in teaching rhetoric, grammar, syntax, and writing often are vague and numerous, some courses listing as many as thirty aims. One feels, too, that courses of study, too often vague and theoretical, do not necessarily show what is going on in the classroom; yet eighty-five to ninety percent of them show similar features in subject matter, aims, purposes, and educational theory. They indicate, indeed, little real progression of subject matter in terms of "ascending value or increasing differences." Many courses show a trend toward remedial rather than systematic instruction. Few show the practice in writing in step with the study of grammar. Since many of the same errors appear as minimum essentials in each grade, the chances are that writing was occasional and the correction of it superficial. With teaching loads as high as they are, and with the heavy schedules given English teachers, it is not surprising that too few themes are assigned, that teachers' corrections are made hurriedly, and that often the student is not required to rewrite papers or correct the errors in them. The same heavy teaching schedule makes conferences almost an impossibility; one questions how many of the after school remedial classes really are held. No English teacher should be compelled to assume the many responsibilities assigned her in our schools.

A survey of 79 colleges and universities in 40 states shows that 54 have no program in which they co-operate with high schools to secure a continuity in the language arts; seven, however, co-operate with high schools through state English associations, state universities or state officers of public instruction; 18 have English programs in which they co-operate with high schools. Like high school teachers of English, college professors feel that students do not speak and write fluently or well. To aid those students whose English is faulty, 41 colleges and universities have special remedial programs. Others have tutorial aid, reading clinics, and special conferences for those who need aid. Since English teaching loads in institutions of higher learning are lighter than those in high school, teachers usually have time to give to those students whose English preparation is faulty. Most college and university teachers of English spend from nine to twelve hours a week in the class room; some teachers' colleges, however, report teaching fifteen hours each week. In a considerable number of colleges, a twelve-hour schedule means nine hours of teaching and three hours of conference work. Four-fifths of the colleges report that English schedules are lighter than those in foreign language and science.

Especially fine work in articulation between high school and university as well as within the university is done by the New England Conference of Teachers of English, the Kansas English Association, University of Illinois, Stanford University, the University of Washington, the University of Wisconsin, the Ohio College English Association, the University of Ohio, Rutgers, Washington University, and the University of Michigan.

Almost every college and university feels grave concern because students as a whole are not proficient in the language arts. The remedy for the situation, many see in remedial courses in the Freshman year; yet doubtless some of these same students had remedial courses in high school in the tenth or twelfth year. As the same types of errors that are listed in high school are listed as errors in college, one suspects that the college remedial courses will not prove any more effective than those did in high school. With lighter teaching schedules, teachers in college should be able to give individual help to students; yet statements like "This is a light teaching load in order that the professor may have more time for his research" or "We have a nine hour teaching schedule in order that instructors may devote time to their graduate studies" occur frequently enough for one to question whether the student who suffered as a result of his high school teacher's heavy schedule may not also suffer because of the professor's interest in research. A few colleges, it is true, are genuinely interested in working with high schools for a better articulated language arts program. The great majority, though far from complacent about the student's inability to express his ideas coherently, have done little to get at the source of the trouble. Furthermore, once the student has passed or failed his Freshman English course, college professors seem to do little except lament his ignorance in use of the spoken and written word.

In conclusion, I believe that many courses of study in the language arts should be revised to permit a steady progression or continuity in the teaching of the structure and function of language. In the words of Professor Clarence D. Thorpe, "Let us avoid the confusion of a multiplicity of goals. Instead of talking in terms of fifteen hundred aims let us limit ourselves, say to competence in conveying ideas, observance of the decencies in expressing ideas. . . ." This will demand a clear understanding of the relationships of vocabulary, syntax, grammar, and sentence structure. Word study, no longer taught in some schools, should be reintroduced. Students should acquire the habit of speaking and writing sentences carried through to meaningful completion; they should have respect for phrases and clauses in relationship to what they modify; "they should be taught the manners of discourse: the right verb and the right noun usage"; they should be taught to speak and write coherently. There should be *definite, specific* courses from kindergarten through college. Through cooperation of teachers, there should emerge uniform nomenclature in grammar, uniform symbols and abbreviations, and a clear definition of minimum standards. There should be a tightening of grading in all courses and a refusal to give passing marks to written work which does not reach minimum requirements. There is grave doubt whether courses in dramatics, journalism, and the like should be accepted as substitutes for required English.

At the present time, the National Council of Teachers of English is working out an articulated program in English. Regardless of the type of curriculum proposed, however, unless teaching loads in English in junior and senior high school are lightened, there can be little hope of our students speaking, reading, and writing better than they do. I realize, of course, that there is a critical shortage of teachers in our school systems, but I believe that important factors contributing to that shortage are excessive teaching loads and the resultant inability of the most conscientious teachers to do the thoroughly professional job their pupils need.

I realize also that to ask for lighter teaching loads means not only employing more teachers but also an increased school budget. I believe, however, that this additional expense is essential in a democratic society where each member should be educated to speak, read, and write well.

AMANDA M. ELLIS
Colorado College

G. A. Yoakam

WHAT MAKES PEOPLE READ.

IT must often have occurred to you that reading is an extremely artificial process. A page of print is an arbitrary
arrangement of curious little signs on a piece of paper
which would be entirely meaningless to a savage. It is made
up of row upon row of symbols that represent meaning only
to those who have been initiated into the art of reading. At
times reading is a very difficult process. To read requires that
one shall remain in more or less a fixed position for hours at
a time. Certain kinds of reading require a large expenditure
of energy and the exertion of the will. Yet many thousands
persist in reading for a lifetime, devoting many hours each
week to the companionship of books, an isolated companionship that shuts out other human beings and closes the door
upon sociability and good fellowship. What is there about
reading that keeps generation after generation breathlessly
poring over the pages of books, lying awake nights with them,
sacrificing the companionship of people to read them, and
believing so firmly in the worthwhileness of reading that they
spend a great deal of money, no end of time, and considerable
trouble in acquiring a stock of books so that they may indulge
their peculiar taste? Curiosity has led me to think a great deal
about the matter, investigate what others have written about
it, and make and direct some original investigations which
help me to understand, "What makes people read." Those

who like reading and books may take some pleasure in comparing their own experiences with what has been found about others. Of course, the subject has a great interest to those who are engaged in either the writing or printing of books. If one knew for a certainty just why people read, he would know exactly what kind of books to make to satisfy their needs.

TWO MAJOR USES FOR READING

It is now being said that there are two major uses for reading: (1) reading for recreation; and (2) reading for practical or vocational purposes. In modern schools children are being trained in these two kinds of reading. The first is called recreational reading and the second, work-type reading. It is probable that the reading of the majority of adults is more commonly of the recreational type rather than the vocational. And it may be regretted that more people do not advance themselves in life and become more skilled in their occupations through the use of books and magazines which would give them more information about their jobs.

This more serious informational kind of reading does, however, seem to be increasing in amount. The recent popularity of books of information on all kinds of subjects attests to the increasing interest of adults in becoming better informed about their world. The many "outlines" of this and of that during the last few years and the great popularity of biography and books about science, art, music, economics, psychology, and all sort of things, suggest the possibility that people are becoming more serious about their reading and that while they may read a great deal for sheer amusement, many are turning to a more or less practical kind of reading which they

[226]

think may get them on in the world by making them more efficient in their work. Much emphasis is being placed upon this kind of reading in many of our schools today, with the idea that such reading will meet the needs of life and make the next generation more capable in what they do because they will be better informed on all sorts of practical subjects. History and geography, biography, science, and travel are receiving increasing emphasis on this account. It is believed that there are values in many kinds of books which may not properly be classified as literature and that the values of these books will be more fully realized when people learn how to read them better.

This increasing interest in what may be characterized as factual reading does not mean, however, that reading for recreational purposes in the realm of literature proper and in more or less popular books which are neither permanent nor artistic enough to be classed as literature is on the wane. The number of newspaper, magazine, and novel readers is evidence of the fact that purely recreational reading has a tremendous popularity, just as it has had for generations.

These two types of reading are neither opposed to each other, nor even separate and distinct. Many readers obtain all their recreational reading from more or less serious and heavy books about various kinds of subjects that would not interest the ordinary reader or appeal to him as recreational. I know many who enjoy reading more or less technical magazines and books that would appeal to the ordinary reader as dry and laborious. The chief distinction between reading which may be classed as recreational and that which is practical or vocational, as near as I can see it, is that the reader who is reading for sheer enjoyment has no serious purpose, no drive to his reading; but that the reader who reads books for values other than entertainment, may have specific practical needs which drive him to read systematically even though he receives no recreation from such reading. That is the difference between my own recreatory and practical reading. Sometimes I work all day, reading and analyzing a serious educational book. I derive a certain pleasure from this work because of my interest in education, but I would not call the reading recreational. The same day, however, I go home at night and read the newspaper for pure relaxation, rather than for any serious purpose; or I pick up a magazine and read an exciting story with no serious thought, entirely for recreation. And the interesting thing about it is, that even though I may have become fatigued reading for practical purposes, the recreatory reading relaxes me and that through it I find pleasure and well-being. It seems, therefore, that reading among adults may be regarded as either play or work. There are two major motives that lead people to read, just as there are probably two major motives in most life activities. People read because in reading they live vicariously. Books make possible the recording of human experiences of all kinds, and reading makes these experiences available to those who have mastered the interpretation of the printed page.

SATISFACTIONS ARISING FROM RECREATIONAL READING

Just to understand that people read for recreation, however, does not throw much light on the whole matter. It is necessary to know what specific kinds of satisfactions they get out of this process in order to understand it better. Writers about literature have often described what literature can do for the individual reader. The values of books have been so often acclaimed that I need not attempt to review them here. Rather, I shall give an account of some original investigation in which I had a part which endeavored to find out just what motives lead people today to read for recreational purposes. Not all the data that are being gathered under my general direction are now available, but a sufficient amount is already collected to show that people read in general for two principal reasons: (1) to relax, and (2) to satisfy curiosities.

Reading for relaxation is one of the commonest practices among certain classes of people. It has been found that all classes of people read more or less for this purpose but that certain groups upon whom life makes many demands find little time for it. People get this relaxation in various ways and read all sorts of things in satisfying this need. Great men of affairs sometimes have tastes in reading that may seem peculiar to the unthinking person. It is said that a certain great president read detective stories for relaxation at night before going to sleep, and another great president was a voracious reader of history and natural science for this same purpose. An investigation now going forward shows that men in all professions have their peculiar tastes in reading of this sort. A busy physician may find relaxation in reading the most frivolous kind of fiction; another may get relief from the pressure of his work by reading scientific articles related to it. A busy lawyer may get relaxation by reading the great classics. It is likely, however, that a great majority of readers get relaxation from reading fiction, and find relief from real life by living in an imaginary world with the characters and events of a book that represents life only in an idealized form. Studies of withdrawals from libraries bring out this possibility. The great popularity of story magazines also attests to the probability that thousands read stories for relaxation with little thought of deriving from them anything except a temporary pleasure and a sense of relief from responsibility of any kind. Certain serious-minded folk who were questioned by one investigator, however, would not acknowledge that they ever had time for this kind of reading, and some testified that they thought it a waste of time. Others were frankly in favor of it and considered it just as legitimate a way of getting relaxation from work as playing golf or chess, or in social contacts.

It is difficult to deny that some people who have very busy lives in the business world or who work in factories where machines are a constant source of noise, need the complete relaxation that comes from being alone in some quiet place. It is hard to see what better way there may be of getting this complete relaxation than in the companionship of books in the atmosphere of home. And in spite of the many forms of amusement now available to people, it does not seem that this form of relaxation is less popular or that it is likely to become so in the very near future. Not even the fascination of the movies, with the added attraction of the reproduction of sound and words, seems likely to wean people of certain temperament away from much quiet leisure reading.

The second in popularity of the types of recreational reading is the satisfaction of curiosity. In his psychology man resembles the monkey in one important respect at least, and that is in his insatiable curiosity. One sure way of getting people to read is to arouse their curiosity about books. Those who advertise books for sale are well aware of this fact and millions rise to the bait of a cleverly advertised book only later to be disappointed that it does not live up to its advance notices. Thousands read books just because they have heard others speak of them or because they have seen a review of the books which arouses their curiosity.

This same motive of curiosity, however, leads many consciously to seek books about persons, events, or things that have interested them. They look for books about strange lands and strange peoples and derive from them a satisfaction that they could never get from things more familiar. By this means they live vicariously the lives of many people and become acquainted with parts of the world they could not otherwise know. This reading may be very profitable, if the reader is discriminative, for by it he may indirectly be gaining much valuable experience while, at the same time, deriving a great deal of pleasure.

While need for finding relaxation and satisfying curiosity are the most frequent reasons given by a large group of readers for engaging in recreatory reading, there are other motives common enough to be significant. One of these is reading just to pass the time. Much of this goes on in railroad stations, on trains, and in other places where people are forced to physical inactivity. I have known people who would read almost anything for this purpose, even the "want ad" columns in a newspaper in which they had little direct interest, or the catalogs of certain ubiquitous mail-order houses which could never have been designed for such purpose.

There are occasions on which people would give a great

deal for the privilege of reading. Once I met two young men on a transcontinental highway in the Mohave Desert who were forced to complete inaction miles from a railroad because an axle of their automobile had broken. The plight of these young men was pitiable. There they sat in the hot sun with nothing to do until a new axle was forthcoming. When they were offered a copy of a certain popular magazine, the eagerness with which they seized it testified to the fact that reading would aid them considerably to pass away many idle hours before they were released from their predicament. I saw also on a transcontinental highway a young man in a car, on the road from the east to Los Angeles. A conspicuous part of his load, and it was a large one, was a cardboard box filled with the back files of a popular pulp magazine. I do not think that he was carrying the magazines for ballast, for he had enough of that. Reading sometimes enables people who ordinarily do not choose to read to relieve unbearable monotony.

Another motive for recreational reading is the need that many find for emotional stimulation. Life becomes dull, dreary, and monotonous. People find in books emotional stimulation that enables them to go on with life even though the daily grind may be stale and unprofitable. They get various kinds of emotional stimuli from reading. Some read to cry and thoroughly enjoy a tale in which misery is the lot of all. The endless difficulties of human beings as portrayed in the soap operas on the radio appeal to the same interest. It is said that women are particularly addicted to this form of reading. Others read to laugh and look everywhere for humorous matter. The great popularity of humorous books and magazines attests to the need for this kind of emotional escape. Children particularly need books full of wholesome humor. It is unfortunate that there are not more of them.

Some find life so monotonous that they read to find a thrill. There are, of course, many ways to get it, but perhaps the most common is to read romantic fiction, detective stories, and adventure tales of all sorts. "Western" books have had an immense popularity because of the adventure element and there are thousands of easterners in the more remote parts of the land beyond the Mississippi who still believe that Iowa and Nebraska constitute the frontier and that beyond the Mississippi Indians still bite the dust and the six-gun is more common than a taxicab on Broadway.

A type of reading for emotional stimulation which may not perhaps be so universal as many would desire but which is doubtless still very common, is that for spiritual strength and guidance. It may at first not be thought of as recreational reading. Yet since in the original sense it is for the re-creation of spiritual strength and well-being, it may well be conceived as one of the most worthy kinds of recreation as well as one of the best motives for reading. There is a great interest in religious books, in books on the development of the will, in popular psychology of the kind that attempts to smooth out the various complexes that Freud discovered. Such books have had a tremendous popularity in recent years. The reading of them attests to the need of humanity for spiritual and moral sustenance and testifies to the great value placed upon reading as a means of attaining the satisfaction of this need.

Another kind of emotional stimulation is gained from the sensory enjoyment derived from reading books in which

[233]

beauty of sound and color—sensory imagery of all sorts—is present. Many people seek such books and enjoy them very much. They revel in imagery. Beautiful illustrations as well as beautiful thoughts and artistry in expression attract people and fill a human need; for thousands are condemned to live in unlovely environments and must obtain the beauty that their souls crave indirectly through the eyes of others from the pages of books. Few will be unwilling to accord them this opportunity.

There is still another kind of purpose leading people to read that should not be forgotten: the sheer joy of handling and seeing beautiful books. Unfortunately such books are generally expensive and are not available for many who would like them. Libraries, available to all, however, do contain limited supplies of such books and bookshops exhibiting them are becoming more and more common. The one who admires and gets pleasure from seeing and examining copies of the bookmakers' finest work, will generally find a sympathetic friend in the keepers of such books and may at times be allowed to examine books that in former days only a king could have known.

This discussion of recreational reading and the purposes which lead people to engage in it would be incomplete if I did not mention a completely unselfish purpose which leads many to read; that is to give pleasure to others. Many have found their greatest reading pleasure from discussing what they have read with others or from reading aloud to children and to invalids from books which they have enjoyed. This socialized reading is probably all too uncommon today. When the home boasted few books and only an occasional magazine, family reading aloud was the usual thing. Many feel that a great deal has been lost in family life because there is not more such reading nowadays. It was good for the family to be together in the companionship of good books. The modern practice of each member of the family doing his own reading provides for individuality of taste, but it also tends to lessen the benefits that come from interchange of ideas and from group interest and concern in a common activity.

Recreational reading, then, takes place in response to many human needs. People find in books relaxation of various sorts. Reading is one of the means whereby people find relaxation from the affairs of life and by which they are enabled to live more broadly and more sympathetically.

MOTIVES LEADING PEOPLE TO READ FOR PRACTICAL OR VOCATIONAL PURPOSES

The second of the major types of reading; namely, practical or vocational reading, has been so little investigated that, unfortunately, little is known about it. People have demanded reading for recreational purposes to so much greater extent that it is only recently that an interest in practical reading has manifested itself. The most common motive that leads people to work with books is that of preparing for a vocation. The student at school or college is the best example of one so motivated. Unfortunately, all too often, as soon as school or college is finished, the student leaves off all effort to advance himself and does not keep up with his vocation. He neglects to read and study further the valuable books and magazines that might keep him up with progress in his field. There is, however, an increasing number of serious-minded persons, handi-

capped by not having had the advantages of schools and colleges, who are following courses in reading on their own ini-
tiative, which sooner or later ought to enable them to progress.

In reading for purely vocational purposes, the reader often
wishes to obtain knowledge of his profession or vocation, to
keep up to date with its development, to learn how to carry
on some activity which has been newly developed, such as how
to raise some new kind of plant, how to use a new technique
in medicine, or dentistry, or what not. The various purposes
which might lead one to read are probably as numerous as the
professions, occupations, and vocations, and so cannot be enu-
merated here. But the general principle that reading can advance the individual in a material way is important to note.
The many practical books and the many training courses for
people who wish to get ahead in the world by home study,
testify to this growing need.

There is another personal kind of practical reading, however, which is probably of more general interest than purely
vocational reading. Many people have an intense desire to
keep up with the times, to be well informed about people and
events. It is said that in the evening classes for adults in certain colleges in New York people are curious about all kinds
of subjects and will study almost anything. Probably the motive which urges many adults to do a great deal of practical
reading of this sort is the desire to avoid ignorance. Many
adults undertake a long course of general reading in history,
economics, sociology, or science in order to experience the
satisfaction of saying that they know about the great developments in the history of mankind. Such reading may be difficult for them. They avoid distractions of a lighter character

in order to indulge in it. It may become highly pleasurable, but pleasurable or not, they persist because they have a pride in knowing and in being well informed.

Some specific examples of motives leading to practical reading may be suggestive. Analyses show that people read for the following purposes, other than that of avoiding ignorance:

1. To find the answer to some question or problem which they have met in their affairs.

2. To find directions for making something, going somewhere, playing some new game, and so on.

3. To broaden their experience in a general way; that is, to get new ideas about new people, places, and things.

4. To support an argument or a cause; as, for instance, in a political campaign when they desire to uphold their choice of a party or a candidate as right.

5. To verify a fact or an opinion. People often seek to verify the pronunciation or meaning of a word by consulting a dictionary or encyclopedia. They read other types of books for the same purpose.

6. To find new problems or interests. People often seek subjects for conversation or discussion, for new problems to attack in their reading, and the like.

These and many other motives lead many readers to read for practical reasons that cannot be classed as purely recreational. The unfortunate part of it is that more people do not take advantage of the opportunities offered in books to develop their general knowledge. Life can be made much richer and more satisfying by reading.

I should like to advise my readers to go to the nearest public library or book store and learn about the many serious books that are available to further their welfare in various ways—books on gardening, home decoration, painting, music, art, inventions, animals, pets—all sorts of useful books which deal in an interesting way with this most fascinating world. A great deal of good can be derived from practical books by any reader who will take the time to investigate their possibilities.

In closing, let me say that people read from almost as many motives as they live. Reading helps one to pass away the time, it satisfies his sense of curiosity, it provides him with an emotional outlet, it gives relaxation, it allows the reader to fill his mind with great thought. Beautiful books satisfy the sense of sight and touch. Through reading one can find support and strength for living. And finally, there are many practical ways in which books may be used to enrich and enlarge life. Silently, on the shelves of bookshops and libraries await a host of willing friends, some to delight you, some to strengthen you; and then there are an increasing lot of just good practical books about all sorts of things which will be glad to help you in the ordinary affairs of life from telling you how to remove ink-spots from a favorite tablecloth to how to fix that leaky water faucet without calling in the plumber.

G. A. YOAKAM
University of Pittsburgh

Richard Murphy

ALEXANDER SMITH ON THE ART OF
THE ESSAY

SHOULD you look up Alexander Smith's biography, as
Christopher Morley once threatened to do in prefacing
an edition of *Dreamthorp*,[1] you discover he was a "Scottish poet, one of [the] chief representatives of the spasmodic
school,"[2] who lived from 1830[3] to 1867. So has the author
of *Dreamthorp* been tagged and stored away by the literary
classifiers. But meanwhile, in defiance of canon and syllabus,
Smith's *prose* works have been widely reprinted and selected.
A Summer in Skye[4] has been issued in half a dozen editions
in this century, and *Dreamthorp*[5] in a dozen. His edition of
Burns,[6] distinctive for its biographical essay, has been continuously in print since 1868. A voluminous collection[7] of

---

[1] (Doubleday, Doran & Co., Garden City, 1934.) Morley has often sponsored Smith.
One of the "writers in English who have given me the greatest pleasure in twenty
years of mature reading," he testified [*Saturday Review of Literature*, VIII, No. 22
(Dec. 19, 1931), 394].

[2] *Webster's Biographical Dictionary* (1943).

[3] *Webster's* is in error on the date of birth, as are the *Dictionary of National Biography*, the *Cambridge History of English Literature*, and many other sources. Alexander Smith was born December 31, 1829. (For confirmation of the date, see the author's thesis, *Alexander Smith: Man of Letters*, University of Pittsburgh, 1939.)

[4] 2 volumes (London, Alexander Strahan, 1865).

[5] (London, Strahan & Co., 1863.) Both *Skye* and *Dreamthorp* were printed by Ballan-
tyne in Edinburgh.

[6] *Poems, Songs and Letters*, being the *Complete Works of Robert Burns* (London,
Macmillan, 1868); *Globe Edition*. This work is not to be confused with Smith's edi-
tion of *The Poetical Works of Robert Burns*, 2 volumes (Cambridge and London,
Macmillan, 1865); *Golden Treasury Series*.

[7] Harrold, C. F. and Templeman, W. D., *English Prose of the Victorian Era* (New
York, Oxford, 1938), p. 1743.

[239]

Victorian prose includes Smith's essays among those of thirteen enduring writers of the period. *Eminent British Writers of the Nineteenth Century* draws upon Smith for parts of its eminence, and compares him with "Lamb, De Quincey and Stevenson." [8] If you would seek Smith's monument today, look in the prose anthologies. There one discovers not only the essays of Smith, but essays in appreciation of him.[9] A worthy essayist has been retrieved from the categorizers. Many readers of essays can say today what Professor George Carver said years ago: "When I read Smith the first time, I knew that for me a new name had appeared among the essayists whom I must reckon as the elect." [10]

If one seeks the vortex of Smith's distinction, it is to be found not in his skill as essayist, but in his ability as a critic, an illuminator of the essay as literary genre. It is in this realm that superlatives most abound. In the "theory of the essay," says Hugh Walker, "Smith is unsurpassed." [11] "No better view can be offered of the significance of the essay," declare Scott and Zeitlin.[12] "Alexander Smith's *Dreamthorp* contains the best definition of the personal essay," write Allen Tate and A. T. Johnson.[13] Frederick Mayer thought "no better introduction" could be found for his treatment of *Victorian Prose*

---

8 Withington, R. and Van Winkle, C., 2 volumes (New York, 1934), I, xii.

9 See, for example, B. C. Williams, *A Book of Essays* (Boston, 1931). The collection includes Smith's "On the Writing of Essays" and "In Praise of *Dreamthorp*" by Joseph J. Reilly.

10 "Alexander Smith," *Of Essays and Essayists* (University of Pittsburgh, 1929).

11 Introduction to *Dreamthorp with Selections from 'Last Leaves'* (*The World's Classics*, Oxford, 1914), p. xiv.

12 Scott, F. W. and Zeitlin, Jacob, *Essays—Formal and Informal* (New York, 1930), p. 150.

13 *America Through the Essay* (New York, 1938), p. i.

than Smith's "essay upon essays." [14] Indeed, Smith's comments upon the essay have become so interwoven with critical theory that some authors draw upon him without acknowledgement.[15] A contemporary of Smith was puzzled that an essayist should be so introspective concerning his art. In reading "essays upon essayists by an essayist," he experienced "the sort of feeling we have in a room with mirrors upon opposite walls." [16] But today we appreciate Smith as a craftsman able to understand and articulate the theory of his art.

His theory comprehends the genesis, development, form and style of the essay. "The essayist does not appear early in the literary history of a country," [17] he says. When the essayist emerges: [18]

. . . the national temper has cooled down—men no longer stand blinded by the splendours of sunrise. The air has been emptied of wonder. The gods have deserted earth, and men only remain. . . . Before the Essayist can have free play, society must have existed long

---

[14] (New York, 1935), p. 1. The essay reprinted is Smith's "On the Writing of Essays."
[15] Three samples follow: (1) A. C. Baugh, P. C. Kitchen, and M. W. Black, in *Writing by Types* (N. Y., 1925, p. 221) quote six lines by Smith, but identify them only as views of "an interesting essayist." (2) In *Modern Familiar Essays,* edited by W. M. and D. B. Tanner (Boston, 1927, p. 3 f.), Smith's ideas of the essay are used with and without quotation marks, but with no acknowledgment. (3) *Cf.* Smith's "The essayist . . . lies upon the idle grassy bank, like Jacques, letting the world flow past him, and from this thing and the other he extracts his mirth and his moralities" (*Dreamthorp*, p. 26); "The familiar essayist is a veritable Jacques upon a mossy bank, who, while he watches the world go jostling its way down the river of life, extracts from its seemingly confused and meaningless tumbling bits of living wisdom and quaint chuckles of fun" [Sister M. Eleanore, *The Literary Essay in English* (Boston, 1923, p. 199)].
[16] *London Quarterly Review,* XXI, No. 61 (Oct., 1868), 157. Reference is to Smith's "Essayists, Old and New," which was collected by Smith's friend, Patrick Proctor Alexander in *Last Leaves* (Edinburgh, W. P. Nimmo, 1868). The review, a very discerning one for the times, was by [James Smetham].
[17] "On the Writing of Essays," *Dreamthorp,* p. 30.
[18] "Essayists, Old and New," *Last Leaves,* p. 245 f.

enough to have become self-conscious, introspective; to have brooded over itself and its perplexities. . . .

For the essay as we know it, we are indebted first of all to Montaigne, "the creator of a distinct literary form." [19] Montaigne demonstrated that personal experiences can be "employed to illustrate and set off . . . [a] subject." [20] Although he himself was the concern of his essays, he considered the events in his life as facts of nature.[21] He was "avowedly an egotist," but an egotist "consumed by a hunger for truth." [22] He wrote about himself because he had nothing else so interesting to write about, and because he had no public to please.[23] Montaigne is not only the first of the essayists, but "the greatest of the garrulous and communicative." [24] Bacon contributed profundity; he is "the greatest of the serious and stately essayists." [25] The "satirists of society," Addison and Steele, "brought style to perfection." [26] In the nineteenth century, the scope of the essay was further enlarged. "Lamb extended the sphere of the essay, not so much because he dealt with subjects which till his day had been untouched, but because he imported into that literary form a fancy, humour, and tenderness." [27] Carlyle perfected the critical and biographical essay. He was an artist able to "brood over the abysses of being"; he revealed "that the poorest life is serious enough

[19] *Dreamthorp,* p. 39.
[20] *Op. cit.,* p. 37.
[21] *Ibid.,* p. 34.
[22] *Ibid.,* p. 35 f. Smith's meaning in *egotist* is akin to current usage of *egoist.*
[23] *Last Leaves,* p. 222 f.
[24] *Dreamthorp,* p. 39.
[25] *Loc. cit.*
[26] *Last Leaves,* p. 223 f.
[27] *Ibid.,* p. 227.

when seen against eternity." [28] Macaulay "is the creator of the Historical Essay." He contributed to the essay a pictorial quality; he painted "historical pictures" in a "wonderful splendor and pomp of colour"; "every figure . . . is finished down to the buttons and the fingernails." Unlike Carlyle, he could not "take hold of an individual and view him against immensity"; but he showed us how to delineate a man against the backdrop "of contemporary events." [29] So did Smith perceive the origins and the history of the essay to be: a literary form which began in Montaigne's introspective egoism, and developed and matured, as society became more complex and sophisticated, into the socially critical egoism of Macaulay and Carlyle.

Although Smith provided [30] for classification of essays by types, he sought not fine lines of demarcation, but rather the essential similarity in all forms. He excluded incidental aspects in searching for the essence. The essay is: [31]

. . . neither a dissertation nor a thesis; . . . it is a work of art, and must conform to artistic rules. It requires not only . . . intellectual qualities, but unity, wholeness, self-completion. It must hang together. It must round itself off into a separate literary entity. When finished, it must be able to sustain itself and live.

The essay "bears the same relation to the general body of prose that the lyric bears to the general body of poetry." [32] In this comparison, Smith finds the key to the essay as form: [33]

---

[28] *Ibid.*, p. 238 f.
[29] *Ibid.*, p. 240 f.
[30] See *Last Leaves*, p. 249.
[31] *Op. cit.*, p. 248.
[32] *Ibid.*, p. 247.
[33] *Dreamthorp*, p. 25.

The essay, as a literary form, resembles the lyric, in so far as it is moulded by some central mood—whimsical, serious, or satirical. Give the mood, and the essay, from the first sentence to the last, grows around it as the cocoon grows around the silkworm.

In the author's mood we find the essay's intrinsic nature.

But not all men have the necessary intellectual qualities, the "constitutional turn of mind" [34] required for writing essays. The true essayist's "habit of mind is leisurely—he does not write from any special stress of passionate impulse"; [35] he is not a pamphleteer. He must have "a quick ear and eye, an ability to discern the infinite suggestiveness of common things, a brooding meditative spirit." [36] If he wishes to follow Montaigne's example, the essayist must be frank, "perfectly tolerant of himself and of everybody else," but able to "laugh at himself and his reader." [37] If the essayist has these qualities, even a trivial subject will "lead him away to the great questions over which the serious imagination loves to brood." [38]

But to produce an artistic essay, the writer must have *style*. Since he is a "kind of poet in prose," [39] he must depend upon style for his success. Although Smith makes style the final test, he shies away from any technical analysis of its elements: [40]

To define the charm of style is as difficult as to define the charm of

[34] *Op. cit.*, p. 38.
[35] *Ibid.*, p. 30 f.
[36] *Ibid.*, p. 25.
[37] *Ibid.*, p. 34 f.
[38] *Ibid.*, p. 26.
[39] *Ibid.*, p. 25, 44.
[40] "Literary Work," *Last Leaves*, p. 131. The parallel with Buffon's "style is the man himself" (*Discours sur le Style*, 1753) is apparent, but Smith seems not to have read the earlier work.

beauty or of fine manners. It is not one thing, it is the result of a hundred things. Everything a man has is concerned in it.

Consistently Smith maintains that an author's situations and responses, and the kind of man he is, determine style. "Emotion and utterance are twin-born, consentaneous, like sorrow and tears." [41] He calls attention to Bacon's sentence; it "bends beneath the weight of his thought, like a branch beneath the weight of its fruit." [42] Sentences worthy of a profound man. He cautions against mere "facility in writing." [43] As the literary skill of a man increases, so must his "intellectual resource increase at the same ratio." [44] One must beware "artifices to fillip the dull spirit of the reader." [45] If the writer resorts to tricks, he becomes a " 'base mechanical,' " [46] and "his successes are not much higher than those of the acrobat or the ropedancer." The stylist is not "a lapidary coldly polishing a gem." [47] Style is the "amalgam and issue of all the mental and moral qualities in a man's possession." [48]

Although Smith exalted style, he also had profound respect for substance. [49] If he had to choose between weight of idea and *mere* form, he chose idea. He heard Mr. Gladstone, marvelled at his "clear and bell-like cadence," yet found him to be "an

---

[41] "Men of Letters," *Dreamthorp*, p. 165.

[42] *Dreamthorp*, p. 31.

[43] *Op. cit.*, p. 151.

[44] *Ibid.*, p. 150.

[45] "Scottish Ballads," *Last Leaves*, p. 14.

[46] *Dreamthorp*, p. 151. The phrase is from Shakespeare, 2 *Henry VI*, I, iii, 196.

[47] *Last Leaves*, p. 18.

[48] *Dreamthorp*, p. 43.

[49] "You cannot make ideas; they must come unsought if they come at all" (*Dreamthorp*, p. 166).

elocutionist" rather than "an orator or a thinker." [50] But he was moved by Carlyle's speech, though given in "low, wavering, melancholy tones," because he had "gone to the bottom of things and knows." [51] To the writer, thought and its expression are of one piece. For the essayist, "style [is] as much an element of his success as his thought." [52] But if the reader evaluates qualities in a finished literary work, style rather than content is the distinguishing element. Smith supported his position with two reasons. One, style not only gives life to ideas, but it gives to them immortality. It is true indeed that "thought is the material on which expression feeds," [53] but: [54]

Thought, if left to itself, will dissolve and die. Style preserves it as balsams preserve Pharaoh. . . . The enamel of style is the only thing that can defy the work of time.

It is in this sense that "style, after all, rather than thought, is the immortal thing in literature." [55] Smith held it to be high literary service that: [56]

. . . when thought grows old and worn with usage, it should, like current coin, be called in, and from the mint of genius, [be] reissued fresh and new.

Age does not invalidate a worthy idea, and it may gain by being recast: [57]

---

50 "Mr. Carlyle at Edinburgh," *Last Leaves*, p. 97 f.
51 *Op. cit.*, p. 105 f.
52 *Last Leaves*, p. 248.
53 *Dreamthorp*, p. 151.
54 *Last Leaves*, p. 130 f.
55 *Dreamthorp*, p. 43.
56 *Op. cit.*, p. 44.
57 *Last Leaves*, p. 127.

To make a fine modern statue, there is a great melting down of old bronze.

Secondly, Smith venerated style as the personal, distinctive quality in literature. Style is: [58]

. . . a secret window through which we can look in on the writer. A man may work with ideas which he has not originated, which do not in any special way belong to himself; but his style—in which is included his way of approaching a subject, and his method of treating it—is always personal and characteristic. We decipher a man by his style, find out secrets about him, as if we overheard his soliloquies, and had the run of his diaries. . . .

Because style gives life to thought, and because style is the personal, "peculiar" [59] element in literature, Smith could say in good conscience: [60]

In reality, it is not of so much consequence what you say, as how you say it.

In regarding literature as "pure," [61] Smith anticipated the aesthetic concepts of the later Victorians. His theories appeared in the 1850's and the early sixties, a time usually described in literary histories as one of high didactic purpose and social responsibility. As Hardin Craig and J. M. Thomas say, it was not at the mid-point, but "toward the close of the century" that literature came to be regarded as not "merely an instrument for instructing or moving men but an art which is to be exercised for the pleasure it gives both to the writer and to his readers." [62] *The Yellow Book,* in an article written

[58] *Op. cit.,* p. 131 f.
[59] *Ibid.,* p. 230.
[60] *Dreamthorp,* p. 43.
[61] *Ibid.,* p. 25.
[62] *English Prose of the Nineteenth Century* (New York, 1929), p. 5 f.

by James Ashcroft Noble, hailed Smith as "a Stevenson born out of due time." Readers of *The Yellow Book* were told: [63] Smith provided

. . . what is probably the first statement by an English writer with any repute of the famous doctrine "Art for art's sake" to which Smith seems to have worked his own way without the prompting of Gallican suggestion.

Although Smith was a precursor, he cannot accurately be classified among the advocates of *l'art pour l'art*. He disparaged neither social reform nor the study of human affairs. And he shunned aesthetic intensity. The essayist and the poet, he maintained, may "inform" and "cancel abuses," although reform is not their "duty." [64] He enjoyed Bunyan's "sermonising in disguise." [65] For Cowper's muse he had admiration: she "does not sit apart in sublime seclusion—she comes down into the ways of men, mingles in every-day concerns." [66] On his shelf of selected books, Smith had room for Ebenezer Elliott, "a monomaniac on the Corn-laws" and "poet of the poor." [67] Succinctly Smith put his theory on art: [68]

What in a work of art is really valuable is the art. The statue that is only worth the weight of its metal is a very poor statue indeed.

---

[63] Vol. IV (January, 1895), 121–142. The highly appreciative article was titled "Mr. Stevenson's Forerunner." It was reprinted by Thomas Bird Mosher in his *fine* edition of *Dreamthorp* (Portland, Maine, 1913).

[64] *Dreamthorp,* p. 25.

[65] *Divine Emblems,* or *Temporal Things Spiritualized*—with Preface by Alexander Smith (London, Bickers and Son, [1867]), p. x.

[66] "William Cowper," by Alexander Smith. *Encyclopaedia Britannica,* 8th ed., VII (1854).

[67] "A Shelf in My Bookcase," *Dreamthorp,* p. 206 f.

[68] "Literary Work," *Last Leaves,* p. 128. This essay was first printed in *Good Words,* IV (1863), 740–742.

Walter Pater's later phrase, "art for its own sake," [69] revealed the trend toward aestheticism, and Oscar Wilde's "joy in art—the flawless beauty and perfect form of its expression," [70] records its culmination.

Since Alexander Smith's theories are egoistic, they can best be understood in relation to the man himself. He was a simple man who read widely and recorded his appreciations. His father was a pattern designer in Kilmarnock when Alexander was born on December 31, 1829. His family hoped they might educate him for the ministry, but they were poor; so it seemed best that Alexander follow his father's vocation. At twelve Smith was a child-worker in a Glasgow warehouse, tracing designs on muslin.[71] As he developed into youth he turned to the world of books, that "finer world within the world," [72] and the realm to which he devoted the rest of his days. He tried writing verse, and sent a packet of his youthful pieces to George Gilfillan of Dundee, then at the height of his influence in Scottish letters. Gilfillan encouraged Smith, hailed him as a "sun-buried Mercury," called upon all lovers of poesy to intervene lest Smith "pine away amid mechanical drudgery," and printed four pages of his verse.[73] In 1853, Bogue of London issued *Poems,* which, within three years, went through four London and twenty Boston [74] editions. At twenty-five Smith was famous, but needed a means of livelihood. The

[69] "Conclusion," *The Renaissance* (dated 1868).

[70] "The English Renaissance of Art" (1882).

[71] The Rev. T. Brisbane, one of Smith's close friends in the warehouse days, has written intimately of him in *The Early Years of Alexander Smith* (London, Hodder and Stoughton, 1869).

[72] *Dreamthorp,* p. 144.

[73] *Eclectic Review,* II, n. s. (July–December, 1851), 447–462.

[74] The early American editions were by Ticknor, Reed, and Fields.

town council of Edinburgh, in 1854, responded by electing him Secretary of the University of Edinburgh, a position he held until his death.

With his induction as secretary, Smith began a regimen little varied through the rest of his life. Days went on university records, evenings in reading and writing. The holidays were spent at his wife's home in Skye. *City Poems*[75] and *Edwin of Deira*[76] were published but indifferently received. The charges of "spasmodity"[77] which had been brought against "A Life Drama," in *Poems,* persisted, and a new attack, plagiarism,[78] was raised. Sensitive to the charges made against his verse, Smith turned to writing reviews and essays. He had found his *metier*. At thirty-four, in retreat behind a full beard, he was the tolerant old gentleman of *Dreamthorp*. He wrote a novel, some tales, edited and reviewed as opportunity came his way. At thirty-seven he died, of typhoid. Fine phrases, he thought, are more desirable than banknotes, and the only fame he cared for was to be quoted occasionally.

RICHARD MURPHY
University of Illinois

---

[75] (Cambridge, Macmillan, 1857.)

[76] (Cambridge and London, Macmillan, 1861.)

[77] The term was used by W. E. Aytoun to describe poets guilty of romantic excesses. Whatever the merits of the word, it can apply to no more of Smith than his first youthful work.

[78] Time has dealt kindly with Smith in this regard. That his early work has echoes of the romantic poets is clear enough, but the charge of literary thievery soon ran itself out.

Elizabeth Johnston

FREEDOM IN RESTRAINT

"Poor man! That is no poor man. That is the great Mr. Pope."

IN poetry especially, of all the arts, judgments are relative. The critic is forced to put a value upon four great intangibles: emotion; thought; workmanship done with symbolic tools; and taste. He who undertakes the task must approach it with awareness. Emotions elude one; thoughts change; approved methods of workmanship vary; taste shifts. A fair consideration of the poetry of Alexander Pope, written at the height of Neo-Classicism, hinges on the recognition of these fluctuations. Pope wrote in a manner which the nineteenth century, dominated by the Romantics, did not admire. We of the twentieth, bred in the tradition of our immediate predecessors, have hardly questioned their verdict. But here and there, one among us is beginning to wonder whether those urbane couplets, undulled after two centuries of weathering, might not be purer poetry than we thought. Before we say that Pope, so inadequate by modern standards, failed as a poet, we must be sure that what we take for mediocrity is not merely a strangeness thrown over him by the shifting light of poetic fashion. Only after we have accustomed ourselves to the techniques approved by the eighteenth century readers for whom he wrote, can we apply safely the tests by which great poetry in every age can be identified. Then we may be able to decide with equity whether or not Pope is a poet.

Even Pope's detractors admit that he was the greatest verse writer of the eighteenth century. And so the chief complaint is against not the man, but the age. The literature produced in England between the years 1660 and 1800 reflected, as it must, the tenets of eighteenth century thinking. As one critic puts it, "The temperature of the age was steadily declining." People preferred moderation to vehemence, rationalization to zealotry, restraint to enthusiasm. These qualities resulted in the use of generalized treatment, a love of abstractions, which the subjective Romantics deplored. Excellence of expression was thought to lie in a severity of form controlled by intellectual austerity, just as the most exalted attitude was thought to be reached by the domination of feeling by reason. As these traits are more often the equipment of the city-dweller, disciplined into conformity of manners by the necessity of living with others, the Town grew to be the admired emblem of perfection. Elegance, politeness, sophistication became the great virtues. Lytton Strachey thinks that eighteenth century society was perhaps the most civilized that our history has known. In this cultivated atmosphere writers discriminated against "the language of artisans, countrymen, and merchants" as being low and vulgar, and substituted for it, especially in poetry, a diction filled with stock, often trite, phrases and lifeless abstractions. Samuel Johnson, that great shaper of late eighteenth century literary thought, believed that ". . . the most heroic sentiments will lose their efficacy, and the most splendid ideas drop their magnificence, if they are conveyed by words used commonly upon low and trivial occasions, debased by vulgar mouths and contaminated by inelegant applications." It took Wordsworth and Coleridge with their insistence on "the very language of men" to delete eighteenth century diction from our poetry. In judging this period, the critic must remember that Pope's standards, often unpopular merely because they are different from ours, are only the outward signs, not necessarily indicative that the inward grace of poetry is lacking. It is sheer rashness to say that the Muse, divested of her eighteenth century dress, is not the Muse still, until we have examined the realities of the poetry.

A great many judgments have been passed on Pope for what he was not. Wordsworth condemns him for not referring more often to external nature; Leslie Stephen and many others deplore his "lack of variety," which they say makes him monotonous. By some he is charged with not using the material of poetry. Others disparage him for not being emotional. All these accusations must be reviewed in the light of his age. Some crumple in complete falsity. Some are true only when qualified. Regardless, however, of their validity, they are negative bases for judging. Proof by elimination is not proof at all; it simply points the way to verification. To judge Pope for what he is not is as foolish as condemning Thackeray because he did not write plays, or Shakespeare for not being a novelist. That man is indeed reckless of his reputation who attempts to criticize the books which were never written. No writer, Shakespeare excepted, has been equally rich in all the gifts of greatness. It is decidedly uncritical to base an estimate of Pope on anything but his positive performance.

One of the bitterest battles has been waged over the kind of ideas he thought worth writing about. Matthew Arnold felt that his subjects have not the "high seriousness" which that critic considers essential to great poetry. Samuel Johnson discredited his material as not being fresh and new. The *Essay on Criticism* is, as it claims to be, a catalogue of critical facts; the *Essay on Man,* a similar collection of philosophical principles. Pope himself calls them "essays." Neither poem represents his best work. The *Essay on Criticism* he wrote in his experimental period. Whether or not the *Essay on Man* stands up as a system of philosophy is beside the point. No sensitive critic discredits the first chapters of Genesis because they are not scientifically accurate. Hazlitt, considered by many the most astute critic of the *Rape of the Lock,* called that poem a "triumph of insignificance." In it Pope combines an empty-headed suitor, a vain debutante, a passing flirtation, and a card game into what Robert Kilburn Root describes as a "great masterpiece of poetic art, one of the permanent achievements of English poetry." The *Homer* is a free translation. In the *Dunciad* the poet complains against Dullness, which to him is a serious lapse not in morality but of "right reason and good taste." The *Satires* are almost perfect reworkings of Horace. Little besides the *Epistle to Arbuthnot* and the *Epilogue* is, in substance, his own. Predominantly intellectual material, if it becomes poetry, it does so in the poet's appropriation of it.

Because Pope uses intellectual themes and develops them with more restraint than is usual with poets, it is erroneously thought that he lacks emotion. In the *Imitations of Horace* he says clearly that emotion is a quality essential to the poet:

> 'Tis he, who gives my heart a thousand pains,
> Can make me feel each Passion that he feigns;
> Enrage, compose, with more than magic Art,
> With Pity and with Terror, tear my heart.

But being the spokesman for an age of reason, and being, temperamentally, Alexander Pope, he relies for the emotional effect, in the "more than magic Art," on this same intellectual quality. He uses ideas rather than pure sense impressions, transmuting them, by the force of his fervor, into poetry. They reappear in various forms: in the *Rape of the Lock,* as the airy, exuberant laughter of light satire; in the *Dunciad,* in sneers; in the *Essay on Man,* as an enthusiasm for a way of life; in the *Universal Prayer,* devotion. That so much of Pope's poetry is animated by the desire to satirize his contemporaries, and thus is dependent on material which must be reinterpreted to us, is regrettable. But the warm-hearted love he professes for Martha Blount, for Swift, Gay, Arbuthnot, Bolingbroke, and other friends balances it. The thing that saves it, satirical or affectionate, is what saves all poetry that is to be saved: honest, convincing sincerity. It produces in us its counterpart, an exhilaration which springs from the transmission of his feelings over the limitations of time and space. That is what was happening to Charles Lamb, who, Hazlitt tells us, was reading Pope's "list of his early friends" in the *Epistle to Arbuthnot* "with a slight hectic on his cheek and his eyes glistening," when "his voice totally failed him, and throwing down the book, he said, 'Do you think I would not wish to have been friends with such a man as this?' " That Pope was properly emotional about his art is evident in this description of himself:

> Not fortune's worshipper, nor fashion's fool,
> Not lucre's madman, nor ambition's tool,
> Not proud nor servile;—be one poet's praise,
> That if he pleas'd, he pleas'd by manly ways:

That flatt'ry, e'en to kings, he held a shame,
And thought a lie in verse or prose the same;

The genuineness of the emotion in Pope's poetry should dispel the doubt about his being a real poet. For many people it does not. Those who continue to question it base their stand upon his almost invariable use of the heroic couplet. It is not that others have not used one form as exclusively. Many poets have written entirely in blank verse. But the heroic couplet seems to have very slender possibilities. It has the closest limitations of pattern in English verse: two iambic pentameter lines, rhymed, and enclosing a single, unified, complete thought. In structure that is all there is to it. How could anyone achieve true variety within such narrow boundaries? The only answer to that Pope knew. In his hands this hedged-in, thin, little verse took on astounding depth. He became so unerringly sensitive to its possibilities that he could say anything he wanted, and go on saying it unendingly. The *Ode on St. Cecelia's Day* and the *Universal Prayer* are the only poems of quality in which he forsook it. He could even write spontaneous, unaffected conversation in couplets:

'Let spades be trumps!' she said, and trumps they were.
. . . .
And thus broke out, 'My Lord, why, what the devil!
Z——ds, damn the lock, 'fore God, you must be civil!
Plague on't! 'tis past a jest—nay, prithee, pox!
Give her the hair.'—He spoke, and rapp'd his box.

Other men had to get out of this form occasionally, using instead blank verse, the heroic quatrain, the triplet, or the twelve-syllabled Alexandrine. These escapes Pope used very sparingly. Yet so acute a critic as Lamb declared that he could read Pope "over and over forever." Whether or not most of his readers see the sublimity of his execution, it is there. Pope knew that within the most highly regarded law lies the greatest freedom. It is only inside a closely regulated society that a man can move about freely, without restriction and without fear. The same is true, Pope reasoned, in poetry. Its fundamental element is rhythmical repetition. In English poetry the most universally accepted form of this repetition is the iambic pentameter line. The most effective method of highlighting regularity of repetition is rhyme; the most regular rhyme, the couplet. Pope's contemporaries got this far. By his sheer genius he went ahead into unthought-of degrees of simplification, of which Lytton Strachey has described precisely the process and extent:

He saw that regularity implied balance, that balance implied antithesis; he saw that balance also implied simplicity, that simplicity implied clarity and that clarity implied exactitude. The result was a poetical instrument contrary in every particular to Blank Verse—a form which, instead of being varied, unsymmetrical, fluid, complex, profound and indefinite, was regular, balanced, antithetical, simple, clear, and exact.

Pope was satisfied that in this logical conclusion of method lay all the perfection to be gained from the practice of Walsh's advice, "I recommend you to make your leading aim correctness." To many people, correctness has a very circumscribed interpretation—all body and no soul. But to Pope it meant a great deal more than slavish obedience to arbitrary rules. Again Lytton Strachey has defined the poet's conception:

. . . it means that the system of versification of which the principle is regularity reached in Pope's hands the final plenitude of its nature—its ultimate significance—its supreme consummation.

[257]

Obviously such verse is artificial; that is, put together by art. "But then," as Strachey reminds us, "there is only one kind of verse that is not artificial, and that is, bad verse." Pope made no claim to naturalness; he believed, he says, in "nature methodized." We all do. No one thinks jungles, swamps, deserts, oceans beneficent. Why is the artificiality of Pope not monotonous? Because we soon learn to look constantly *within the couplets* for each variation, each new use of balance, of antithesis, or of simple clarity, for each amazing evidence of exactness; or for his unbelievable combinations of them. The profusion of effect becomes a source of ever-astonishing surprise. In such demands upon our alertness there can be no monotony. Geoffrey Tillotson recognizes the essence of this faultless handling: "Pope's practice is to provide expectation rather than surprise. But the expectation is expectation *of* surprise." That the reader may be receptive to this intrinsic quality, he must have an awareness of the technique by which the poet gained his effects.

This technique Pope perfected to a miracle by relying on every conceivable device of texture-making. In the early *Pastorals* he tried only for simplicity:

> But see, the shepherds shun the noon-day heat,
> The lowing herds to murm'ring brooks retreat,
> To closer shades the panting flocks remove;
> Ye Gods! and is there no relief for love?

Compounded of eighteenth century cliches, unbroken regularity of meter, and sentimentality, it still pleases by its very lack of cleverness. Having achieved his first aim, Pope went on into all kinds of complexities. The rhyme and the closing of the thought within two lines insure the integrity of the couplet. That was not enough. He mastered the precision necessary for making the single line complete the thought:

> Swift to the lock a thousand sprites repair;
> A thousand wings, by turns, blow back the hair;
> And thrice they twitch'd the diamond in her ear;
> Thrice she look'd back, and thrice the foe drew near.

Not satisfied with that, he often, by the use of antithesis, balanced the single line, thus completing a unit of the idea in half a line. Hundreds of his lines, thus built, are made of four important words in a double antithesis:

> Caps on their heads, and halberts in their hand.
> . . . .
> If wrong, I smiled; if right, I kiss'd the rod.
> . . . .
> Willing to wound, and yet afraid to strike.

He reaches the highest intensity in the economy of lines which have not a useless syllable:

> Alive ridiculous, and dead forgot!
> . . . .
> To err is human, to forgive divine.

Conciseness becomes a passion with him. He can vary the structure of a line without sacrificing one jot of exactness. It is hard to imagine greater concreteness within smaller scope than his description of a playing card:

> The embroider'd king who shows but half his face.

or the picture of a spider at work:

> The spider's touch, how exquisitely fine!
> Feels at each thread, and lives along the line.

With this exactness he couples musical quality far beyond mere sonorous rhythm. It, too, he produces by every possible means. It is hardly believable that he can create so wide a range of effects in modulation simply by shifting pauses (indicated in the following example by z), the lengths of which he varies by skillful combination with long vowels and stop consonants:

> Of these am I, (z) who thy protection claim,
> A watchful sprite, (z) and Ariel is my name.
> Late, (z) as I ranged the crystal wilds of air,
> In the clear mirror (z) of thy ruling star (*only run-on line*)
> I saw, (z) alas! (z) some dread event impend,
> Ere to the main (z) this morning sun descend,
> But Heav'n reveals not what, (z) or how (z) or where!
> Warn'd by the sylph, (z) O pious maid beware!

Here the pauses are frequent and heavy:

> Sooner let earth, air, sea, to chaos fall,
> Men, monkeys, lap dogs, parrots, perish all!

He can use liquid consonants in the "sylph-woven nets of dew" with almost the grace of Shakespeare:

> Some to the sun their insect-wings unfold,
> Waft on the breeze, or sink in clouds of gold;
> Transparent forms, too fine for mortal sight,
> Their fluid bodies half dissolved in light.
>   . . . .
> While ev'ry beam new transient colours flings,
> Colours that change whene'er they wave their wings.

There is an even richer, softer tone-quality in such combinations of l's, m's, and n's as these:

> And parti-coloured troops, a shining train,
> Draw forth to combat on the velvet plain.

and in the matchless use of long vowels and liquid consonants of this line:

> Die of a rose in aromatic pain.

Contrast with these the tonal coldness in the couplet which best pleased Pope himself:

> Lo! where Maeotis sleeps, and hardly flows
> The freezing Tanais thro' a waste of snows.

We say that the use in "lo" and "Maeotis" of the long o of the rhyme, and the repetition in "freezing" of the long e in "sleeps," added to the smooth softness gained by the prolixity of liquids, gives us the effect. In reality, lines like these baffle analysis. They repudiate the idea sometimes put forward that Pope cannot reach the majestic in tonal quality. So do these:

> Lo! thy dread empire, Chaos! is restored;
> Light dies before thy uncreating word;
> Thy hand, great Anarch! lets the curtain fall,
> And universal Darkness buries All.

Whether or not the acid in satire stung him into higher excitement, Pope is at his musical best in it. In the following lines he combines the explosives with an ingenious arrangement of long and short vowels to produce what could have become the thunder of tragedy. But this is the gentle irony of the *Rape of the Lock*. It must have only sharpness, with an airiness of tone corresponding to the mood. See the antidote: a joke in the last line, cast in the lightness of short vowels weighted only by one long e; even it is softened by a liquid before and a voiceless th after it:

[261]

> Then flash'd the living lightning from her eyes,
> And screams of horror rend the affrighted skies.
> Not louder shrieks to pitying Heav'n are cast,
> When husbands, or when lap dogs breathe their last.

When Pope really wants to shriek, he does not lack the art to do it. No more terrible "trumpet-screams of rage" have ever been blasted at an enemy than his against the hated Lord Hervey:

> Let Sporus tremble—

These lines have the rise and fall of extreme emotion. With magnificent scorn he deprecates the weakling:

> What? that thing of silk,
> Sporus, that mere white curd of ass's milk?
> Satire or sense, alas! can Sporus feel,
> Who breaks a butterfly upon a wheel?
> Yet let me flap this bug with gilded wings,
> This painted child of dirt, that stinks and stings;
> Whose buzz the witty and the fair annoys,
> Yet wit ne'er tastes, and beauty ne'er enjoys:

Then he changes effects. After using together numerous multiple-syllabled words, he settles down into the destructive blast of the explosive monosyllable, by its very contrast more violent than ever, rises to a climax of sound and fury at the beginning of the second couplet, and winds up with a double trick: a four-syllabled word in a triplet rhyme:

> Or at the ear of Eve, familiar toad,
> Half froth, half venom, spits himself abroad,
> In puns, or politics, or tales, or lies,
> Or spite, or smut, or rhymes, or blasphemies,
> His wit all see-saw, between that and this,

> Now high, now low, now master up, now miss,
> And he himself one vile antithesis.

Edith Sitwell's "fluttering dirtiness" aptly describes the next see-saw:

> Fop at the toilet, flatterer at the board,
> Now trips a lady, and now struts a lord.

The passage closes with withering contempt:

> Beauty that shocks you, parts that none will trust,
> Wit that can creep, and pride that licks the dust.

We reach the end of it convinced that in this man's reach lie all the tools for perfect craftsmanship.

What then can be said for Alexander Pope as a poet? He worked almost wholly in a form unpopular in every age but his own, rejected by many brilliant writers for its limitations and found entirely inadequate by the mediocre. He depended for his emotional effects on intellectual themes, which ask more effort and intelligence than many readers will or can give. He was his best in satire, a medium dependent on contemporary allusion. From these unpromising materials he molded an exactness of idea into such harmony of form as to make him admired not only by many of the best literary and critical minds, but by the stream of unknown men and women in whose discriminating taste lies every writer's immortality.

ELIZABETH JOHNSTON
California State Teachers College

Mary Martha Purdy

POLITICAL PROPAGANDA IN BALLAD
AND MASQUE

A S Queen Elizabeth's secretary, Walsingham, put it, she
was "the best match in her parish"; [1] and all the
youths in Europe with any pretensions to royalty recognized that fact, as did their parents and guardians. Her no-
bles, too, and not least Gloriana herself, realized that her hand
was a choice "titbit"; [2] and so it is not strange that, the queen
continuing what Marjorie Fleming scornfully called "a cross
old maid," the negotiations for her marriage not only covered
fifty years but gave rise, especially during the latter half of her
reign, to much imaginative literature. *The Faerie Queene,* in
which various scholars have found references to one or more
of her suitors and their courtships, is only the greatest of doz-
ens of works of all types which treated of her marriage. The
importance of the matter, both from the staudpoint of popular interest and from that of patriotism, fully justified these
writers, ranging from a fourteen-year-old Winchester College
student, George Coryat, [3] to Shakespeare himself.

---

[1] ". . . the Queen of England's marriage had become the absorbing topic from
Stockholm to Constantinople," Milton Waldman, *Elizabeth and Leicester* (Boston:
Houghton Mifflin Company, 1945), 58.

[2] "The greatest diplomatic game ever played on the world's chessboard was that
consummate succession of intrigues which for nearly half a century was carried on
by Queen Elizabeth and her ministers with the object of playing off one great continental power against another for the benefit of England and Protestantism, with
which the interests of the queen herself were indissolubly bound up." Martin
Hume, *The Courtships of Queen Elizabeth* (New York: Brentano, n.d.), 97.

[264]

As the ambassador De Feria early wrote to his master, Philip II, ". . . I see that all will turn on the husband which this woman will choose." [4] He did not overstate the matter. If she wed a Protestant, England might become the champion of Protestantism against mighty Spain, a bulwark which Scotland, the Hollanders, and the decentralized German states could cling to; but if she chose a Catholic for her "brid-bed," [5] the Reformation was perhaps doomed not only in England but in Europe. Politically, her choice of either a Spaniard or a Frenchman would destroy the near balance of power between the two great continental states, perhaps with momentous results for Scotland and for England itself, which was trying to maintain its independence and to work out its own solution to the religious problem. Moreover, the queen of this potentially rich land was young, handsome, and pleasure-loving, an attractive wife for the man who would, quite properly, everyone thought, be the real ruler.

But, whatever the reason, the queen postponed marriage year after year; and so the question of the succession, in everyone's mind when the last of Henry's children came to the throne, became almost an obsession with Englishmen, who could not forget the horrors of civil war. Her naming a suc-

---

[3] Father of Tom Coryat, who wrote one of the strangest of all travel books, *Coryat's Crudities.*

[4] James Anthony Froude, *History of England from the Fall of Wolsey to the Death of Elizabeth* (New York: Charles Scribner's Sons, 1906), VII, 27.

[5] English Protestants especially feared her marrying a foreign Catholic. In the first sermon Bishop Latimer preached before the solemn little boy, Edward VI, he said, "Well the kynges grace hath systers, my Ladye Mary, and my Lady Elizabeth . . . Who yf they shulde mary with straungers, what should ensue God knoweth." *Seven Sermons Preached before Edward VI* (London: *English Reprints*, ed. Edwin Arber, 1869), IV, 34.

cessor would have helped the situation,[6] but her bearing children would have solved many problems; and so many an Englishman used his pen either to capitalize on public interest in the subject or to try to influence the queen.

The twenty-year courtship of the Earl of Leicester, her "sweet Robin," as early as January, 1560, called "the king that is to be," naturally occupies a larger place in that literature than that of perhaps any other suitor, not only because of its length but because Leicester was "the most prominent, most powerful and most famous man in all England." [7]

Leicester's character is a sixteenth century conundrum,[8] partly because he was a representative man of the Renaissance, and so embraced in himself all sorts of apparently contradictory traits and passions; partly because he aroused both violent enmity and the most enthusiastic devotion. According to *Leycester's Commonwealth* there was little to choose between him and the Borgias, yet Spenser, disagreeing with his friend Raleigh, wrote of Dudley as a true gentleman who

Right and loyall did his word maintaine.

Chivalrous knight or treacherous villain—and modern historians have differed as much in their estimate as did his con-

---

6 She evidently agreed with Fulke Greville, who said in his play *Mustapha,* IV, 3, "A fatall winding sheet succession is."

7 Frederick Chamberlin, *Elizabeth and Leycester* (New York: Dodd, Mead & Company, 1939), VII. As Milton Waldman puts it, "Round the queen's favourite were to gather all the gifted, impetuous young men whose exuberant enterprise led to the destruction of the Armada and the penetration of the New World—Walsingham, Raleigh, Francis Bacon, Essex, Sir Philip Sidney—and though he was not the greatest of them they acknowledged him as their political leader." *England's Elizabeth* (Boston: Houghton Mifflin Company, 1933), 78.

8 "Of all the prominent Elizabethans he was the most enigmatic and elusive." Milton Waldman, *Elizabeth and Leicester* (Boston: Houghton Mifflin Company, 1945), Foreword.

temporaries—this "first of Roberts" was the queen's favorite, the noble whom she delighted to honor, and long a leader of "this gang of heretics," as the very astute Spanish minister, De Quadra, called the Protestant party. Probably the queen liked him, perhaps loved him, partly because he was also "a man very well versed in the more delightfull sort of Studies, as Musick, Love-toys, and other Courtly Dalliances," and a patron of the theater and of literature.[9]

Probably it was inevitable that the courtship of so powerful and many-sided a man should be recorded in ballad and epic, in drama and tract, by anonymous writers and by Sidney and Spenser. It is the purpose of the remainder of this study to link with Leicester's courtship two writings which seem never to have been identified as relating to it.

I. *A Strife betwene Appelles and Pigmalion*

Early in 1566 was published "A Strife betwene Appelles and Pigmalion," [10] a curious ballad by Bernard Garter, described variously as "a not unknown writer" [11] and as "the well-known versifier." [12] In this poem Garter not only encour-

---

[9] Leicester's men formed the first theatrical company under the protection and patronage of a great personage; and the earl as a well-known patron of literature had many books dedicated to him.

[10] The text I have used is that of *A Collection of Seventy-nine Black Letter Ballads and Broadsides, Printed in the Reign of Queen Elizabeth, between the years 1559 and 1597* (London: Joseph Lilly, 1867); the poem starts on page 151. It is included also in *Ancient Ballads and Broadsides* (London: Whittingham and Wilkins, 1667), starting on page 222. According to the *Stationers' Register*, this poem, fully signed by Garter, was one of several poems on a broadside printed by Alexander Lacy.

[11] By the anonymous writer of the introduction to *Ancient Ballads and Broadsides*, page xv.

[12] By W. C. Hazlitt in his edition of Warton's *History of English Poetry* (London: John Russell Smith, 1871), IV, 301. Warton mentions Garter briefly, but Courthope does not. Additional entries about him are found in Allibone, Lowndes, Hazlitt (in his *Handbook*), especially Collier and Ritson. The account in the *D. N. B.* is extremely scanty.

aged his "most gracious and popular princess" [13] to marry, but urged her to wed the Earl of Leicester.

Garter used the old Pygmalion subject—a subject which had appeared in *Tottel's Miscellany* nine years before. The poem begins with the lines,

> When that Appelles liued in Grece,
> Pigmalion also raigned than:

and proceeds to tell of the rivalry between the two artists in the shaping of a woman's figure, of their combining the results of their labors to produce a woman so beautiful that Pigmalion went mad for love of her, and of the figure's being taken up into the sky, where Dame Nature treasured it in a chest

> To pleasure him that shee loued best.

Appelles, though discouraged, made another "pece,"

> Which long time did hold great renowne,
> For Venus all men did it call;
> Tyll in our dayes gan Nature growne,
> And gaue the workemannes worke a fall;
> For from her chest, t'avoyde all stryfe,
> Shee tooke the pece, and gave it lyfe,
> And for a token gave the same
> Unto the highest man of state,
> And said, Since thou art crowned by Fame,
> Take to thee here this worthie mate,—
> The same which kyld the carvers strife,
> Before that Nature gave it life.

---

[13] As Naunton called her in *Fragmenta Regalia*.

Lord! yf Appeles now did know,
Or yf Pigmalion once should heare,
Of this their worke the worthie show,
Since Nature gave it life to beare;
No doubt at all her worthie prayse
Those selic Grekes from death would rayse.
Then those that daylie see her grace,
Whose vertue passeth everie wight,—
Her comelie corps, her christall face,—
They ought to pray, both day and night,
That God may graunt most happie state
Unto that Princesse and her mate.

Finis.

Ber.Gar.

Surely the woman

Whose vertue passeth everie wight,

the woman called a princess in the last line, was Queen Elizabeth. It is unlikely that any other woman would be described in quite such flattering terms, unless, as often happened later in the reign, an exception was made in the queen's favor; [14] but there is no such exception here. "Her grace" of the "comelie corps" for whose welfare all who had the privilege of seeing her were to pray, was evidently the queen herself, Garter's poem being, then, one of the early tributes to her fame and beauty.

But even the anonymous editor of *Ancient Ballads and Broadsides,* who in his introduction speaks definitely of the

---

[14] Says Dr. Grosart, "The potentiality, the momentum of the great Queen comes out . . . in hardly anything more strikingly than in the semi-scared note when laudation of any sort of any other seems to touch her supremacy."—Harvey's *Works* (London: Huth Library, 1884–1885), III, XXIV. Thus in his *Cynthia's Revels* Ben Jonson makes Anaides say of Arete that she "is held the worthiest lady in court, next to Cynthia. . . ." Act IV, scene 1.

lady as Elizabeth,[15] has nothing to say about the man so strongly praised. Evidently this "highest man of state" was an Englishman, and apparently the one whom Froude called the queen's evil genius. Leicester was not so high in birth as Norfolk, nor did he influence his sovereign in serious matters so deeply as did Cecil; but no other man at court combined in himself birth and ability (of a sort, at least) and influence as he did. He was a picturesque noble, whereas Cecil and Walsingham, although perhaps more substantial and public-spirited than he, were neither picturesque nor noble; and the fact that the queen liked Leicester best of all her courtiers was not only well known, but notorious; "he was ex primitiis, or of her first choice," as Naunton put it.

Leicester, as the man whom his sovereign had delighted to honor, might well be called "the highest man of state." Having begun to heap honors upon him in the first year of her reign by making him Master of the Horse and appointing him to the Order of the Garter, she had made him high steward of Cambridge in 1562, and in 1564 chancellor of Oxford, as well as "Erle of Leycester, Barron of Denbich, with gret solemnite at Westmester," [16] he receiving "Denbigh, with large Possessions thereunto belonging." [17] Early in 1566 he received a signal honor; for when Charles IX of France sent two ensigns of the cockleshelled Order of Saint Michael for the queen to bestow upon two of her noblemen, she chose

---

[15] "This loyalty, which led Elizabeth's subjects to employ the extreme of flattery. . . ." And again, "The pious Englishman of that day imagined, in his devotion, that no beauty could surpass that of the great champion of Protestantism."

[16] Sir James Melville, *Memoirs of His Own Life* (Edinburgh: Maitland Club, 1833), 119.

[17] William Camden, *The History of the Most Renowned and Victorious Princess Elizabeth* (London: M. Flesher, 1688), 73.

"Leicester as most dear unto her, Norfolk as most noble.
. . ." [18] Indeed in this year (1566) Leicester was so strong that
he could afford to quarrel with Norfolk, who had repri-
manded him for continuing to court the queen, and to quarrel with his inveterate enemy, Sussex, who struck him at the
very council table.

As a candidate for the queen's hand he was strong partly
because the always grave matter of the succession had become
acute. Elizabeth's first parliament had confidently discussed
the rank to be conferred upon her husband; yet though she
had dallied for years with the Archduke Charles of Austria,
and other suitors had come and gone, some to wed elsewhere,
she "had now in full eight years time thought nothing seriously of a husband." [19] The land having been alarmed when
she had smallpox, the Commons in 1563 had importuned her
to wed. But the little people, too, were bold enough to urge
upon her some kind of settlement: when she visited Coventry
while on progress during the summer of 1565, the Recorder
frankly urged marriage upon her for the good of the realm,
"that, like as you are a mother to your kingdom, . . . so you
may, by God's goodness and justice, be a natural mother." [20]

Moreover, Mary Stuart, who married Lord Darnley that
same summer, was gaining in popularity, and when the ballad
was issued it was known that in June she was to bear a child,
the son who immensely strengthened her position in England.
But though the Lords favored Mary's claim to the succession,
the Protestant Commons favored the Lady Catherine Grey

---

[18] *Op. cit.,* William Camden, 82.
[19] *Ibid.,* 83–84.
[20] John Nichols, *The Progresses and Public Processions of Queen Elizabeth* (London:
John Nichols and Son, 1823), I, 197.

and her sons; must there be a new War of the Roses when
Elizabeth died? The young men of Oxford were so much concerned that when the queen in August of 1566 made her first
visit at their university they thrust upon her the subject which
she called her death-knell; for they declaimed on the old *Gorboduc* theme, the dangers of a disputed succession.[21]

In a few months the queen's proud tutor, Roger Ascham,
who years earlier had likened her to Hippolita rather than to
Phaedra, was gracefully to urge marriage upon her in his dedi-
cation to *The Scholemaster;* and at the same time Parliament
was meeting in an angry mood, agreeing with Bishop Latimer
that "a woman is frayll and proclive unto all evels," [22] especially procrastination and evasion. The Lords urged her to
marry "whomsoever, wheresoever, and how soon soever" she
would. There was a succession ferment in England during the
reign of this last of the Tudors, and it was at its height in
1566; for "that Princely Lady," as Fulke Greville called her,
seemed to her people to be "over cairles what mycht com efter
hir anent the weall and qyetnes of hir contre." [23]

Moreover, if the woman mentioned in the poem is the
queen, the man can be no other Englishman than Leicester,
for no other Englishman was courting her in 1566. Those who
"at home also . . . feigned unto themselves vain Dreams of
marrying with her . . ." [24] had long since been disillusioned;
even the persistent Arundel had lost hope as well as fortune

---

21 James Anthony Froude, *History of England* (New York: Charles Scribner's Sons,
1906), VIII, 301.
22 "The First Sermon" from *Seven Sermons before Edward VI*, English Reprints, ed.
Edwin Arber (London: 1869), IV, 34.
23 The Duke of Norfolk to the Scottish Regent, according to Melville's *Memoirs*, 207.
24 Camden, *op. cit.*, 44.

by this time, and for several years past no one else had seen any chance of his succeeding. Then too, Leicester was a noble, a Protestant, a man of splendid bearing, and long the queen's trusted favorite; was he not the most likely candidate to be urged upon her—the one she could be persuaded to accept if she wed at all? Hume thinks that after Mary Stuart's rejection of Leicester and her marriage to Darnley, Elizabeth considered accepting Leicester; [25] in fact De Silva, the Spanish ambassador, thought they were already married. Surely, as Hume says, the Dudley star "was distinctly in the ascendant during the spring of 1566." [26]

Weak as the poem is in many ways, its makes several points very clearly: the queen is destined by Nature to wed Leicester; he is worthy of such a bride; and those in authority should not only permit the union, but call down the blessings of heaven.

Everyone, it seemed, was eager that she should wed, and this poem is interesting first as one link in the long and varied series of works concerning the queen's marriage, especially as it is, so far as I have yet discovered, one of the few printed ballads on the subject, and the earliest in time. Moreover, there was little attempt in the literature this early in the reign to persuade the queen to accept any particular suitor; and thus Garter's ballad is not only an early plea for Leicester, but an early piece of special pleading in connection with the courtships.

It would be interesting to know more about Garter and his relations with Leicester. The earl, unlike the queen's very last

---

[25] Martin Hume, *The Courtships of Queen Elizabeth* (London: Eveleigh Nash, 1904), 89.
[26] In the Brentano edition, 103.

suitor, James Stuart, unlike the queen herself, seems to have written no amorous verses, although he took all other means of wooing Elizabeth. May he have hired Garter to write this ballad, just as nine years later he hired George Gascoigne and others to urge his cause at Kenilworth? Leicester had already used literature to aid him in his suit, for only a year before, in 1565, a comedy of unmistakable meaning had formed part of a splendid entertainment he had given at Court. In a lively discussion Juno had advocated marriage, whereas Diana had championed virginity; and after Jupiter, serving as arbiter, had decided in favor of Juno, Elizabeth had turned to the Spanish ambassador and said, "This is all against me." [27] Probably it was not merely Leicester the patriot but also Leicester the suitor who had seen that Juno won the victory.

Then too, Garter was interested in the literature of love and courtliness, for his first work, published in 1563, was a verse imitation of Arthur Broke's *Romeus and Juliet,* and in 1578 he worked with Arthur Goldingham on a masque presented during the queen's progress at Norwich. Perhaps Garter was a dependent of Leicester; he may even have produced this poem with the same honest enthusiasm which went into the making of Gabriel Harvey's *Gratulationes Valdineneses* ten years later.

Or possibly Garter wrote the ballad because of the same anti-Catholic attitude which expressed itself in his *A New Gifte, dedicated to the Popes Holiness and all Catholikes addicted to the Sea of Rome,* a work licensed in 1565, but

---

[27] T. S. Graves, "Some Allusions to Religious and Political Plays," *Modern Philology,* IX (1911–1912), 550–551, from *Span. Cal.,* 404–405. May not this play have given Gascoigne the suggestion for the Zabeta "shew" at Kenilworth in 1575?

not published until 1579. A staunch Protestant himself, he
may have found the vacillating Leicester from the standpoint
of religion a far from satisfactory candidate for the kingship,
but so much to be preferred to Mary Stuart, wars of succession, or a foreign king that, seeing no chance of the queen's
marrying any other Englishman, he accepted the favorite and
made the most of him, the chief need being that the queen
marry, and marry soon.

Whatever Bernard Garter's reason for writing this ballad
may have been (and very possibly it was a combination of
reasons), because of it he can claim membership in the famous company, including not only Gascoigne and Harvey
but also Sidney and Spenser, which tried to encourage a marriage between queen and favorite.

II. SIR PHILIP SIDNEY'S *The Lady of May*

"Therefore o Lady . . . vouchsafe our cares such happinesse, and
me that particular favor, as that you will judge whether of these two
be more worthy of me, or whether I be worthy of them; and this I
will say, that in judging me, you judge more then me in it."

This being said, it pleased her Majesty to judge that Espilus did
the better diserve her: . . .[28]

These lines present the climax of Sidney's pastoral masque,
The Lady of May, given in Queen Elizabeth's honor at Wanstead, probably the latter part of May, 1578,[29] and first pub-

---

[28] Sir Philip Sidney, *The Lady of May,* in the *Complete Works of Sir Philip Sidney,*
ed. Feuillerat (Cambridge: at the University Press, 1922), II, 337.

[29] E. K. Chambers, whom one hesitates to question, after mentioning that Nichols
in his *Progresses* assigns this date, says, "But it might also belong to that [the prog-
ress] of 1579, and possibly to that of 1582." *The Elizabethan Stage* (Oxford: Hum-
phrey Milford, 1923), II, 89. Yet the *D. N. B.,* Courthope, Gregg, Parrott, Thorndike,
and many biographers—Symonds, Fox-Bourne, Wallace, Wilson, Denkinger ("prob-

lished in 1598. The Earl of Leicester had greatly improved
and adorned this new home he had recently acquired in Essex, and now was host to Elizabeth, who had begun her progress early that year. The earl had not provided such elaborate
entertainment as his famous one at Kenilworth three years
before, but because of custom and because of the thorough
enjoyment both he and his royal guest took in spectacle and
pageantry, it was natural that such amusement should be
planned.³⁰ *The Lady of May* is only part of the entertainment
provided, apparently the only part which has come down.

Almost without exception critics of this short play have discussed it from one or more of these points of view: (1) as the
first literary attempt of a gifted and scholarly young man who
was to become a versatile and attractive writer; (2) as an early
and rather unusual form of the masque;³¹ (3) as a more or

---

ably 1578"), and Bill—all use 1578. Fulke Greville names only the *Arcadia* from
among Sidney's works; nor does another contemporary biographer, Thomas Moffet,
mention *The Lady of May*. The *Oxford Companion* does not consider it important
enough for inclusion anywhere.

This study is based upon the majority acceptance of 1578 as the date of presentation; but much of any validity the argument has holds at least partially for 1579,
and perhaps more forcefully. It does not hold, however, for 1582, when all real
threat of the French marriage probably had passed.

30 Professor Schelling says, "Elizabeth was a devoted lover of every form of the ceremonies of homage, hospitality, and compliment." Felix Schelling, *Elizabethan Play-
wrights* (New York: Harper and Brothers, 1925), 42.

31 Professor Thorndike in his *English Comedy* calls it the first English pastoral; Professor Parrott says that "although equipped with masqueing properties of music,
dance, and contest, [it] is essentially a little pastoral play" . . . , "not, properly
speaking, a Court masque at all." T. M. Parrott, "Comedy in the Court Masque: A
Study of Ben Jonson's Contribution," *Renaissance Studies in Honor of Hardin Craig*
(Stanford University Press, 1941), 237. He stresses the mock fight which often occurs
(as in *The Lady of May*) as an adaptation of the mediaeval tournament; elsewhere
it has been described as a development from the dèbat. Professor Greg lists as the
first mask "the masquerade in which Henry VIII appeared disguised as a shepherd
at Wolsey's feast, which, according to Shakespeare, was the occasion of his first meeting with Ann Boleyn." He goes on to call Sidney's play, presented before Anne's
daughter, "the first literary specimen of the kind." W. W. Greg, *Pastoral Poetry and
Pastoral Drama* (London: A. H. Bullen, 1906), 370, 371.

less graceful attempt at compliment and polite entertainment, with some originality.[32] But whether critics take the patronizing, almost contemptuous attitude of John Addington Symonds ("How it came to be written we know not; per adventure at two sittings, between the evening's dance and retirement to bed. The thing is slight and without salt. . . . why it ever was printed I am unable to conjecture" [33]) or the more generous attitude of A. W. Ward ("Sidney's own high-spirited mask" [34]) and Professor Schelling ("only rarely does coherency emerge, as in the lively little pastoral"),[35] all agree in calling it slight; that is the adjective most commonly used in describing its contents and its form. But however slight it perhaps is as a literary production, it seems to this writer to be much more than a polite trifle—to be, in fact, perhaps as definitely political in intention as *Comus* is ethical, yet puzzling because of its courtly cloudiness.[36]

As Swinburne said in his "Astrophel,"

---

[32] As Bill puts it, "that originality which great talent brings to the performance of the most trivial tasks." Alfred H. Bill, *Astrophel* (New York: Farrar and Rinehart, 1937), 193.

[33] *Sir Philip Sidney* (New York: A. L. Fowle, 1905), 50.

[34] *English Dramatic Literature* (London: Macmillan, 1899), I, 268, N. 1.

[35] *Op. cit.*, 43. Taine calls it "a flattering and comic pastoral; a genuine 'jewel of the court.'" H. A. Taine, *History of English Literature* (Philadelphia: Henry Altemus Company, 1908), I, 262.

[36] Halpin thought the masque a plea that the queen permit the marriage of some young woman of high birth, saying, "Without some such meaning, the piece were a tissue of insipid rusticity and idle buffoonery." He believed that the queen had probably taken part extempore. See N. J. Halpin, *Oberon's Vision in the Midsummernight's Dream*, etc. (London: Transactions of The Shakespere Society, 1843), 99–100. Halpin's interpretation seems to me possible but not very convincing. J. M. Purcell in his "A Few Notes on Sidney's 'Lady of May,'" *Modern Language Notes*, XLVII, (1932), 386, says, "it is possible that the Lady stands for Queen Elizabeth who was present and judged between the two lovers." So far as I have discovered, no one else has seen any double meaning in the pastoral.

Mary Martha Purdy

The letters and lines on the pages

. . . .

Wax faint as the shadows of ages
That sunder their season and ours;

Without looking for allegory or political implication behind every wood pile, the modern reader must move warily through Elizabethan literature, so often less simple than it seems. Dryden's famous statement about *The Faerie Queene* may well be kept in mind as he reads plays, especially; for as John Dover Wilson says, "Nothing is so remarkable about the Elizabethan stage as the secret understanding which almost invariably existed between the dramatist and his audience. . . . The spectators were always on the alert to detect some veiled reference to prominent political figures or to current affairs." [37] This was certainly true of dramatic entertainments given before the court and when the queen was on progress; [38] in one "shew" after another the queen, for instance, had been represented or referred to, as at Kenilworth and Woodstock.

One may ask, too, whether or not grave Sidney, especially at that time and that place, was likely to write a mere court

[37] *John Lyly* (Cambridge: Macmillan and Bowes, 1905), 102.

[38] According to Professor Edith Rickert, "in the sixteenth century the play and the masque did the work of the modern newspaper in guiding opinion" ("Political Propaganda and Satire in 'A Midsummer Night's Dream,'" *Modern Philology* (1924), 139; and Professor Manly says, "The value of literature for those who were then trying to transform the world, to rebuild it and themselves nearer to the heart's desire, was of course best recognized by the finest spirits of the age, men like Erasmus, Thomas More, Walter Raleigh, Edmund Spenser, Philip Sidney. . . ." "The Influence of the Tragedies of Seneca upon Early English Drama," in Frank Justus Miller's *The Tragedies of Seneca* (Chicago: The University of Chicago Press, 1907), 3–4.

trifle; for as Symonds interprets it, "his position at this time was well-nigh intolerable." [39]

Since his return from his long and leisurely first trip to the continent his life at Court had been pleasant, perhaps, but inactive [40] at a time when the Protestant cause on the continent was not thriving.[41] In a letter written to his older friend, the German scholar Languet, on March 10 of that year, he spoke with discouragement of the lack of unity among continental leaders, and of the fact that "from this the Queen has taken occasion to defend her tardiness in executing her designs, against Leicester, Walsingham, and others who had persuaded her to a more active course; which I much regret." [42] Sidney had been zealous about the formation of a Protestant league, with England as supporter of the Low Countries against Spain; but now he continued, "For my own part, unless God powerfully counteract it, I seem to myself to see our cause withering away, and am now meditating with myself some Indian project." [43]

There were family troubles, too, that winter and spring. Ormond and his friends had accused Philip's admirable fa-

---

[39] *Op. cit.,* 50.

[40] As Sidney's best friend wrote years later—and he knew from experience—"how mild soever those mixtures of favours, and corrections were in that Princely Lady: yet they fell heavy in crossing a young man's ends. . . ." Fulke Greville, *Life of Sir Philip Sidney* (Oxford: At the Clarendon Press, 1907), 146.

[41] "To unite the Protestant powers against Rome and Spain was the cause for which Sidney lived and died. . . ." "This is the note of Elizabethan literature, the motive of Spenser's *Faerie Queene,* England the champion of Protestantism—'to Hell with the Pope'—of Shakespeare's historical plays, of Drayton's *Poly-Albion.* . . ." Herbert J. C. Grierson and J. C. Smith, *A Critical History of English Poetry* (New York: Oxford University Press, 1946), 84 and 100.

[42] *The Correspondence of Philip Sidney and Herbert Languet,* ed. William Aspenwall Bradley (Boston: Merrymount Press, 1912), 163.

[43] *Op. cit.,* 163.

ther, Sir Henry, who was Lord Deputy of Ireland, of being extravagant, unjust, and dishonest, and the queen talked of removing him from office, besides refusing to refund £3000 he had forwarded for necessary expenses and now needed as a dowry for his daughter Mary. Philip persuaded his faithful and distressed father to put aside his idea of resigning in disgrace near the end of his term, and he intervened rather rashly when he believed his father's correspondence was being tapped.

And a cloud much larger than man's hand boded trouble to England itself; for Catherine de' Medici's youngest son, the pock-marked but fluent and gracious dwarf Alençon, had renewed his courtship of the queen, which had been in abeyance since 1576. The vigorous letter which Sidney wrote Elizabeth a year later shows his fears for his beloved country if such a fateful marriage occurred. Such a union, too, would mean not only loss of power and influence for Leicester and the family of which Leicester was the head, but perhaps even danger for the beloved uncle whose guest "our Philip" was.

But has not Sidney himself given us a key in "and this I will say, that in judging me, you judge more than me in it"?

But to a summary the masque itself, ten pages of prose interspersed with many lyrics:

The Lady of May, a beautiful country girl, has two faithful lovers, Espilus and Therion, and is in a quandary to know which to accept. Her mother is very much disturbed over the situation. Several shepherds create a suitable pastoral atmosphere, and humor is produced by a pedantic schoolmaster, Rombus, said to be a pattern for Shakespeare's Holofernes. Finally the May Lady turns to the queen and tells her to judge between the two suitors, adding, "in judging me you judge more than me in it," all of which would seem to indicate that Elizabeth is really judging for herself—that she is the May Lady.

True, Rixus, in his praise of a forester's life, has already made a conventional reference to the queen's cruelty:

What life is to be compared to ours where the very growing things are ensamples of goodnesse? We have no hopes, but we may quickly go about them, and going about them, we soone obtaine them; not like those that have long followed one (in troth) most excellent chace, do now at length perceive she could never be taken: but that if she stayed at any time neare the pursuers, it was never meant to tarry with them, but only to take breath to fly further from them.[44]

Does this mean that Sidney had lost all hope of the queen's marrying, or is it merely a graceful compliment to her general desirableness and chaste self-sufficiency? Probably the latter, in which case the anxious mother is England, just as the May Lady is the queen.

The mother says in the very beginning, as she lays her case before the queen,

One onely daughter I have, in whom I had placed all the hopes of my good hap, so well had she with her good parts recompensed my paine of bearing her, and care of bringing her up: but now alas that she is come to the time I should reape my full comfort of her, so is she troubled with that notable matter, which we in countrey call matrimony, as I cannot chuse but feare the losse of her wits, at least of her honesty.

---

[44] The shepherd Dorcas, too, has spoken of "how many courtiers . . . I have heard under our field in bushes make their wofull complaints, some of the greatnes of their mistrisse estate, which dazzled their eyes and yet burned their harts; some of the extremitie of her beauty mixed with extreme cruelty, some of her too much wit, which made all their loving labour's folly"—a vivid and properly complimentary picture of the English Portia and her suitors.

For there are two suitors, "both loving her, both equally liked of her, both striving to deserve her." Therion, a forester, and Espilus, a shepherd. They hold a singing contest to justify their respective claims to the lady, after which the forester group and the shepherd group almost come to blows.

Rombus says the question is "whether the many great services and many great faults of Therion, or the few small services and no faults of Espilus, be to be preferred, incepted or accepted the former." The queen decides upon Espilus; whether it is an actual decision, or merely an announcement by one of the actors without consulting her, is not clear from the passage which follows Rombus' speech. "This being said, it pleased her Majesty to judge that Espilus did the better deserve her: but what words what reasons she used for it, this paper, which carieth no base names, is not worthy to containe."

If the May Lady is the queen, whom do these suitors represent? Espilus, "a shepheard very long even in love forsooth," seems to be Leicester, who had been in The Tower at the same time as the Princess Elizabeth, who had courted her before the death of Amy Robsart, and who in all the twenty years since she had come to the throne, many thought, had been the cause of her not marrying.[45] "Shepherd" may refer to his being, like the queen herself, a true born Englishman who was looking after the interests of his people and of

---

[45] "Without Leicester as a permanent matrimonial possibility to fall back upon, the endless negotiations for marriage with foreign princes would soon have become pointless and ineffectual and the balance would have been lost." Martin Hume, *The Courtships of Queen Elizabeth* (New York: Brentano's, n. d.), 98. "Courtship was to her a diplomatic asset of the first importance." Conyers Read, "Good Queen Bess," *American Historical Review*, XXXI (1926), 655. If she never intended to marry a foreigner, and there had been no English favorite, her bluff would have been called early in her reign, and English history might have been quite different.

the true religion.[46] The few small services may well mean the various offices he had held and his courtly and political usefulness to the queen.[47] The no faults perhaps means his being no foreigner or Catholic or commoner but a well-born and able English Protestant—a fit father of kings as his loyal nephew saw it.[48]

Who is Therion, or is he any person in particular? Before hazarding a guess (and certainly there is no proof) one will do well to notice the political situation at the time.

The preceding February Alençon had escaped the guards placed over him by his mother and his brother, Henry III of France, and had fled a safe distance from Paris. As Hume explains,[49] all Europe knew that he would soon be in Flanders leading the Hollanders in their struggle against Spain; and Europe knew that Elizabeth did not want him there unless he was working with, and under, her. Alençon realized he needed her support; and so in March he sent envoys to England, probably to open negotiations for his marriage with the queen. Soon the union was again talked of, and on May 16 Stafford was sent to the French king and his brother to report that Elizabeth favored resuming the negotiations. The same month Alençon sent her a loving letter, to which she returned a favorable reply. This was the status of the French match when *The Lady of May* was given.

Little had yet happened; but the political situation being

---

[46] In much the same way as Spenser called Raleigh the shepherd of the ocean.

[47] Espilus also speaks of himself as rich. Leicester was, or at least was rapidly becoming, the richest man in England. Alençon was very poor.

[48] As Thomas Moffet probably saw it when he called him "the principal Atlas of this realm." *Nobilis or A View of the Life and Death of a Sidney*, ed. H. H. Hudson and V. B. Heltzel (San Marino: The Huntington Library), 87.

[49] In his *Courtships of Queen Elizabeth*.

what it was, and the queen being as fond as ever of the old game of maiden coyness and diplomatic fencing, it was not difficult to foresee the interesting wooing that actually occurred that summer.

May not Therion be Alençon? The prince's "many great faults"—belonging to the evil and physically rotten de Medici family, his rearing at the dissolute French court, his Catholicism, his stature and face, his being more than young enough to be Elizabeth's son—were obvious enough, and were to be specified by Sidney himself a year later.[50] The "many great services" are harder to explain, for the only thing her frog had done for the queen was to write her fervent love letters. But perhaps the expression simply stands for his royal birth and exalted rank in powerful France; perhaps, too, Sidney is referring to Alençon's sympathy for and support of French Protestantism. According to his song in the contest Therion is poor, but rich in being free, and this is not an unsuitable description of the troublesome youngster who had escaped from Catherine de Medici and Henry III, who both hated him, winning more of their disapproval by doing so.

Moreover, it would have been thoroughly in keeping for Sidney to bring his pen to his uncle's support, not only because, to a certain extent, his own fortunes depended upon those of the earl, but because the Dudleys, they of the bear and ragged staff, were a very clannish family. In the early part of the reign Philip's father and mother, persons of special integrity, had yet entered into strange intrigues for the

---

[50] In his famous letter to the queen. In his account of the letter, Greville speaks bluntly of "her comeliness, his disadvantage that way" and of "the very reflection of scorn between youth and age." *Op. cit.*, 59, 60.

sake of furthering Leicester's matrimonial interests. Sir Henry Sidney constantly defended Leicester, the most hated man in England; Leicester's brother Warwick was always friendly to him; and year after year Leicester showed kindness to his father's family. Furthermore, as Wallace says, "Sidney's relation to his uncle . . . seems to have been of the closest, and we frequently find their names associated" [51] (as when Leicester introduced young Philip at court), and it was Philip who in 1584 wrote a vigorous answer to the scurrilous pamphlet against his uncle, *Leicester's Commonwealth*. Sidney was very proud of his Dudley blood; perhaps that was one reason he never seemed to see any faults in his brilliant uncle, the chief representative of the family.

But Dudley loyalty would not have been the only or perhaps the chief reason for Sidney's writing of the political situation in 1578. One remembers Fulke Greville's saying, "That though I lived with him, and knew him from a child, yet I never knew him other than a man. . . . His talk ever of knowledge, and his very play tending to enrich his mind: . . ." [52] Greville goes on to say, "his end was not writing, even while he wrote," [53] "his chief ends being not Friends, Wife, Children, or himself; but above all things the honor of his Maker, and service of his Prince, or Country." [54] Like

[51] M. W. Wallace, *The Life of Sir Philip Sidney* (Cambridge: at the University Press, 1915), 197.

In Sidney's will, prepared after Zutphen, one finds, "*Item,* I give to my most honourable good Lord, the Earl of *Leicester,* an hundred Pounds, as a Token of my devrowed Service, and great Love, which I have ever borne to him in all Duty." Arthur Collins, *Letters and Memorials of State* (commonly called the *Sidney Papers*) (London: T. Osborne, 1746), I, 111.

[52] *Op. cit.,* 6.

[53] *Ibid.,* 18. *Ibid.,* 35.

[54] M. W. Wallace, *op. cit.,* 35.

his sovereign, Sidney had given much time to the study of history, a subject he strongly recommended to his younger brother Robert in a famous letter.[55] Greville speaks of Sidney's serious purpose as he wrote his delicate and wandering *Arcadia;* and others, perhaps especially Professor Greenlaw, have found it definitely a piece of political writing.[56] In his *Defence of Poesie* Sidney was to write his approval of *Gorboduc*, "as full of notable morality, which it doth most delightfully teach, and so obtain the very end of Poesy." The explanation of his father's course in Ireland which he sent the queen has been called a masterly exposition of state policy; and his famous letter to the queen in 1579 about the Alençon match is definite, thorough, and extremely forceful. Then too, Greville, his intimate associate for years, shows in the *Life* itself his own absorbing interest in history, and says

---

[55] Written October 18, 1580. See *Sidney Papers*, I, 285.

[56] "Sidney's book, concrete application of the theories of poetry laid down in his *Defense*, springing out of his interest in the problems of government, the object of his care during the ripest and most thoughtful years of his life, is less truly to be described as a pastoral romance than as an 'historicall fiction,' a prose counterpart of the *Faerie Queene*, having for its object 'to fashion a gentleman or noble person in vertuous and gentle discipline,' and to portray 'a good governour and a vertuous man.'" Edwin A. Greenlaw, "Sidney's Arcadia as an Example of Elizabethan Allegory," *Kittredge Anniversary Papers* (Cambridge: Harvard University Press, 1913), 337. The discussion is continued in his "The Captivity Episode in Sidney's *Arcadia*," in *The Manly Anniversary Studies* (Chicago: The University of Chicago Press, 1923), 56, where he says, "Sidney's intention, at least in part, was not vaguely moral but was intended to apply to political conditions in his own time and to the crisis that he saw coming upon England. That crisis, I believe, was the conflict with Spain, with all that that involved in Sidney's thought. But the French marriage, imminent in 1580, . . . was a phase in the larger conflict." On the next page he continues, "There is abundant testimony to show that Sidney, more than most of his contemporaries, possessed the faculty of visioning the tendencies of European politics not by sections affecting some particular matters of diplomacy but as a whole. He was politically minded."

Marcus S. Goldman, too, in his *Sir Philip Sidney and the Arcadia* (University of Illinois Press, 1933), has material on the allegory. W. S. Briggs, in "Sidney's Political Ideas," *Studies in Philology*, XXIX (1932), discusses the political thought found in the letter opposing the French match.

that the object in his tragedies was "to trace out the high waies of ambitious governours." As one of Sidney's biographers put it, "Sidney did not consider his own writing of any particular importance except when he employed his pen to political purpose." [57]

Moffett, who, because of his attachment to the Earl of Pembroke, Sidney's brother-in-law, probably knew Sidney well, fully agrees with Greville: "The safety and advantage of the commonwealth were so imprinted upon his mind that he expelled concern for private interest"; and again, "He devoted himself wholly to watching over the interests of his fatherland, concerned with nothing but that he might be acceptable to the Queen and to virtue." [58] Sidney wrote to Languet about the time of *The Lady of May,* "For with what end should our thoughts be directed to various kinds of knowledge, unless the knowledge is put to use for the public good"; and the whole Sidney-Languet correspondence shows Sidney's intense interest in politics and his sense of political responsibility—a sense which in his day might naturally express itself in the writing of a polite entertainment, he being "not only the perfect knight, but also the letter courtier. . . ." [59]

Moreover, Sidney had seen many pageants and shews, and knew how Prince Arthur, the Lady of the Lake, and other characters were used to refer to that English history of which Elizabethans in general, not just Spenser and Shakespeare,

---

[57] Emma Marshall Denkinger, *Immortal Sidney* (London: George Allen and Unwin, 1932), 158.
[58] *Op. cit.,* 79, 81.
[59] Emile Legouis and Louis Cazamian, *A History of English Literature* (New York: The Macmillan Company, 1930), 271.

were so conscious. He had returned from the continent in time to share the festivities at Kenilworth in 1575, and probably shared his uncle's chagrin and disappointment over the fact that it was never quite convenient for the royal guest to see the shew of *Zabeta,* in which Leicester quite definitely proposed to the queen. He probably knew, too, how his uncle's enemies had used Woodstock pageant to oppose the message of *Zabeta.* Would it not have seemed natural to him, whether or not his uncle had requested literary support in his courtship, to use the drama of pageantry, however short and simple the play, in his uncle's behalf? Certainly the man who had commissioned and planned to give *Zabeta* would have had no quibbles about the propriety of a host's employing entertainment in his own interest.

As we see it from the perspective of almost four hundred years, Leicester had shot his last bolt at Kenilworth and was not likely to win the queen after that ambitious and sumptuous effort had failed; but his failure did not seem so definitive then as it does now, just as the defeat of the Armada did not seem nearly so decisive to the Elizabethans, who feared and watched Spain for years, as it does to us.

Was Sidney pleading that the queen accept his uncle,[60] or merely that she should not allow a foolish young foreigner

---

[60] The exact status of Leicester's relation to the queen in 1578, as in 1575, probably cannot be determined. Hume claims in his *Courtships,* 347, that "it is evident that from about 1571 or 1572 onwards there was no real question of marriage beween the Queen and Leicester," supporting his view in part by the fact that Leicester had entered into a union with Douglas Sheffield in 1573.

But the historian Freeman, in his article "Queen Elizabeth and Her Favorites," *The Living Age,* XLII (1854), 449, says that Leicester "never appears to have abandoned hope till the crisis of the famous courtship of Alençon, in 1578. Professor Schelling, too, disagrees with Hume, for in his *The Queen's Progress and other Elizabethan Sketches* (New York: Houghton Mifflin Company, 1904), 12, he says, "Leicester was then (during the Kenilworth progress) at the height of the elaborate and to come between her and her old favorite, to say nothing of endangering the land and its religion? But the question must be raised, was Leicester free to wed? And how much did Sidney know about what Camden called "Leicester's Rambling and Inconstancy in his Love," especially about the affair with Lady Essex, mother of Stella and the ill-fated young Essex, and cousin of the queen? The public marriage of Leicester and Lady Essex did not occur until September 20, 1578, at Wanstead, Sir Francis Knollys' solicitude for his daughter's honor (he had none too much faith in his new son-in-law) requiring that her first secret marriage with the earl be repeated in her presence. That private marriage had occurred the preceding year; and Sidney knew of it,[61] for in the letter he wrote Leicester after visiting him in December, 1577, he sent his duty to "my Lady and Aunt."

At first glance it would certainly seem late in the day for Leicester to hope for and Sidney to encourage a marriage with the queen. However, Sir Francis Knollys evidently took no account of the earl's secret and irregular union with Douglas Sheffield (thought by many scholars to be the "little western flower" of *A Midsummer Night's Dream*), and was not satisfied with his own daughter's private marriage; hence it seems likely that the almost-secret union with Lady Essex would not have stood in the way of Leicester's wedding the queen (excepting that the reactions of the lively and in-

---

subtile courtship which he paid to his sovereign through several years, sanguine of success, and eager in pursuit of the most difficult mistress that ever bade lover hope only to play with his despair." I believe the courtship continued at least into the summer of 1578, very possibly to 1583.

[61] Further proof of the close relations between uncle and nephew, since it is likely that very few were in the secret.

dependent Lady Essex would have been most interesting, not
to say trying, to everyone concerned). The general laxity of
sixteenth century marriage arrangements inevitably brings
to mind Mexican marriages, frequent Hollywood matrimonial shuffling, and Reno and Mexican divorces. Even after
the public marriage with Lady Essex some legal flaw might
easily have been found if the queen, supported by all those
who insisted upon her marriage at any cost, had wished to
wed Leicester. Sidney himself would probably have supported a divorce in the interest of strengthening Protestantism and assurring the succession.

However, Sidney may well have been working against the
Alençon marriage rather than for the Leicester marriage,
Alençon seeming as contemptible and dangerous to him as
to Spenser himself, and anything which diminished his great
uncle's power and influence inimical to England and to the
Protestant cause for which both young poets were so zealous.
Certainly *The Lady of May* is perplexing out of all propor-
tion to its length.[62]

Did the young maids of honor, dressed in white and sur-
rounding their great queen, nudge each other expectantly
and watch to see how their mistress was taking it all? And how
did she take *The Lady of May?* We do not know. If she was
provoked by its advice and special pleading, she may have

---

[62] It is interesting to notice that Leicester and his friends did not remain inactive,
especially after the coming of Alençon's able friend and agent Simier, in January,
made the French courtship at least appear to thrive. On February a "history" was
"provided to have been shewen at Whitehall . . . by the Earl of Warwick's players,"
but the queen "wold not come to hear the same." As Graves suggests, this history
probably dealt with the marriage situation at that time. Later, on Innocents' Day,
the favorite's players were perpared to give a history, but the queen "couldne not
come forth." *Op. cit.*, 551, as quoted from Feuillerat's *Documents of the Revels*, 303
and 320.

concealed her disfavor because of her liking for the author and because of his youth; perhaps she complimented him graciously on his first literary attempt. If she herself spoke the decision, she may have chosen Espilus out of good nature, the desire to tease Leicester and keep every one else guessing, or the feeling that she must be gracious and do what her host expected her to do this time, since she had been rather hard upon him at Kenilworth.

Yet the Alençon negotiations went on, and very likely Sidney felt that his masque had been a practical if not a literary failure. A letter from Languet written October 22, 1578, suggests much about his young friend's mood that summer: "I am especially sorry to hear you say that you are weary of the life to which I have no doubt God has called you, and desire to fly from the light of your court and betake yourself to the privacy of secluded places to escape the tempest of affairs by which statesmen are generally harassed." [63]

If one accept *The Lady of May* as containing political propaganda, several interesting conclusions seem to follow:

1. Instead of being written so casually and gaily as Symonds has suggested,[64] the masque probably was earnestly planned and carefully written, the young writer trying to achieve a skilful balance between propaganda and entertainment—"to teach delightfully."

2. Sidney began writing of government and public affairs a year earlier than has been thought; indeed, his first work was political as well as polite. Thus the amount of his politi-

---

[63] *Op. cit.*, 78.

[64] Was he not forgetting the gravity of Sidney, his great veneration for the queen who was to be entertained, and a young writer's struggles over the first work to be presented to the public?

cal writing is increased, as well as the portion of that writing which is imaginative (if one accept the *Arcadia* as having political implications, even to the extent that Cecropia is Catherine de Medici, "that subtile old woman").

3. The play presents another proof of the solidarity of the Dudleys.

4. Unconscious of the fact as Sidney was when he wrote it, it served as a modest dress rehearsal for the patriotic and bitter attack on Alençon he was to make in his letter to the queen in 1579.

5. This masque adds another link to the long and interesting series of political entertainments—pageants and plays— during Elizabeth's reign.

6. It shows that the pastoral was being used for political purposes before *The Shepherdes Calender* and Lyly's court plays were written, before the *Arcadia* itself.

7. *The Lady* may have influenced Lyly; for if Bond be correct in thinking that Lyly in his *Endymion* intended the hero to represent Leicester, and Eumenides Sidney, the dramatist may have had Sidney's masque in mind as well as his defense of his uncle against *Leicester's Commonwealth*.

8. The brilliant but gauche Gabriel Harvey's *Gratulationes Valdinenses,* produced and hastily published after he had met "the excellent knight and my inestimable dear friend, Sir Philip Sidney," perhaps for the first time, may have been written in part because of Sidney's play. The queen had come on progress to Audley End, that eventful summer of 1578, and Harvey was one of the Cambridge men chosen to dispute before her. Harvey had been trying diligently and by no means secretly to advance the marriage of

his patron, Leicester, with the queen; now he dedicated to Leicester the first part of his book in which he advocated the union. To be sure, Harvey was trying to gain preferment for himself; but if, as seems likely, he had heard of *The Lady of May,* is it not possible that he wrote his book in part because as a loyal Englishman and Protestant he was glad to continue Sidney's literary attempt to influence events?

9. Possibly Spenser, too, at least in his attitude towards Alençon, was influenced by Sidney when he wrote *The Shep- herdes Calender* the next year, and even in *The Faerie Queene* itself, and perhaps in his attitude toward Leicester and Leicester's relations with Gloriana.

MARY MARTHA PURDY
Westminster College

Five hundred copies of this book have been printed in Baskerville type on Worthy Permanent Book, all rag paper, by the Lancaster Press, Inc., Lancaster, Pennsylvania. On the title page the line drawing was made by George Stout of the Worcester Art Museum, and the hand lettering by Wendell Gullion and Theodore Bowman. The editor was Agnes Lynch Starrett; the literary adviser, George Carver; and the publisher, the University of Pittsburgh.